Edward Wilmot Blyden and the
Racial Nationalist Imagination

Rochester Studies in African History and the Diaspora

Toyin Falola, Series Editor
The Frances Higginbotham Nalle Centennial Professor in History
University of Texas at Austin

(ISSN: 1092-5228)

White Chief, Black Lords: Shepstone and the
Colonial State in Natal, South Africa, 1845–1878
Thomas V. McClendon

Narrating War and Peace in Africa
Edited by Toyin Falola and Hetty ter Haar

Ira Aldridge: The Early Years, 1807–1833
Bernth Lindfors

Ira Aldridge: The Vagabond Years, 1833–1852
Bernth Lindfors

African Police and Soldiers in Colonial Zimbabwe, 1923–80
Timothy Stapleton

Globalization and Sustainable Development in Africa
Edited by Bessie House-Soremekun and Toyin Falola

The Fante and the Transatlantic Slave Trade
Rebecca Shumway

Western Frontiers of African Art
Moyo Okediji

Women and Slavery in Nineteenth-Century Colonial Cuba
Sarah L. Franklin

Ethnicity in Zimbabwe: Transformations in Kalanga and Ndebele Societies, 1860–1990
Enocent Msindo

A complete list of titles in the Rochester Studies in
African History and the Diaspora series, in order of publication,
may be found on our website, www.urpress.com.

Edward Wilmot Blyden and the
Racial Nationalist Imagination

Teshale Tibebu

UNIVERSITY OF ROCHESTER PRESS

First published 2012

University of Rochester Press
668 Mt. Hope Avenue, Rochester, NY 14620, USA
www.urpress.com
and Boydell & Brewer Limited
PO Box 9, Woodbridge, Suffolk IP12 3DF, UK
www.boydellandbrewer.com

ISBN-13: 978-1-58046-428-4
ISSN: 1092-5228

Library of Congress Cataloging-in-Publication Data

Teshale Tibebu.
    Edward Wilmot Blyden and the racial nationalist imagination / Teshale Tibebu.
        pages cm. — (Rochester studies in African history and the diaspora,
        ISSN 1092-5228 ; v. 56)
    Includes bibliographical references and index.
    ISBN 978-1-58046-428-4 (hardcover : alk. paper) 1. Blyden, Edward Wilmot,
1832–1912. 2. Black nationalism. 3. Pan-Africanism. 4. Liberia—Intellectual life.
5. Africa, West—Intellectual life. 6. Intellectuals—Liberia—Biography. 7. Intellectuals—Africa, West—Biography. I. Title.
    DT634.3.B58T47   2012
    320.54'6092—dc23
    [B]

                                                                          2012038658

A catalogue record for this title is available from the British Library.

This publication is printed on acid-free paper.
Printed in the United States of America.

To my family, my wife, Zewditu, and my children, Christian and Ewqat

Contents

Acknowledgments

My interest in Edward Wilmot Blyden grew out of a larger concern regarding Eurocentrism and how it negatively affected perceptions of Africa. In my book *Hegel and the Third World*, I provide a critical inquiry into the origins of Eurocentrism by focusing on Hegel's works. Among African intellectuals, Blyden stands as one of the few who addresses the problem of Eurocentrism, although the term did not exist then.

I want to express my sincere thanks and appreciation to Toyin Falola, the editor of the Rochester Studies in African History and Diaspora series, for his promptness, professionalism, and support in expediting the process for the publication of this book.

Suzanne Guiod, the editorial director at the University of Rochester Press, lightened the anxiety of the publication process and made the worries that go with the craft manageable. She was always courteous, prompt, and full of support and encouragement as I moved through the various stages of publication. And she was always available to answer my questions. I thank her deeply.

I thank Ryan Peterson, the managing editor at the University of Rochester Press, for his help in expediting the publication process. I thank Susan Silver for her superb job in the copyediting of the manuscript.

I express my gratitude to the Temple University College of Liberal Arts for providing me with the Research Incentive Fund Grant awards in fall 2005 and summer 2008. These grants helped me to cover expenses while conducting the research on this book. I also thank the staff at the Schomburg Center for the Study of Black Culture in New York City for their help in making available Blyden's writings in their possession.

My friends Fikru Bekele, Tilahun Afessa, Abye Assefa, Pietro Toggia, and Haimanot Wudu were always there to provide me with their unswerving moral support and encouragement during my research and writing.

As always, I thank friends and colleagues in the Department of History at Temple University for their moral support and encouragement in my academic career. They are too many to mention, but I want to specially thank Nugyen Thi Dieu, Wilbert Jenkins, Peter Gran, Bettye Collier-Thomas, Kenneth Kusmer, Susan Klepp, Arthur Smith, Phil Evanson, Kathleen Uno, Kathleen Biddick, Bryant Simon, and David Waldstreicher. Gratitude is also due to the external readers of the manuscript for their suggestions and comments, which helped me improve its quality.

Blyden used to repeatedly invoke the biblical adage, "Ethiopia stretches its hand unto God!" Yet this is the first book about him written by a person of Ethiopian origin!

Introduction

A true respect for the past—a consciousness of a real national
history—has not only a binding force but a stimulating effect,
and furnishes a guarantee of future endurance and growth. That
which has been achieved in the past is a prophecy of what may
be done in the future.

—Blyden, *Christianity, Islam, and the Negro Race*

This book offers a critical reading of the works of Edward Wilmot Blyden, a
seminal figure in modern transnational African thought. It aspires to map
the contours and configurations of Blyden's appraisals of the encounter
between the black world and the Western world in modern times. It is an
undertaking in intellectual history.

Long before the deconstruction discourses of Michel Foucault, Jacques
Derrida, and others in the West rocked the boat of Western hegemonic
hubris, black men and women on both sides of the Atlantic were cultivat-
ing alternative paradigms from the one informed by the self-images of the
Western world regarding modernity. The incisive pens of David Walker and
Frederick Douglass wrote against the dehumanization of enslaved black
humanity. The powerful voice of Sojourner Truth journeyed through the
"land of liberty" speaking truth to power.[1] Harriet Tubman, born in slavery,
made certain that she was not born for slavery. She traversed long stretches
of the land of slaveholders, snatching her people from the inferno of American slavery. She helped overturn the ground of slavery's hold through her
underground activities. Harriet Jacobs, born in slavery, exposed the cruel,
hypocritical, and dehumanizing world of slavery in her narrative *An Incident
in the Life of a Slave Girl*. Anna Julia Haywood Cooper, born in slavery, earned
a PhD in history from the Sorbonne in France and authored *A Voice from the
South*, published in 1892, in which she articulated black feminism.[2] There
were many outstanding black leaders in nineteenth-century America that
defied the paradigm of white supremacy.[3]

Frederick Douglass, whom Orlando Patterson called "undoubtedly the
most articulate former slave who ever lived,"[4] wrote extensively about the
despotism of the American slave-holding system. Born in slavery, Douglass
penned critical treatises against the slaveholding system, its ideologies, and
social practices, and he exposed the hypocrisies of the religious institutions in America that embraced slavery. His was a critique of slaveholding

modernity, as well as of the subsequent virulent racism. In their place, he advocated a democratic, humanist alternative.

Black people in America were not Thomas Jefferson's helpless wretches groaning under crouching submission to the slaveholder. The author of the Declaration of Independence, and one of the most sophisticated American intellectuals of his time, would write in his *Notes on the State of Virginia* in 1782, "The whole commerce between master and slave is a perpetual exercise of the most boisterous passions, the most untrammeled despotism on the one hand, and degrading submissions on the other." Jefferson's view on master-slave relations become even clearer a few lines later: "Indeed I tremble for my country when I reflect that God is just; that his justice cannot sleep forever." Jefferson foresaw "a revolution of the wheel of fortune, and exchange of situation, is among possible events; that it may become probable by supernatural interference!"[5] Indeed, this revolution did take place in America, but it did not result in the "exchange of situation" between master and slave. Instead, at least six hundred thousand American lives were needed to bring down the house of slavery, the same number as that of Africans who landed in America to become enslaved. As Jefferson intimated in his "trembling" state of mind, enslaved Africans challenged in a variety of ways the wrongs of the slaveholder world, and the racism that followed the demise of the "peculiar institution."[6]

African American women played a critical role in challenging slavery and racism in America.[7] As historian Bettye Collier-Thomas shows in her magisterial work, *Jesus, Jobs, and Justice: African American Women and Religion*, African American women subverted the ideology of the slaveholding, Jim Crow-enforcing paradigm of the white churches by reinterpreting the teachings of Jesus. Similar to many oppressed peoples around the globe who were introduced to Christianity, African American women activists saw in Jesus the moral voice of justice, universal fraternity, and human decency. Like Frederick Douglass's critique of American Christianity in his *Narrative of the Life of Frederick Douglass*, African American women activists redefined Christianity.[8] They read Jesus's moral philosophy as transcending color, class, and gender, and his teachings as entailing concrete, universal humanism. Moses and Jesus were the heroes of African American Christianity; Paul, on the other hand, was the source the slaveholding class cited ad infinitum for rationalizing slavery.[9] There were few white churches in America that stood up against slavery, including the Quakers, but theirs was not the dominant voice in the white churches supporting the widespread perjuries, prejudices, and perversions of slavery. African-descended intellectuals in the Caribbean confronted and challenged the racism of their "masters," slaveholder and colonial alike.[10] Enslaved Africans in Brazil defied the power of the slaveholding class in a variety of ways, including creating independent black states and polities, the Quilombos.[11] There was then that unique event in the history of revolutions, the first ever successful slave revolt in world history, the Haitian Revolution. The Haitian Revolution was more radical and more antisystemic than the French Revolution. Enslaved Africans buried a civilization based on the barbarism of commoditized chattel slavery.[12] Enslaved black women in the French Caribbean fought Napoleon's army, which came to reinstate slavery abolished by the French National Assembly in the aftermath of the French Revolution. Present in the thick of battles, they defied as they celebrated death. Their slogan was a declaration of supreme courage: "*Vive la mort!*" (Long live death!).[13]

W. E. B. Du Bois, Eric Williams, and Oliver Cox, among others, were working with approaches similar to Immanuel Wallerstein's world-systems perspective, only earlier.[14] Du Bois's *The World and Africa*, was first published in 1946, while Eric Williams's *Capitalism and Slavery* was first published in 1944.[15] Both books were published three decades before Wallerstein's first volume of *The Modern World-System*, which came out in 1974.[16] Walter Rodney's famous work, *How Europe Underdeveloped Africa*, was published the same year as the first volume of *The Modern World-System*.[17] Oliver Cox's works were published between 1959 and 1964. Indeed, it has been persuasively argued that the black Trinidadian intellectual Oliver Cox was the founder of world-system theory.[18]

More than a century before the current buzzwords of globalization and transnationalism, black Atlantic intellectuals saw their predicament on global, interconnected terrains. Western-educated Africans in South Africa were privy to events in Jim-Crow America, and vice versa. Modern black thought was born out of the hierarchical, racially bipolar world order. Black Atlantic intellectuals spoke with one voice in their condemnation, and their indictment against this world was contained in one word: hypocrisy! They zeroed in on the double standard and cried out loud that such hypocrisy is heresy to truth, justice, and human decency. Like Native Americans, their peers in suffering, they decried in the like of the Amharic adage: *baand ras hulat melas* (two tongues in one head).

The black diaspora is among the few in the modern world that invented transnationalism. African-descended people in the Americas, living in precarious homelessness, claimed the entire continent of Africa as their singular national origin. Africa is not a nation but a continent of many nations, a transnational entity. By definition, modern black thought cannot be anything but transnational, and the same is true for African history.

Out of the deeply hurt heart, the open wound festering for centuries, African descendants in the land of their exile created the bonding that bondage made possible. Out of this bonding came the racial identity "African" or "black." Prior to their violent encounter with Western modernity, the peoples of the continent we now call Africa were neither "African" nor "black." They were instead a mosaic of different self-defined identities with no need of a common bond to unite. After all, they were not in common bondage to make them search for bonding. The African diaspora in the Islamic world melted away in the larger society. As such, it did not become a distinct racial category seeking a common cause. Western Christian bourgeois modernity hurt the African heart twice: by religion, and by race. The first justified slavery, the latter racism. The world of Islam did not invent race or abhor blood mixing with Africans. It has color consciousness but is open to many colors mixing.[19]

Africans in the diaspora imagined Africa as their home, from where their ancestors were snatched away by force.[20] Out of sight, Africa became indelibly inscribed in their mind and memory. Indeed, it was this African diaspora that coinvented African identity, alongside the modern West.[21] Continental Africans were the last to be drawn into the racial nationalist imagination of an Africa they live in and an African identity they supposedly belong to.

It was in the land of their exile that Africans could conceptualize the modern racial dichotomy of identity and difference: Africans versus Europeans, black versus white, slave versus master, non-Christian versus Christian, and so on. In Africa, African identity became the self-conscious expression of Africans during European colonial rule in the twentieth century, somewhat earlier in places of significant European settlement such as South Africa.

Africa is a concept created by the modern West in the age of empire. It is made into a reality in conformity with the concept. Africa and African identity were both "invented" at the lower deck of the transatlantic slave ship.[22] The ethnic, linguistic, and religious mosaic that filled the Atlantic slave ship was fused, confused, and compressed into one dark mass of people and transformed from names to mere numbers. Then race was "invented." As Bruce Baum notes, "The 'race' concept itself was introduced by European elites only near the end of . . . the seventeenth century, after the rise of the Atlantic slave trade and massive enslavement of 'black' Africans." By extension, the "'Caucasian race' category was a product of the European Enlightenment and late-eighteenth-century natural history."[23]

As the Caucasian race was meant to imply whiteness, purity, innocence, and transparency, the "black" race was meant to represent its extreme opposite. In David Brion Davis's words, "In all four languages [Spanish, Portuguese, French, and English] the word carried connotations of gloom, evil, baseness, wretchedness, and misfortune. Black was the color of death, . . . of the devil; it was the color of bad magic and melancholy, of poison, mourning, forsaken love, and the lowest pit of hell." In addition, there "were black arts and black humors, blackmail and blacklist, blackguard and black knights, the Black death."[24]

The invention of an African race was an act of "con-fusion." Culturally meaningful and significant names of peoples in Africa were replaced by meaningless, abstract numbers. This racist numerology that erased the identity of real people was the first act of the Western cultural genocide against

Africans. As Marcus Rediker tells us in *The Slave Ship* of the horrendous barbarity and savage terrorism of the European Atlantic slave trade, those dragged into the lower deck of the slave ship tasted the dual whip of race and religion long before they left the shores of Atlantic Africa. The only name assigned to the captives on those European ships was as foreign as it was racial and totalitarian: African. Those on the upper deck of the slave ship were the Europeans, in contrast with those whom they kept in shackles in the lower deck, whom they called Africans or Negroes. The longest and most horrendous undertaking in modern history, the Atlantic slave system, created the categories in its despotic adventures on the high seas: black and white, African and European. The former was deemed inferior, lazy, heathen, savage, and animal-like; the latter praised as superior, civilized, Christian, rational, handsome, and humane.

We may be more correct to say that the time of Africa's invention was the time of the second invention of European identity. Europe had its first identity not in relation with Africa but rather with Islam. During the eighth century, Europe was considered identical with Western Christendom. By the time Europe came to define itself in relation with the non-European world at large, it had a second identity. Post-Columbian Europe was what made the identities of Africa and African possible.

Historically speaking, the first distinct European identity was born at the Battle of Tours and Poitiers in the year 732 CE At that time Charles Martel stopped the relentless drive of the new faith that intruded on European soil, Islam. Overrunning North Africa from 639–711 CE, the army of Islam crossed into Spain in 711 CE. Two decades later, it was in the land of the Frankish Kingdom. "It was indeed on this occasion that the very notion of Europe as an entity which could be threatened or saved appeared for the first time."[25] In the literary beauty that made his pen immortal, Edward Gibbon wrote,

> A victorious line of march had been prolonged above a thousand miles from the rock of Gibraltar to the banks of the Loire; the repetition of an equal space would have carried the Saracens to the confines of Poland and the Highlands of Scotland; the Rhine is not more impassable than the Nile or Euphrates, and the Arabian fleet might have sailed without a naval combat into the mouth of the Thames. Perhaps the interpretation of the Koran would now be thought in the schools of Oxford, and her pulpits might demonstrate to a circumcised people the sanctity and truth of the revelation of Mohammed. From such calamities was Christendom delivered by the genius and fortune of one man.

That one man was Charles the Hammer. From that historic encounter of two world religions, Europe saw the world as a Manichaean contest between Christendom and the impostor "Moor." So was born Christian Europe's other, Islam. The "Saracens"—as Christian Europe called the conquer-ing Muslim forces—became a name that "every Christian mouth has been taught to pronounce with terror and abhorrence."[26] Charles the Hammer charted and hammered out the moment that gave rise to the birth of West-ern Christendom as a unified conceptual category.[27]

As a geographical space, Africa once denoted a name of a North African Roman province, today's Tunisia. It was, however, during the modern age of empire that Africa became a single continent, the habitat of the "Negro." Africa's spatial boundaries were determined and defined by European car-tography. But even then, pace Hegel and others like him, the northern area was set apart from the rest of the continent.[28] As a concept, Africa is repre-sented as the extreme other of the West. Africa is the West's alter ego. By not being like Africa, the West ascribes its superiority. Africa and the West are mutually inclusive, complementary, oppositional categories. Whoever speaks of Africa speaks of the modern West; and vice versa. Africa is an "idea," as it is an "invention."[29] The West has had the power of inventing and naming geographies, concepts, and peoples around the globe.[30]

Africans incorporated into the rational discourse of the Enlightenment project, the Western-educated elite, challenged Africa's place in the grand project of Western modernity. A good many of these Western-trained African intellectuals represented the deep resentment, rage, and anger felt against the racialized episteme of the modern Western discourse, as well as its lived material realities. They became its negation.[31]

Modern African thought is the representation of Africa by those Africans intellectually incorporated in the cultural discourses of Western modernity during the nineteenth and twentieth centuries.[32] It belongs in part to the global family of revolt against Western imperial hegemony. Yet this revolt stems to a significant degree from within the intellectual and cultural domain premised on validating some critical elements of Western rational-ism, including the idea of progress.[33] This is so in part because the non-Western other finds its identity in the identity of the modern West, which constitutes its difference. It is not a case that the West defines itself first and the non-Western other came later. To the contrary, in the beginning was the simultaneous creation of the West and its non-Western other. Their relation-ship has been in part one of oppositional complementarity.

The term "West" is a conceptual category, not a descriptive term of refer-ence. Eurocentrism created the West as a conceptual field to bracket itself in its alleged distinctiveness from the non-Western other. The West has been presented as on the higher plane of civilization in the scientific, technologi-cal, artistic, and literary realms. The rest of the world is told to catch up or perish. Those that caught up are called modernized, westernized; those that could not or did not catch up are looked down upon and called traditional, exotic, inert, and barbarous.

The relation between the West and the non-Western other is not one where the former is active, the latter passive. On the contrary, as Frantz Fanon clearly saw it, the West is a creation of the non-Western world, that is, without this other, there is no West by whose difference it finds its own identity. And this difference is one of dependence. As Hegel has it in the *Science of Logic*, "Something *preserves* itself in the negative of its determinative being. . . . It is essentially *one* with it and essentially *not one* with it. It stands, therefore, in a *relation* to its otherness and is not simply its otherness. The otherness is at once contained in it and also still *separate* from it; it is a *being-for-other*."[34]

As Orlando Patterson discusses in his works *Slavery and Social Death* and *Freedom*, it was the enslaved Africans' lack of freedom that instilled the idea of the importance of freedom among Europeans, especially in the Americas. It was in relation to the unfree African that the European cherished freedom. It was by reducing Africans to the degradation of slavery that Europeans could brag about how much they value freedom. Enslaved Africans and free Europeans were two of the many agents in the making of the modern world. They both made each other, with unequal power relations, of course. There are not many Enlightenment thinkers who did not comment somehow on African slavery and European freedom. In James Thomson's rendition, the "guardian angels" of Britain sung, "Rule, Britannia, rule the waves / Britons never will be slaves."[35] Blyden's prodigious intellectual productions, spanning over half a century, and their historical significance need to be appraised from the vantage point of such larger global theoretical contexts, concerns, and configurations.

Edward Wilmot Blyden was one of the most sophisticated black intellectuals of the nineteenth century. Hollis Lynch, author of the most important work on Blyden, calls him "the greatest Negro champion of his race in the nineteenth century." Blyden was also perhaps the greatest inconsistent black thinker of modern times. Valentin Mudimbe charged him of "unbelievable inconsistency."[36]

Although Blyden was a seminal figure in the history of black racial nationalism, and although many of his ideas were incorporated later in the writings and perspectives of his intellectual descendants in Africa and the black diaspora in the Americas, there are few books about him. The most learned account of Blyden's life and works to date is Hollis Lynch's 1967 book, *Edward Wilmot Blyden: A Pan-Negro Patriot, 1832–1912*. A year earlier, Edith Holden published her work on Blyden, *Blyden of Liberia: An Account of the Life and Labors of Edward Wilmot Blyden, LL.D. as Recorded in Letters and in Print*. Mudimbe devotes a long brilliant chapter on Blyden in his influential work, *The Invention of Africa*. There are also some articles and dissertations written about Blyden. Yet it is not an exaggeration to say that such a significant figure in the history of black racial nationalism as Blyden has been marginalized and forgotten in the voluminous literature on the subject. There are allusions to him, comments here and there, but not many book-length engagements. In this book, I intend to bring Blyden back from oblivion and engage in an intense critical evaluation of his written works. Along with Lynch and Mudimbe, Wilson Jeremiah Moses is a prominent scholar who has made extensive commentaries on Blyden's intellectual vocation. I begin with Moses, as he provides the historical background and context of Blyden's thought.

In *Classical Black Nationalism: From the American Revolution to Marcus Garvey*, Moses writes, "The essential feature of classical black nationalism is its goal of creating a black nation-state or empire with absolute control over a specific geographical territory, and sufficient economic and military power to defend it."[37] Moses identifies the different spectrums in understanding classical black nationalism as follows:

> In its strictest form, classical black nationalism must be defined as the effort by African Americans to create a modern nation-state with distinct geographical boundaries. In a broader sense, it may indicate a spirit of Pan-African unity and an emotional sense of solidarity with the political and economic struggles of African peoples throughout the world. In a very loose sense, it may refer simply to any feelings of pride in a distinct ethnic heritage. (20)

Moses points out a critical element in classical black nationalism at the heart of the Blydenian paradigm: "Black nationalism during the classical period was invariably obsessed with uplifting and 'civilizing' the race. Black nationalists defined their mission as a movement for 'African civilization.'" He adds, "Pan-Africanism always revealed a concern for the universal cultural improvement of all African peoples, and the desire to bring modern economic, industrial, and military development to the African continent" (20–21).

Central to classical black nationalism, a theme of critical significance in Blyden's paradigm as well, was the role and place of God in history. Moses writes, "The major proponents of classical black nationalism in the nineteenth century invariably believed that the hand of God directed their movement. Their religious beliefs led to a black nationalist conception of history in which Divine Providence would guide the national destiny to an early fulfillment, once the work was taken up" (2–3).

Moses points out to the historic rationality of classical black nationalism: "to its adherents it provided a means of preserving shreds of dignity and self-respect in the face of the almost universal military, technological, and economic domination by whites over blacks. With its religious optimism, black nationalism met the need for psychological resistance to the slavery, colonialism, and racism imposed by Europeans and white Americans." Regarding the cultural terrain of classical black nationalism, Moses identifies a very important point, one that was shared to a great degree by Blyden himself: "Ironically, the cultural ideals of nineteenth-century black nationalists usually resembled those of upper-class Europeans and white Americans, rather than those of the native African or African American masses. Classical black nationalists were quick to claim an ancestral connection with Egypt and Ethiopia" (3).

Moses distinguishes between nineteenth-century classical black nationalism from that of the late twentieth century. The "nationalism of Alexander Crummell and Marcus Garvey was situated in a 'high culture' aesthetic, which admired symbols of imperial power, military might, and aristocratic refinement." By contrast, "Post-Garveyite nationalism . . . has tended to idealize African village life, sentimentalize the rural South, and romanticize the urban ghetto" (3).

As we are to see in this book, Blyden combines both aspects of cultural nationalism: the version of what Ali Mazrui called "romantic gloriana," awe-struck and proud of African "high cultures" like Egypt and Ethiopia, and "romantic primitivism," the "simple" life of the African.[38] Blyden is too complex, too contradictory, and too stretched out in many directions to be wrapped in a single package. Harold Cruse writes in *The Crisis of the Negro Intellectual*, "American Negro history is basically a history of the conflict between integrationist and nationalist forces in politics, economics, and culture, no matter what leaders are involved and what slogans are used."[39] Without getting into a debate with Cruse about this sweeping statement, we can say that Blyden was both: an "integrationist" who believed in the need for the black race to appropriate the positive aspects of Western modernity, and a "nationalist" who was an ardent and indefatigable champion of black racial nationalism.

Moses singles out Blyden among all the classical black nationalists: "Classical black nationalism has its most influential defender in Edward Wilmot Blyden."[40] In his *Afrotopia: The Roots of African American Popular History*, Moses writes that Blyden was a "true Afrocentrist. He was not, however, an Egyptocentrist, although he did believe that the pyramid builders had been black. But among the voluminous writings of Blyden, we find very little about Egypt." Moses explains, "His Afrocentrism was far more concerned with promoting the Back to Africa movement, the establishment of Liberia and Sierra Leone, and the study of West African peoples and customs. Blyden devoted far more energy to mastering contemporary African languages than to rhapsodizing on pharaonic glories."[41]

Moses finds Blyden a man of contradictions, torn between the defense of African cultures on the one hand and the belief in the ideology of progress on the other:

Among the Afrocentrists who had come to prominence in the mid-nineteenth century, he was among the few who had demonstrated an interest in the systematic study of African cultures, and only he seemed to be on the road to discovering relativistic multiculturalism. His view was seemingly contradicted by his belief in progress, but that did not seem to bother him; like most of us, he contained many contradictions. He was a cultural relativist who apologized for tribal polytheism, but he never completely repudiated the Protestantism of his youth. And he remained highly respectful of Islam, which he considered a progressive force. . . . Society, in his view, was advancing inexorably, like a railroad, whose steel rails and telegraph wires must meet on the horizon of a progressive utopia with no place for racism.

Moses pursues the line that Blyden, like his contemporaries, was not a cultural relativist but rather a believer in societal gradations of high and low cultures. Blyden and his "Afrocentric" peers "were committed to a civilizing mission. They made references to Egyptian civilization hoping to focus the minds of black folk on noble and uplifting universal values. . . . They were not cultural relativists; they believed that some cultures are better than other cultures."[42]

Moses turns Blyden around again, this time highlighting his embrace of cultural relativism:

Blyden, unlike Douglass, did not view progress as synonymous with the advancement of science, and was even willing—like the negritude poets of the 1920s—to abandon the field of modern science to the European. Blyden believed that progress for Africa and the black race must be developed along African lines. This was the reason for his defense of African "communism," and, to the disapproval of African American feminist intellectuals like Anna Julia Cooper, polygyny and clitorectomy.[43]

While it is true that Blyden defends polygamy in his *African Life and Customs*, he does not defend clitorectomy. Moses seems to make such statement by deduction: if Blyden defends African customs, he must also have defended clitorectomy. Blyden does not say anything regarding the practice, at least not in *African Life and Customs*, which Hollis Lynch identifies as Blyden's "most significant work after *Christianity, Islam, and the Negro Race*." It is "the first attempt at a sociological analysis of African society as a whole."[44]

In Moses's major study, *Alexander Crummell: A Study of Civilization and Discontent*, he compares Blyden with Crummell regarding the question of cultural relativism. He states that Blyden "had far greater tolerance for African traditions and customs than Crummell could ever muster." He adds, "While Blyden never completely abandoned the Eurocentric and Christian biases of his youth, he recognized that it would be impossible to develop a West African civilization if one did not cultivate an appreciation for the indigenous languages and cultures. To this end, he busied himself with the study of African languages. As many as forty have been attributed to him."[45] Moses's statement,

"Blyden never completely abandoned the Eurocentric and Christian biases of his youth," is a theme critical to my appraisal of Blyden in this work.

While both Crummell and Blyden see the need for the assimilation of Africa to Western modernity, "Crummell saw assimilation as a one-way street. Africans, like Afro-Americans, must become Europeanized. Blyden was no less 'Civilizationist,' no less 'Europhile,' than Crummell, but neither that, nor the fact that Blyden was an ordained Christian minister, prevented his recognizing the importance of Islamic or indigenous tribal culture to the future of Africa."[46] In this sense, Léopold Sédar Senghor is undoubtedly closer to Blyden than Crummell. As is covered in the epilogue, he raises this same question of one-way assimilation, opting instead for a two-way assimilation between Africa and Europe. Overall, Moses's reflections on Blyden show us the many contradictions that undergird Blyden's worldview.

In *Edward Wilmot Blyden*, Hollis Lynch identifies the historical conditions that undergirded Blyden's paradigm: "perhaps the greatest wrong inflicted on the Negro race in the nineteenth century was the successful building up of a myth that the Negro was inherently inferior to other races—a myth that had been originally elaborated in an attempt to justify Negro slavery, and later, European imperialism in Africa." He locates Blyden in this context of contempt and degradation, and in his struggle to overcome it.[47] Lynch identifies what "Blyden's philosophy of history was: the inscrutable working of a Divine Providence for the ultimate good of the Negro Race." This position, which Lynch calls "theocratic determinism," has made Blyden "maintain ridiculous positions," such as the role of divine providence in the enslavement of Africans in the Americas (79–80).

Lynch sees Blyden as being more than a "Negro" prophet. He is above all a first-rate intellectual. "Blyden was one of a few Negroes to make a significant impact on the English-speaking literary and scholastic world in the nineteenth century" (54). He goes on to say,

> More than any other Negro in the nineteenth century, Blyden's writings and scholarship had won him widespread recognition and respect in the English-speaking literary world, as well as acclaim in the Muslim world. His outstanding literary reputation, his vast learning and catholicity of interest, his charm and sophistication, his brilliance in conversation, and eloquence as a speaker, combined to create a great demand for him as a lecturer, contributor to learned journals, or as the honoured guest of litterateurs on his visits to Britain and America, particularly after the publication of *Christianity, Islam, and the Negro Race* in 1887. (81)

In *The Invention of Africa: Gnosis, Philosophy, and the Order of Knowledge*, Mudimbe devotes one long chapter to Blyden, calling him "one of the most careful students of African affairs."[48] (98–99). For Mudimbe, Blyden was "a strange and exceptional man, who devoted his entire life to the cause he believed in" (129). He refers to Blyden's "paradoxical and romantic paradigm" (109), "complexity" (110), and "originality" (124).

Mudimbe focuses on Blyden's racial views, which at times he calls "racist." As an example, he refers to Blyden's views regarding "mulattoes" (104–5). He further charges, "Blyden simply opposed one racist view to another racist view, precisely by emphasizing anti-mythologies on Africans, their cultures, and the necessity of unmixed Negro blood" (130). He writes that "Blyden's theory of race makes excellent sense" when it relates to the views of Arthur Gobineau and others (119). Mudimbe retorts, "The frame of his [Blyden's] thinking was a 'traditional' one and may be summed up in three propositions: a racial opposition (white vs. black), a cultural confrontation (civilized vs. savage) and a religious distance (Christianity vs. paganism). His racial theory was simply a relativization of the supposed superiority of the categories white, civilized, and Christian" (129).

But Blyden's "race theory" is not a "simple" case of relativization. Yes, he took his ideas about race from the worldview of his time, primarily from whites. But, there was no "Negro" intellectual of Blyden's time that did not use the race category to fight against racism. Just as much, feminists fight gender oppression by rallying behind their gender, as workers fight for their rights around their common identity, class.

Mudimbe provides us with an assessment of Blyden that belies a simple labeling. From Mudimbe's own admission, we see how Blyden was both an inheritor of racial views that sprouted before, during, and after his lifetime. Per Mudimbe, Blyden was in the company of powerful black names and republics. "Blyden worked on racial issues in the nineteenth century. In order to oppose racist mythologies, he focused on 'the virtues of black civilization' and promoted the concepts of 'blackness' and 'Negro personality,' thus inventing positive new myths about race and the black personality." Blyden's ideas "were incorporated in W. E. B. Dubois's Pan-Africanist ideology, and in the 1930s they were important in the genesis of the negritude movement in Paris" (131).

Mudimbe identifies what makes Blyden's idea of race distinct: "Blyden's perspective is particular. His political ideology arose as a response to racism and to some of the consequences of imperialism. It represents an emotional response to the European process of denigrating Africa and an opposition to the exploitation that resulted from the expansionism of Europe from the fifteenth century." He states that Blyden's thesis, "distinct but equal," was "the first articulate nineteenth-century theory of 'blackness'" (132). He rightly adds, "The fundamental theme in Blyden's writings is that Africans, from a historical point of view, constitute a universe apart and have their own history and traditions. This point is worth analyzing, since the European nineteenth-century literature on Africa emphasized this point too, but in a different way" (107).

He sees Blyden's political philosophy and historical project as having been affected by African enslavement in the Americas. "Blyden's ideology is, however, mostly determined by a profound understanding of the burden of slavery. It is as a negation of this experience that Blyden recommends a role for Black Americans in the modernization of Africa" (132). Yet Blyden himself was not affected by slavery. Indeed, he was "of relatively privileged birth. Both his [parents] were free and literate."[49]

In *Invention of Africa*, Mudimbe identifies three major themes in Blyden: "the basic organized community under Muslim leadership, the concept of the African nation, and, finally, the idea of the unity of the [African] continent" (114).[50] He would still say, "The concept of the African nation is perhaps the most puzzling, but also the most original one, in Blyden's writings" (115). He agrees with the view that Blyden was "the founder of African nationalism and Pan-Africanism" (117) and that Blyden's "Pan-Africanism is a sort of prophetism" (116). He closes, "Despite its inconsistencies, Blyden's political vision is probably the first proposal by a black man to elaborate the benefits of an independent, modern political structure for the continent [of Africa]" (117–18). Overall, he finds Blyden's works to be "contradicting each other and accounting for philosophical inconsistencies, racist propositions, and political opportunisms" (130).

Blyden was a pioneer in the ideology of black racial nationalism, including Pan-Africanism.[51] Nowadays, it is also known as black internationalism.[52] His is a discourse of racial nationalist imagination, wherein race and nation were imagined as being congruent.[53] For Blyden, Africa is the site of the black race nation, and the African American is the historic agent making the project of the black race nation feasible.

Blyden's racial nationalist paradigm did not sprout out of nowhere, nor did it develop out of the mind of a solitary thinker. Instead, Blyden's paradigm has a long historical grounding. Although this historical grounding is not covered in this work, I refer to an example of one significant figure in the history of nineteenth-century black nationalism whose ideas found fertile reception in Blyden: Martin Delany.[54]

Delany presented a fascinating and quite sophisticated paper titled "Political Destiny of the Colored Race, on the American Continent," at the National Emigration Convention of Colored People, held on August 24, 1854, in Cleveland, Ohio. There he proclaimed the central paradigm of black nationalism:

> Let it then be understood, as a great principle of political economy, that no people can be free who themselves do not constitute an essential part of the *ruling element* of the country in which they live. . . . The liberty of no man is secure, who controls not his own political destiny. What is true of an individual, is true of a family; and that which is true of a family, is also true concerning a

whole people. To suppose otherwise, is that delusion which at once induces its victim, through a period of long suffering, patiently to submit to every species of wrong. . . . This delusion reveals the true secret of the power which holds in peaceable subjection, all the oppressed in every part of the world.[55]

Delany further reveals his lucid intellectual sophistication when he states, "A people, to be free, must necessarily be *their own rulers*: that is, *each individual* must, in himself, embody the *essential ingredient*—so to speak—of the *sovereign principle* which composes the *true basis* of his liberty. This principle, when not exercised by himself, may, at his pleasure, be delegated to another— his true representative." Delany makes it abundantly clear that there can be no political right that is not based on freedom and sovereignty. As he eloquently puts it,

> No one, then, can delegate to another a power he never possessed; that is, he cannot *give an agency* in that which he never had a right. Consequently, the colored man in the United States, being deprived of the right of inherent sovereignty, cannot *confer* a suffrage, because he possesses none to confer. Therefore, where there is no suffrage, there can neither be *freedom* nor *safety* for the disfranchised. And it is a futile hope to suppose that the agent of another's concerns, will take a proper interest in the affairs of those to whom he is under no obligations. Having no favors to ask or expect, he therefore has none to lose.[56]

For Delany, black nationalism means black power, and black power means first and foremost black sovereign political power, nothing short of black independence. The idea of sovereign black power was Blyden's central, life-long political project. In this, Blyden was a follower of Delany. For both Delany and Blyden, an inseparable link was established between the black race and the black nation such that their nationalism becomes black racial nationalism.

Delany, like Blyden, was vehemently opposed to the hierarchical gradations of racial classification into superior and inferior races. In *The Origin of Races and Color*, first published in 1879, Delany critiques the theory of multiple origins of the human species. He reiterates the unity of the human species and accepted racial distinctions within the human family, but not the racist ascription of one race as essentially superior and another inferior.

Like Blyden later, Delany penned powerful indictments against American civilization for its treatment of the "Negro." In his most famous work, *The Condition, Elevation, Emigration and Destiny of the Colored People of the United States, Politically Considered*, published in 1852, Delany deconstructs the amorphous, ambiguous, and hypocritical underpinnings of the American social order:

The United States, untrue to her trust and unfaithful to her professed principles of republican equality, has also pursued a policy of political degradation to a large portion of native born countrymen, and that class of people is the Colored people. Denied an equality not only political but of natural rights, in common with the rest of our fellow citizens, there is no species of degradation to which we are not subject.[57]

Like Blyden's observations later on, Delany critiques the white cultural hegemony under which black people were ruled, including the sphere of historical knowledge: "The colored people are not yet known, even to their most professed friends among the white Americans; for the reason, that politicians, religionists, colonizationists, and abolitionists, have each and all, at different times, presumed to *think* better what suited colored people, than they knew themselves; and consequently, there has been no knowledge of them obtained, than that which has been obtained through these mediums."[58]

Delany, leaving the focus on the black race, makes the case that the "colored races" have a major role to play in the future of world history. Theirs was unique, one that the materially driven Western world was unable to accomplish:

That the colored races have the highest traits of civilization, will not be disputed. They are civil, peaceable and religious to a fault. In mathematics, sculpture and architecture, as arts and sciences, commerce and internal improvements as enterprises, the white race may probably excel: but in languages, oratory, poetry, music and painting as arts and sciences, and in ethics, metaphysics, theology and legal jurisprudence; in plain language—in the true principles of morals, correctness of thought, religion, and law or civil government, there is no doubt but the black race will yet instruct the world.[59]

Three decades after Delany's death, and three years after that of Blyden, the most brilliant black intellectual of the twentieth century, W. E. B. Du Bois, echoed Delany's writings. In his work, *The Negro*, published in 1915, he wrote, "Most men in this world are colored. A belief in humanity means a belief in colored men. The future world will, in all reasonable probability, be what colored men make it."[60] As far back as 1915, Du Bois had the "prophetic" brilliance of seeing that the "racial" themes in the "colored" peoples' struggles were anything but racist. Perhaps his most famous quote in *The Souls of Black Folk*, published in 1903, reads, "The problem of the twentieth century is the problem of the color-line,—the relation of the darker to the lighter races of men in Asia and Africa, in America and the islands of the sea."[61] As I write, the son of an African scholarship student from Kenya to America is presiding over the United States. Needless to say, the son of an

African sitting in the White House is an important event in American history. Perhaps, it is time that the White House is called the Grey House. We are in many ways still ensnared in the color code, the color line. Postracial America is a project for the future; it is not a reality, yet.[62]

Blyden is perhaps the most pertinent expression of the contradictions and paradoxes of the encounter of the black world with Western white Christian bourgeois modernity. His voluminous writings laid the groundwork for some of the most important ideas of black intellectuals in the twentieth century, including Fanon, Nkrumah, Nyerere, Cabral, Senghor, Garvey, and Césaire, to cite but a few, and he himself is one of the few original and provocative black Atlantic thinkers of modern times.

Blyden's prodigious intellectual labor spans nearly six decades. In the larger contour of modern black world history, it covers the period from Dred Scott in America (1856–57) to the founding of the African National Congress in South Africa (1912). In 1855–56, Blyden was the editor of the *Liberia Herald*, and in 1856 he wrote that heart-wrenching piece on black suffering, *A Voice from Bleeding Africa on Behalf of Her Exiled Children*. Blyden lived and wrote in one of the most crucial periods in the history of the modern world, especially that relating to Africans and the African diaspora.

Blyden had a deep reverence for the historical. As he puts it, "A true respect for the past—a consciousness of a real national history—has not only a binding force but a stimulating effect, and furnishes a guarantee of future endurance and growth. That which has been achieved in the past is a prophecy of what may be done in the future."[63] This historicized epistemology undergirds Blyden's perspective of the most important vocation of his life, the "uplifting" of the Negro race.

Two momentous events that had tremendous and life-changing experiences for the black world took place during Blyden's life: the US Civil War and the European colonial scramble for and occupation of Africa. Blyden was a contemporary of some of the most prominent black Atlantic intellectuals on both sides of the ocean. He was the intellectual and temporal peer of such people as Alexander Crummell, Martin Delany, Henry McNeal Turner, Booker T. Washington, and Frederick Douglass in the Americas, and Samuel Ajayi Crowther and J. E. Casely Hayford in West Africa.[64] He crossed swords with almost all these names from the American side of the Atlantic.

Blydenism is the most sophisticated articulation of black racial nationalism. As in all forms of nationalist discourses, Blyden's racial nationalism is replete with strongly conceived convictions, contradictions, allusions, emissions, silences, and, of course, illusions. After all, what is nationalism without a certain degree of illusion, of beliefs worth living by and, if need be, dying for? Whatever variations of nationalist articulations prominent black intellectuals may have held since Blyden's death, the overarching ideological and philosophical underpinnings were Blydenian.

Blyden articulated the idea of Africa as a single race nation. For him, Africa is the natural home of the black race, the natural grounding of African nationalism. To speak of African nationalism may be problematic, since Africa is a continent, not a nation. Nevertheless, as prominent scholars on nationalism such as Ernest Gellner and Benedict Anderson inform us, it is not nations that create nationalism, but nationalism that imagines and creates nations and national identities.[65] It is in that sense that black intellectuals imagined, elaborated, and formulated the African nation, and thus African nationalism, articulating the idea of an African identity.[66]

At the conceptual level, African nationalism is the articulation of a compressed identity of disparate but similar experiences of the oppression of Africans due to their location in the modern world-system in general and in the racial colonial context in particular. African nationalism as expressed in the words and actions of intellectuals such as Blyden is an articulation of oppressed, repressed, and suppressed identities. By expressing oppressed identities, African nationalism itself suppresses other subidentities within. African nationalism is a giant compressor valve; it crushes non-African individualities, derogating them to the ignoble status of tribalism. After all, how can African nationalism be African without violating the legitimate voices from within, voices of otherness, be they based on regional, religious, ethnic, clan, gender, class, or other identities within Africa? As African nationalism winds down, other subidentities can raise their distinct voices. These national identities are what are mistakenly called "tribalism."

In Blyden, the distinct and different voices of Africa are muzzled for the good of a higher universal singular unity, pan-Africanism or pan-Negroism. To be heard in the world, to find a place for Africa under the sun of modern civilization, Blyden underplays the distinct voices within Africa and creates one single African voice, demanding, "Here we stand. Count us as one among humanity's many faces!" Blyden is the most systematic blender of Africa's internal distinctions. He places the canon of Africanity in the framework of modernity discourse. Blyden's paradigm is totalizing; it transcends nonracial difference just as it builds on racial totalization. Blyden downplays distinctions within the black race as much as he highlights distinctions among the various races. He is adamantly opposed to anything that blends races; in the same way, he is for the transcendence of ethnic and regional differences for the sake of a higher calling, the well-being of the black race. I call Blyden's perspective "black racial nationalism," a project of black racial totalization.

What is remarkable about Blyden is that he was not just a black racial nationalist. More than any other black intellectual born in the Americas who made Africa his home, he took deep interest in the prolific mosaic of differences that was Africa. He spoke dozens of African languages, including Arabic, so that he could communicate with Africans in their own tongue.

For Blyden, Africa is not an idea suspended in midair. Africa is, rather, Africas, in the plural. Africa is a continent of linguistic, cultural, religious, and regional differences, and he studied these differences. Just as he indefatigably fought for the racial dignity of the African race, he never fell into the lazy temptation of collapsing all Africans into the simplistic category of being just one people. Blyden wanted and succeeded in having it both ways: he identified what makes the African one but also acknowledged that this oneness contains the beauty of multifarious differences.

Blyden's pan-Africanism, his black racial nationalism, was not abstract but informed by the recognition of the concrete, lived experiences of the African peoples. For Blyden, Africans inhabit two domains: (1) as one people, they belong to the same "Negro" race, spread out around the globe, with Africa as their home base; and (2) Africans are Temne, Mandingo, Fulah, Asante, Fanti, and so on. They are Muslim, Christian, or followers of traditional African religions. Part of his acrimony against the "mulatto" in Liberia was that they declined to link up with the people of the interior. Unlike the later-day black nationalists who could not see beyond Africa in its undifferentiated abstraction, Blyden could not only spell the names of Africans but also speak many West African languages, the best testimony to his willingness to know Africans in their actual, concrete human diversities, not as a mere aggregate united by a common race category. In short, Blyden's black racial nationalism can better be called "concrete black racial nationalism."

Another pertinent issue that undergirds Blyden's grand opus is the black diasporic imagination, a longing for the ancestral home from which the American black was snatched away by force. That home was Africa, which without further determination, becomes the abstract universal home of the black diaspora. The black diasporic imagination claims the whole continent of Africa as the home of the "homeless," of black exiles forced to cross the Atlantic by brute force. This imagination is a project of rejecting the native homeland in which one was born and raised, with the longing after a homeland one does not know. It is a rejection of lived nativity and the longing for the ancestral nativity. It is a sort of reverse "natal alienation." To the natal alienation that accompanied enslavement, this reverse natal alienation rejects its homeliness in the Americas and aspires for a home away from home, Africa.[67] It aspires for a reversed Middle Passage. This time, unlike the earlier Middle Passage that was nothing but a scene of unimaginable horror, it was to be a happy one—a voyage back to the land of the ancestors.[68] It may come as a surprise, even a painful shock, to discover that the black diasporic imagination may be in the main a one-way aspiration—from the Americas to Africa.[69] No one addressed the black diasporic imagination and the search for return to the black ancestral homeland more than Blyden, that brilliant, contradictory, and indefatigable "race patriot."[70] Blyden was for the nineteenth century what Du Bois was for the twentieth.

Blyden's paradigm is constructed from three basic ideas: a Jeremiah-like lamentation describing in detail the pains, agonies, sufferings, and woes of Africans and African-descended peoples in the Americas in modern world history; a passionate and unwavering belief in the need for African "upliftment," or development and progress; and the call for the black diaspora to carry out a "civilizing mission" in Africa. These three bases of Blyden's paradigm can be condensed into one overall perspective, black racial nationalism.

The book contains six chapters. Chapter 1 deals with Blyden's notion that throughout their history, the calling of Africans had been to serve humanity. This service had produced suffering and subjection. Yet this was not to be lamented; rather, it was to be appraised positively. To serve humanity is the highest calling. It is akin to Jesus's service of humanity, and his suffering thereof. Such was the philosophical vantage point from which Blyden addressed the monumental sufferings that took place in the Atlantic crimes against African humanity.

In chapter 2, I discuss Blyden's critique of Eurocentrism, especially in the cultural sphere. Although Blyden did not use the term "Eurocentrism," as the term did not exist then, what he critiqued is the same phenomenon. Blyden produced a sophisticated, critical compendium of views and reflections about the black world that anticipated in remarkable depth the writings of such seminal figures as Aimé Césaire, Frantz Fanon, and Amilcar Cabral by many decades.

Chapter 3 covers Blyden's euphoric embrace of Islam, despite his being Protestant. Blyden had a high regard for the religion. He saw it as a "civilizing" force in Africa, one that fit the African character better than Western Christianity defined by missionaries. Blyden's embrace of Islam was not, however, an acceptance of its being equal with Christianity. Like Hegel before him, Blyden saw Islam as being an intermediary between indigenous African religions and Christianity, with Christianity being the highest and most perfect religion.

Chapter 4 addresses Blyden's central political vocation, aspiration, and project—the introduction of "civilization" into Africa through the agency of African American emigration to Africa via the gateway of Liberia. Blyden believed in the "black man's burden," that Africa could not be civilized without outside intervention. He advocated people of African descent in the Americas to be the agents of such a civilizing mission.

Chapter 5 deals with Blyden's other prominent preoccupation, his uncompromising animosity toward the "mulatto," especially in Liberia, but also in the Americas. He tirelessly advanced the ideology that racially mixed people were unsuitable for both Africa and "racial science." He pleaded with the American Colonization Society and other agencies that sponsored African American emigration to Liberia to stop sending mulattoes. His choice was for "full blooded Negroes" like himself. In this chapter, we see the extent to which Blyden embraced the most racist doctrines of his time, including the idea that race mixing leads to degeneration of both races.

In chapter 6 I show how Blyden, at the end of his life, both supported European colonial rule in Africa and defended wholesome African "life and customs." Blyden reasoned that European colonial rule in Africa would dissipate the "darkness" that hitherto engulfed the continent and introduce the light of civilization, Christianity, and commerce. As such, he welcomed it. Nay, he worked for it. The book closes with an epilogue discussing the ideas, imaginations, and political projects of some of the most important African and black diasporic thinkers of the twentieth century: Léopold Sédar Senghor, Kwame Nkrumah, Julius Nyerere, Amilcar Cabral, Chiekh Anta Diop, and Frantz Fanon. The chapter presents the central ideas of these African intellectuals. I highlight ideas articulated by Blyden that are to be discerned in the works of these intellectuals. I show the Blydenian ideas they have embraced, reformulated, or transcended. One of the most important Blydenian idea found in the works of these intellectuals is in the cultural sphere: how Western imperial cultural hegemony has resulted in the cultural deracination of Western-educated Africans from their African roots. This theme is of critical importance in the writings of Fanon, Cabral, Senghor, and Diop. These intellectuals, like Blyden, were formidable voices in articulating ideas in the field of "cultural studies" long before the field bearing that name came to play a prominent role in Western academia.

1

Africa

Service, Suffering, and Subjection

The glory of the African thus far has been the glory of suffering—the glory of the cross—the glory of the Son of Man—the man of sorrows and acquainted with grief. But the future will have a different story to tell. The Cross precedes the Crown.

—Blyden, *Study and Race*

Blyden sees the history of Africans as a history of serving humanity, both materially and spiritually. Indeed, he is of the opinion that the glory of Africa lies in serving humanity.[1] This view is central to Blyden's philosophy of history. As a Christian minister, he draws parallels between the trials and tribulations of Jesus and that of the Africans. He writes, "If service rendered to humanity is service rendered to God, then the Negro and his country have been, during the ages, in spite of unwanted influences, tending upward to the Divine."[2] As such, "Shem and Japheth have largely participated in the guilt of the enslavement of Ham. Shem, having lagged behind Japheth in the march of enlightenment, persists in the perpetration of the hideous wrong. But, under pressure, the dilatory brother is being urged on to his duty" (323).[3] He further states that although all races have passed through the fire of slavery as part of their journey toward civilization, no one had suffered as much from it as Africans. "Africa has been spoiled by all the races alien to her, and, under their stimulating example, by her own sons. Other races have passed through the baptism of slavery, as a stepping-stone to civilization and independence, but none has toiled under the crushing weight of a servitude so protracted and inflicted from so many sources." He adds,

Millenniums mark the period of bondage and humiliation of Africa's children. The four quarters of the globe have heard their groans and been sprinkled and strained with their blood. All that passed by have felt at liberty to contemn and plunder. The oppressors of this race [Negroes] have been men with religion, and men without religion—Christians, Mohammedans, and Pagans. Nations with the Bible, and nations with the Koran, and nations without Bible or Koran—all have joined in afflicting this continent. And now the last of her oppressors, tearing from her bosom annually half a million of her children, are nations with the Koran. (323–24)

Even as he writes about the participation of the descendants of Shem and Japheth in the oppression of the African, Blyden reminds the reader that Africa's blood flows in the veins of many prominent men of religious distinction.

A slave and an African was the mother of Ishmael, the progenitor of the founder and first followers of Islam. Shem and Ham unite in Mohammed. Instances of the union of Shem and Ham are frequent in Holy writ. We have Joseph and the Priestess of On; Moses and the Ethiopian woman; Solomon and Pharaoh's daughter. They have been together in ruling and in serving, on the throne and in the dungeon. (355)

To depict Africa's service to humanity, Blyden compares the African with those who rule, the Anglo-Saxon. "The Negro is, at this moment, the opposite of the Anglo-Saxon. Those everywhere serve the world; these everywhere govern the world. The empire of the one is more wide-spread than that of any other nation; the service of the other is more wide-spread than that of any other people." He further writes,

The Negro is found in all parts of the world. . . . He is everywhere a familiar object, and he is, everywhere out of Africa, the servant of others. And in the light of the ultimate good of the universe, I do not see why the calling of the one should be considered the result of a curse, and the calling of the other the result of a special favour. The one fulfills its mission by domination, the other by submission. The one serves mankind by ruling; the other serves mankind by serving. The one wears the crown and wields the sceptre; the other bears the stripes and carries the cross. (138–39)

To serve others is not demeaning; neither is to dominate.

Africa is distinguished as having served and *suffered*. In this, her lot is not unlike that of God's ancient people, the Hebrews, who were known among the Egyptians as the servants of all. . . . The lot of Africa resembles also His who made Himself of no reputation, but took upon Himself the form of a servant, and, having been made perfect through suffering, became the "Captain of our salvation." And if the principle laid down by Christ is that by which things are decided above, viz., that he who would be chief must become the servant of all, then we see the position which Africa and the Africans must ultimately occupy. And we must admit that through serving man, Africa—Ethiopia—has been stretching out her hands unto God. (139)

The African served in suffering; suffered in serving. He did not dominate. The African's "hands are free from the blood of other men. He has not in any way oppressed other races. He has suffered, *and that is all.* He has been scattered and peeled, despoiled and plundered, abused, persecuted, and down-trodden, *and that is all*" (161).

For Blyden, Africans have nothing in their history to be ashamed of.

> Tell me, now, ye descendants of Africa, tell me whether there is anything in the ancient history of your African ancestors, in their relation to other races, of which you need to be ashamed. Tell me if there is anything in the modern history of your people, in their dealings with foreign races, whether at home or in exile, of which you need to be ashamed? If there is anything, when you compare yourselves with others, to disturb your equanimity, except the universal oppression of which you have been the victims? (186)

Blyden then makes the following philosophical and theological argument: "And what are suffering and sorrow but necessary elements in the progress of humanity? Your suffering has contributed to the welfare of others. It is a part of the constitution of the universe, that out of death should come life. All the advancement made to a better future, by individuals or races, has been made through paths marked by suffering" (186).

Blyden here raises a critical but contradictory point regarding the price Africans pay for progress, both theirs and others they serve. On the one hand, Africans' suffering produces the progress of others. But on the other hand, the suffering of Africans could also lead to their own progress. In many of his writings, he makes the case that African enslavement in the Americas was a school in the civilization and progress of Africans themselves.

Africa's service and suffering under the domination of others took a most dehumanizing form during the era of capitalist modernity. Here Africa served as the pillar on which Western prosperity was built. Africa served by rendering its children to the inferno of American slavery. The "slaves exported to America have profoundly influenced civilisation. The political history of the United States is the history of the Negro. The commercial and agricultural history of nearly the whole America is the history of the Negro" (137). Blyden writes of Africans' contribution to the rise of Western modernity,

> He who writes the history of modern civilisation will be culpably negligent if he omit to observe and to describe the black stream of humanity, which has poured into America from the heart of the Soudan. That stream has fertilised half the Western continent. It has created commerce and influenced its progress. It has affected culture and morality in the Eastern and Western hemispheres, and has been the means of transforming European colonies into a great nationality. Nor can it be denied that the material development of England was aided greatly by means of this same dark stream. By means of Negro

labour sugar and tobacco were produced; by means of sugar and tobacco British commerce was increased; by means of increased commerce the arts of culture and refinement were developed. The rapid growth and unparalleled prosperity of Lancashire are, in part, owing to the cotton supply of the Southern States, which could not have risen to such importance without the labor of the African.[4] (136–37)

In the aftermath of the decimation of Native Americans, Africans provided the labor needed for the development of the Americas. When the "despairing cries of a moribund population reached the ears of the sympathetic in Europe, the Negro with his patience, his stronger physical qualities, and his superior powers of endurance, was thought of." Heeding to this call, "Africa, the grey-haired mother of civilisation," picked up the burden of labor, working the "newly-discovered country, and thus contribut[ing] towards the development of modern civilisation, and towards making this almost boundless territory what it is now." In short, "The discovery of America without Africa," Blyden writes, "would have been comparatively useless" (136). With a trenchant look at the political economy of modern global capitalism, he writes, "And now that Europe is exhausting itself by over-production, it is to Africa that men look to furnish new markets" (137).

Blyden evokes the role of enslaved black women in raising white children in America. They rocked the cradle of some of the most powerful men in American history. "The greatest statesmen whom the United States have produced were produced in the South—men who chiefly governed the country until the great Civil War—George Washington, Thomas Jefferson, James Madison, James Monroe, and all that followed, including Jefferson Davis, John C. Calhoun, and Robert E. Lee." Indeed, "These men all had black 'mammies,' and to this day in the South the traditions of the old 'Aunties' linger among the most cherished memories of the aristocratic families." To highlight the critical significance of enslaved black women in the "cultivation" of such powerful men in American history, Blyden retorts, "But since the Black 'Auntie' has disappeared from her post in the great families, and has ceased to preside at the cradle and in the nursery of the South, no such men have appeared as distinguished the history of that country before 'the late unpleasantness.' The secret of this deficiency is known to the African."[5]

Blyden's grasp of global capitalism is quite sophisticated. Sounding similar to the contemporary discourse of globalization, he writes, "Upon the opening of Africa will depend the continuation of the prosperity of Europe. Thus Providence has interwoven the interests of Europe with those of Africa. What will bring light and improvement, peace and security, to thousands of women and children in Africa, will bring food and clothing to thousands of women and children in Europe."[6]

Blyden was Africa's Jeremiah.[7] He expresses most of Africa's lamentations, the depth of its infinite sorrow. These lamentations come out most strongly in two of his works: a collection of pieces written at different times published under the title *Liberia's Offering* and the powerful, fertile, evocative, heart-wrenching, passionate, and sometime contradictory ideas packed in the compact, brilliant thirty-three-page discourse, *A Voice from Bleeding Africa on Behalf of Her Exiled Children.*

In *Liberia's Offering* Blyden begins his account with the Western concept of Africa, the grounding, so to speak, in which Africa was made the object of systemic contempt. "To the majority of civilized and enlightened men, Africa is hardly ever made as subject of earnest thought. Various interests of more immediate concern crowd out thoughts of a land which is spoken of, perhaps, only when instances of degradation, ignorance, and superstition are referred to." In such views, Africa becomes transformed into a concept of contempt. (It is disheartening that to this day, such images abound in the intellectual and popular depictions of Africa.) Others view Africa from either a commercial point of view or a spiritual point of view, to harvest souls. The former, with "souls more sordid and hearts more various, who are never troubled by any sentiment of humanity, are interested in Africa only as a scene for plunder and carnage." From them, "Africa has had the most frequent and the most constant visits, during the last three centuries. They have spread all along the coast of that peninsula—formerly the abode of peace and plenty, of industry and love—'arrows, firebrands, and death.' In their pursuit of blood—'not beasts but human gore'—they have scattered desolation, and misery, and degradation into all parts of the land whither they have had access."[8] Thanks to the "cruel chase of the slaver," an "insurmountable and impenetrable barrier—some wall of mountain height— might be erected between his [African's] country and all civilized nations." Going to the heart of the racist degradation of African humanity, he notes,

> Only a few, very few, have regarded Africa as a land inhabited by human beings, children of the same common Father, travelers to the same judgment—seat of Christ, and heirs of the same awful immortality. These few have endeavored to hold up that land as the object of the sympathy, the labors, and the prayers of the Christian World. They have held her up as the victim of unfortunate circumstances, which have operated against her progress, and prevented her from keeping pace, in the march of human improvement, with other and more favored portions of the earth. (7)

Blyden admired those "civilized men" who were interested not just in Africa's land but in the African people. He praised their hard work in making the African known to the Western world. "Through their noble efforts, that forgotten country [Africa] is becoming better known. Its inhabitants are receiving more of the sympathy of the enlightened portion of mankind; and efforts are making to introduce among them the blessings of civilization and Christianity—to accelerate the day when 'Ethiopia shall stretch her hands unto God'" (7).

Blyden writes about slavery and the slave trade, whose "names alone are sufficient to call up emotions of sympathy wherever there exist the feelings of humanity." In a powerful rendition of the African predicament, he laments, "The wrongs of the African fill the darkest page of human history." He expresses his rage at "the barbarities which the Christian nations of Europe and of America have inflicted, and are now inflicting upon the negro" (17).

Blyden cites not only the physical sufferings of Africans in the lands of their exile, the "diabolical tortures, and debasing usages" they have been subjected to, but also "those deeper wrongs whose tendency has been to dwarf the soul, to emasculate the mind" (17). He also writes about their "sorrows of the heart." "There are secret agonies known only to God, which are far more acute than external tortures":

> Oh! it is not the smiting of the back, until the earth is crimsoned with streams of blood; it is not the pursuing of human beings with blood-hounds; it is not the sufferings that a people can undergo. Oh! No; these affect only the outward man, and may leave untouched the majestic mind. But those afflictions which tend to contract and destroy the mind; those cruelties which benumb the sensibility of the soul, those influences which chill and arrest the currency of the heart's affections—these are the awful instruments of real sufferings and degradations; and these have been made to operate upon the African. (18)

Blyden states that psychological dehumanization, the consideration of the African as nothing, "the deeper wrongs," is more damaging than that of physical abuse, however horrific the latter might be. But then, every act of physical abuse, such as rape and whipping, produces a "deeper wrong" in the person suffering from the abuse. It is not possible to separate where physical suffering ends and psychological torment begins. Every physical suffering is also psychological torment. Rape is as "physical" as it is emotional; torture is as physical as it is psychological. Every physical torture of Africans in the Americas was meant to make them not only suffer physical pain but also feel less than human; its main intent was degradation, dejection, and dehumanization.

After such powerful indictment of Europe's "sins" against Africa, Blyden slides and falls on the slippery slope of divine providence to explain the phenomenon: "But mark the providence of God in the case of this people [Africans]. The very means which, to all human appearance, seemed calculated to crush them out from the earth, have been converted into means of blessing. In the countries of their exile, they have come under the influences of

Christianity, from which they were debarred in their own country, by physical circumstances" (18). The same religion, he tells us, in whose name their enslavement was rationalized in the first place, is now considered the path to the spiritual salvation and material elevation of the Africans.

Blyden reflects deeply about African enslavement in the Americas and the serving and suffering of Africa's children under the domination of white Christian Europeans. One of his most heart-wrenching writings that expresses the deep hurt felt by African humanity is *A Voice from Bleeding Africa on Behalf of Her Exiled Children*, published in Liberia in 1856. There he called American slavery "that monstrous injustice," the "universal cause of their [Africans'] degradation." The "institution [of slavery] is wrong; and if wrong—then all the good and great and holy in the universe, from Him who sitteth upon the 'burning Throne,' down, through all the various gradations of those high and holy intelligence, to the humblest saint upon the earth, are against it."[9]

He states that the Portuguese were the first modern Europeans to establish commercial contact with Africans. He saw this commercial relation as "lawful traffic." He says the Portuguese "would, probably, not have fallen into the custom of slave holding, had they not found slavery a domestic institution of long standing, and slaves forming an article of trade. This, however, was a species of slavery as widely different from American slavery as light is from darkness."[10] In these few lines, Blyden makes points repeatedly debated among students of the transatlantic slave trade. He refers to both ends of the argument. On the one hand is the Fage and Thornton school that argues slavery was already well established in Atlantic Africa long before the beginning of the transatlantic slave trade, and all the Atlantic trade did was divert the direction of the trade and the destination of those caught in its net.[11] On the other hand is the argument of Walter Rodney, who sees the transatlantic slave trade as the major catalyst for the development of internal slavery in West Africa, which had "other forms" of unfree labor but not slavery.[12] Blyden combines these two views decades before they were to enter the debate regarding the transatlantic slave trade. Moreover, he discusses what is now commonplace among students of African slavery, that domestic slavery in West Africa was fundamentally different from that of American slavery.[13]

Blyden sees that the Portuguese permanent settlement along the coast of West Africa was "exerting a considerably wholesome influence upon the aborigines in their vicinity." More than a century before Walter Rodney's *How Europe Underdeveloped Africa*, Blyden writes,

> And it is very probable that had it not been for the subsequent interruptions occasioned by the foreign Slave Trade, western Africa would, at this time, be enjoying, like the greater portion of South America, the civilization of Catholic Europe, and would not be, as some apologists for the African Slave Trade

contend, "wrapped in the night of impervious darkness"; and the race would have been saved the humiliation and degradation which have entailed upon it by American Slavery.[14]

The reference to Africa as "wrapped in the night of impervious darkness" is quite intriguing. Blyden does not cite the author of these lines. It is Hegel who, in *Lectures on the Philosophy of World History*, calls Africa "the land of childhood, removed from the light of self-conscious history and wrapped in the dark mantle of night."[15] Did Blyden read Hegel? That is the question. If he did, why didn't he identify him by name, as he identifies all those he cited? Yet Blyden did not read German, and Hegel's *Lectures* was not translated into English until long after Blyden had passed away. Be that as it may, Blyden's view that western Africa would have developed along the same path as Catholic South America is akin to Rodney's view that the transatlantic slave trade was the culprit that blocked Africa's potential for development and modernization.

Blyden sees Columbus as the agent who opened the path of the dehumanization and degradation of Africans. Much in line with the arguments of the underdevelopment paradigm over a century later, Blyden judges that Columbus's voyages were "the forerunner of unspeakable blessings to the European, was the precursor of bloodshed, torture and extermination to the Indian, and of suffering, degradation and misery to the African."[16] Blyden brilliantly summarizes the relation between Western modernity and the peoples of the Americas in this one sentence: development for Europe, genocide for Native Americans, and degradation and misery for Africans. This, for Blyden, is the outcome of the Columbian project, a paradigm about modernity, entailing what I called "negative modernity."[17]

Blyden states that the "transportation of Africans as slaves to America was commenced by the Portuguese in the sixteenth century." Later, "nearly all the leading nations of Europe" became involved. They all participated in this "system of enormous outrage and robbery: the whole civilized world agreeing that there was nothing wrong with it." This process was "tearing out the very bowels of Africa. It affected not only those who were its immediate victims, but, on account of the immense profit arising from it, and its consequent powerful appeal to the cupidity of influential chieftains along the coast, was the source of considerable war, carnage, and bloodshed."[18]

He does not put all the blame for Africa's degradation on Europeans alone. He recognizes African agency in making the transatlantic slave trade possible. He distinguishes the victims from those who were active participants in the Atlantic market for human chattel. The denial of African role in the traffic is something Blyden finds ludicrous, and in this he anticipates recent reflections on the topic (11).[19] Focusing on the chiefs and their role, he laments, "These chieftains, for some trifling compensation, consisting of gay and showy articles, which, however they regarded as very valuable, engaged to supply the traders with slaves" (12). Blyden delves deep into the mechanisms of the trade and the role of Africans:

> At first, they [African chieftains] sold only those who for criminal or other offenses, had been reduced to slavery; but when the demand increased, and a supply of persons of this class failed, they made occasions of quarrel with their weaker neighbours, and, under the most frivolous pretenses, attacked their villages and took them prisoners; and, frequently, when they could not succeed in fomenting strife between themselves and their neighbours, they treacherously captured the latter in order to meet the demands of the ruthless and relentless Slave Trader. Thus irreconcilable feuds were engendered; tribe stood opposed to tribe—all social ties were dissevered; and a state of sanguinary and unprecedented warfare ensued. Africa was made to bleed at every pore; nor was there one atoning circumstance amid the horribleness of her condition. Thousands of her sons were annually snatched from her shores, and carried into cruel, degrading and hopeless bondage; while those at home, instead of building up her waste places, were engaged in destroying each other; increasing, by their mutual barbarities, the desolation and ruin over which she mourned and lamented. (12–13)

Even as he conducts such relentless critique of the role of African elites in the Atlantic trade, Blyden does not lose sight of the other picture, the degradation of Africans in America. He takes on those apologists of slavery who came up with two basic ideas to defend the "peculiar institution": slavery is as old as human civilization, and slavery is justified in the Old Testament and not condemned by Jesus in the New Testament. Against the first line of defense of slavery, he simply says, "If from these premises true logic warrants the inference that Slavery is right; then will the same logic warrant the conclusion that polygamy is right; for that practice can be defended on the same grounds." He goes on to cite the patriarchs of the Old Testament—Abraham, Jacob, and David—who were all polygamists, to find biblical corroboration for his argument. Then he asks rhetorically, "But shall we argue from this that polygamy is right?" Relying on the New Testament, which condemns polygamy, he says that what is wrong for polygamy is also wrong for slavery (15). Here Blyden's pen is powerful, his logic impeccable, and his argumentation sound.

Much like Frederick Douglass's critique of American Christianity in his *Narrative*, Blyden makes a fundamental distinction between the teachings of Jesus and the practices of American Christianity and its defense of slavery. He fulminates, "How deplorable is it that some teachers of our holy religion, in order to justify so enormous an iniquity as American Slavery, should distort and pervert that beautiful, consistent, pure and sublime system of morality, which Jesus Christ introduced into world, for the enlightening, improvement and dignifying of man—and which his Holy Spirit seals on every truly awakened heart" (31). The teachings of Jesus could not be any further from that of the practices of American slavery. "Would a system among whose fundamental principles is the sublime precept, 'Love your enemies,' warrant the doing of violence to persons, who have done us no wrong whatever, merely on the ground that they differ from us in complexion." Blyden wonders, "And yet a great many professed Christian men—in the land of boasted liberty and religious light—in the face of this plain injunction, uphold and defend Slavery. But these Christians—if Christians they may be called—are weak and imperfect; their judgement has been warped, their understanding obfuscated, by the powerfully bewitching and blinding influence of self-interest" (16).

Blyden is a true intellectual: he does not discriminate in his critiques. Any fault he sees, he writes about and against it. He does not shrink from critiquing Africans just because they are Africans, or fail to give due to Europeans just because they are European. With the same passion that he condemns African chiefs for their role in the Atlantic slave economy, he praises people such as Mary Kingsley and David Livingston for what he considers their positive contribution to the regeneration and uplifting of Africa.

Blyden critiques the slaveholder ideology that considered enslaved Africans incapable of learning or improvement. Citing prominent proslavery ideologists such as John Calhoun, he states, if indeed the enslaved African is incapable of improvement "why have they made such stringent laws prohibiting the Slave from learning to read?—Why do they so sedulously close against him every avenue to mental development and improvement? Why not regard him as other animals of burden?" He notes that slaveholders knew the "susceptibility of the Slave to improvement; they know he can learn what his rights and privileges as a man are—and that if he should learn them, he will be rendered altogether unfit for a state of bondage." In a biting indictment against the American slaveholding class, he declares that they "debar him [the slave] from all means by which men are improved and elevated above the level of the brute; and, imposing upon him the ponderous weight of barbarous despotism, they expect him to exhibit the same intellectual and moral greatness with other men. How reasonable?" (18–19).

Like Frederick Douglass, who was his contemporary, Blyden sees in American slavery the deepest pit of human degradation. "What under the sun, can be worse than American Slavery, that 'mystery of iniquity?'" (22). The same American slaveholding ideology that saw the enslaved Africans as being incapable of attaining self-improvement made the case that the transportation of Africans to America and their enslavement there was a school for their uplifting, a condition deemed much superior than what they left behind in Africa. This rationalization for slavery did not escape the notice of Blyden's sharp eye. He mocks the idea entertained by a certain reverend

Dr. Parker, whom he sees as one "under the binding influence of the evil which he was laboring to justify." Blyden cites Parker, who wrote regarding enslaved Africans in America, "If they are degraded here they were more so in Africa. *If slavery degraded them it also educated them.*" Blyden comments, "Unfortunate, hapless, suffering lot! What a School have poor Africans been sent to for instruction! What severe discipline! What beating, kicking, brutalizing, in order to Christianize, to elevate, to educate!" He further says, "We must deny most positively that the American Slave was more degraded in Africa than he is in the South. We also deny most emphatically that the education and civilization of the American colored people are attributable to Slavery. They have received these blessings *in spite of* their condition, in spite of the brutifications of that atrocious system" (32).

In *The Negro in Ancient History*, Blyden writes, "Without the foreign slave trade Africa would have been a great deal more accessible to civilization, and would now, had peaceful and legitimate intercourse been kept up with her from the middle of the fifteenth century, be taking her stand next to Europe in civilization, science, and religion."[20] As much as he makes the Atlantic slave trade the culprit for Africa's "backwardness," he still believes that Africa was indeed bereft of civilization and that the agency for its civilization comes from outside Africa. In other words, Blyden rules out the possibility of the "uplifting" of Africa by the indigenous Africans themselves.

Blyden makes another pertinent point. He states that life in West Africa prior to the Atlantic slave trade was more like that of Europe during the Middle Ages. In both cases, there was "the same oppression of the weak by the strong; the same resistance by the weak, often taking the form of general rebellion; the same private and hereditary wars; the same strongholds in every prominent position; the same dependence of the people upon the chief who happened to be in power; the same contentedness of the masses with the tyrannical rule."[21]

Blyden cites two factors that inhibited Africa's development: the "isolation of the people from the progressive portion of mankind" and the "blighting influence of the traffic introduced among them by Europeans." He sees enlightened Europe as the agent producing its exact opposite for Africa, benightedness. He goes on to say, "Had not the demand arisen in America for African laborers, and had European nations inaugurated regular traffic with the coast, the natives would have shown themselves as impressible for change, as susceptible of improvement, as capable of acquiring knowledge and accumulating wealth, as the natives of Europe."[22] This view of how Europe underdeveloped Africa is articulated with such sophistication a century before it was to come from the many pens of the dependency and underdevelopment school.

In his travelogue *From West Africa to Palestine*, Blyden compares Africans with Native Americans:

While the American Indians, who were, without doubt, an old and worn-out people, could not survive the introduction of the new phases of life brought among them from Europe, but sank beneath the unaccustomed aspects which their country assumed under the vigorous hand of the fresh and youthful Anglo-Saxon and Teutonic races, the Guinea Negro, in an entirely new and distant country, has rather delighted in the change of climate and circumstances, and has prospered, physically, on all that great continent and its islands from Canada to Cape Horn.[23]

In his most acclaimed work, *Christianity, Islam, and the Negro Race*, published three decades after *A Voice from Bleeding Africa*, Blyden bemoans the disruptions brought to African life by the transatlantic slave trade:

The slave trade was a serious interference with African life. Before the demand for Negro labour in the Western hemisphere taught the people of the coast to make war upon each other, there was continuous intercourse between Sierra Leone and the interior. An extensive agriculture beautified the landscape on every land. There was gradual, regular growth in the elements of civilisation. But when the necessities of the slave trade spread confusion and disorder through all the maritime regions, legitimate trade retired from this part of Africa, and found its way across the desert to the Mediterranean.[24]

He states that the peoples of West Africa were at an advanced stage of development long before the transatlantic slave trade began. "The ancestors of these people understood the use of the cotton-pant, and the manufacture of the cotton, when Julius Caesar found the Brittons clothing themselves in the skins of wild beasts. . . . Another proof, this, of the connection of the Nigritian tribes with the ancient Egyptians" (225).

Blyden comments, "There is nothing surprising in the fact that . . . Africans sell each other. Who was it that sold those Angles [*sic*] whom Gregory saw in the slave-market at Rome? Is it not well known that Saxon husbands and parents sold their wives and daughters? Did not slavery prevail in every country in Europe?" He further notes, "It cannot have escaped the most superficial reader of African history that the ravages introduced by the slave trade have had a distinctly marked effect not only on the personal or tribal character of the inhabitants, but on their social organisation—on the whole industrial and economic life of the country. Their condition for centuries has been one of restless anarchy and insecurity" (309). Blyden continues:

Among the evils wrought by the slave trade, none has been more damaging to Africa and the Negro race than the promiscuous manner in which tribes have been thrown together and confounded in the lands of their exile. There are Negroes and Negroes. The numerous tribes inhabiting the vast continent of Africa can no more be regarded as in every respect equal than the numerous peoples of Asia or Europe can be so regarded. There are the same tribal or family varieties among Africans as among Europeans. (311)

He further writes,

> The cruel accidents of slavery and the slave trade drove all Africans together, and no discrimination was made in the shambles between the Foulah and the Timneh, the Mandingo and the Mendi, the Ashantee and the Fantee, the Eboe and the Congo—between the descendants of nobles and the offspring of slaves, between kings and their subjects—all were placed on the same level, all of black skin and woolly hair were "niggers," chattels, having no rights that their oppressors were bound to respect. And when, by any course of events, these people attempt to exercise independent government, they start in the eyes of the world as Africans, without the fact being taken into consideration that they belong to tribes and families differing widely in degrees of intelligence and capacity, in original bent and susceptibility. (314)

Blyden does not only make remarks about those Africans forcefully snatched from their homes and delivered to be devoured by the Atlantic economies, if not by the sea first. He also comments on the social origins of those Africans who found themselves on European ships:

> The Africans who were carried into slavery were mostly of the lowest orders—of the criminal and servile classes—the latter of whom had lived for generations at home with "half their worth conveyed away," and who, it was not supposed, would improve in manly qualities under the circumstances to which they were introduced in foreign lands. Only here and there a leading mind—a real Man—was carried into captivity. (312)

Elsewhere, he writes, "The Africans who were carried to the Western world were, as a general rule, of the lowest of the people in their own country. They did not fairly represent the qualities and endowments of the race. Even the traditions of the country they carried away in the most distorted form" (39). His statement that those Africans dragged to their enslavement in the Americas were not "real" men and women is problematic. This view smacks of an elitist perspective where real men are seen as those in positions of high power and authority, while those dirtying their hands in the field or the household were seen as human riffraff. Yet it was to enslaved blacks in the Western Hemisphere that Blyden gave the role of the regeneration of Africa! The reason is quite simply that these "civilized Negroes," as he calls them, drank deep at the fountain of Western modernity and had already become "domesticated" in the "civilized" behavior that Africa needed so badly. It would be foolish to present Blyden as a consistent thinker free of contradictions. But then one needs to focus on the inconsistencies that are more systemic in his paradigm, leaving out the minor irritants. Still, Blyden is empirically correct in stating that only occasionally did Africa lose its elites to the world of the Atlantic slave trade.[25]

Blyden seems to believe that Africans have been slaves for millennia, even in Egypt, which he identifies elsewhere as a "Negro" civilization. He writes, "the African has gone on from generation to generation furnishing, in remote ages, materials to swell the triumphal processions of Egyptian Kings, and, in modern times, strong arms for the plantations of the Western Hemisphere, and is taunted by his persecutors (and his friends) with his inability to rise against this pressure" (320). He sees the slave trade as the main obstacle for the introduction of civilization in Africa. "Next, then, to the exploration of the country, the most important preliminary to the general civilisation of the African tribes is the suppression of the slave trade" (323).

Regarding the impact of American slavery on the enslaved Africans' material and spiritual improvement, he writes, "The Negro, in exile, is the only man, born out of Africa, who can live and work and reproduce himself in this country. His residence in America has conferred upon him numerous advantages. It has quickened him in the direction of progress. It has predisposed him in favour of civilisation, and given him a knowledge of revealed truth in its highest and purest form" (384–85).

Blyden is of the conviction that enslaved Africans were moving in the direction of material and spiritual progress in the land of their exile. But how is this so? He believes that divine providence is the moving hand of history, and this applies to the transatlantic slave trade too. "We believe that the deportation of the Negro to the New World was as much decreed by an all-wise Providence, as the expatriation of the Pilgrims from Europe to America." Knowing well the horrors of the Middle Passage and the ensuing house of bondage, degradation, and dehumanization that awaits the African in America, the "ponderous weight of barbarous despotism," as he calls it, he would not dare say that an all-powerful and merciful Christian God would do such a crime against his own creation. So he twists the story:

> When we say that Providence decreed the means of Africa's enlightenment, we do not say that He decreed the wickedness of the instruments. . . . It was not the first time that wicked hands were suffered to execute a Divine purpose. No special guilt on the part of the African, no special merit on the part of the European, made one the slave and the other the master. Many a wicked man became master, and flourished the rod of the oppressor over the head of his moral and intellectual superior. The good are often in distress; the wicked in prosperity. (385)

Blyden believes that the Atlantic slave trade could be divided into two periods: the initial good, humane time, the time before European avarice; and then the bad times, after such avarice took the good of the European.

Yet the Atlantic slave trade from the very beginning to the end has a single story: the dragging of Africans into the Americas for servile labor. There is no division in periods of the humane and inhumane in this trade. The only possible division is before and after the development of the plantation economy. But this issue deals with the magnitude of the trade, not the change of humaneness on the part of the Europeans toward Africans.

Blyden's statement that it was "not the first time that wicked hands were suffered to execute a Divine purpose" begs the question: Why did providence decide to make Africans slaves, and the Europeans masters? Why not the reverse? He seems to have no answer. But then, he has written extensively that Africans were lost in the darkness of sin, paganism, and superstition. They did not hear the words of the Gospel. If providence was to save them from utter darkness by lifting them up to the light of the Gospel, it was only by making Christians masters and Africans slaves. Despite his racial intention to reject a "special guilt" of Africans and "special merit" of Europeans as the condition for their master-slave relationship, it was exactly what transpired in history. What, we may ask, was the African's special guilt? The tension in Blyden's account here is a tension between his profound belief in racial equality and his belief in religious hierarchy, the absolute superiority of Christianity over African religions, which he, alongside the missionary enterprise, calls paganism. We now know why providence made one the master, the other slave. He made master the one who followed him; slave the one who did even know about his existence. The Christian God practiced apartheid.

Although we may make these assertions, Blyden still has another trick to play on us. This is the whole business of the Christian God testing with fire those he likes, not those he dislikes. But then, does not God know a priori those who would follow him and those who won't? But this issue heads into a path of theological argumentation, one beyond the scope of this book. Blyden writes,

> But the Christian has been taught, that whatever is done, is done, not from the caprice of the gods, but because it seems good in the sight of a merciful Father, infinite in wisdom, power, justice, goodness and truth. No grief, therefore, at the recollection of the ravages in Africa; no memory of the evils [of] "middle passage"; no abhorrence of successful and damnable crime; no indignation at the iniquities of unparalleled oppression in the house of bondage, can prevent us from recognising the hand of an over-ruling Providence in the deportation of Africans to the Western world, or interfere with our sense of the incalculable profit—the measureless gains—which, in spite of man's perversity, cruelty and greed, must accrue to Africa and the Negro race from the long and weary exile. (385–86)

Therefore, what he wrote in *A Voice from Bleeding Africa*, alongside many similar voices, is to be taken not only as so many African "indignations at the iniquities of unparalleled oppression in the house of bondage," but also as acknowledgments of the benefits that accrue despite the wickedness of the methods. Blyden mocks the reverend Dr. Parker, who wrote of enslaved Africans in America, "If slavery degraded them it also educated them." Isn't that what Blyden is saying here? Blyden's soul is tormented, the site of conflict between the two Rs: race and religion. What he agrees with from the angle of religion, he fulminates against it from the angle of race. The reverend Dr. Parker and the reverend Dr. Blyden share the same religious universe; they part company in the abode of race. What they agree in the former, they disagree in the latter. Blyden is the personification of that contradiction.

There is more to the Blydenian appraisal of African enslavement in the Americas. He writes, "Africans were carried away by millions. There is no means of estimating the number. Had they been taken to the foreign school as individuals, and been brought back after their training, the desirable results would not have been attained." Such a situation would have been unable to provide the necessary mass needed for the wholesome transformation of Africa along the lines of the three Cs; Christianity, commerce, and civilization. Had it been the case of individual Africans going to foreign lands and "returning to their country as the prophets of a new era, they would have shared the proverbial fate of the solitary reformer among his own people." Theirs would have been lonely voices in the wilderness. Hence the "need" for millions of Africans to be extirpated from their home, endure three centuries of the inferno of American slavery, all the better to be trained to redeem Africa from itself: "They were, therefore, carried away in such numbers, that, while under the control of a civilised people of a different race, and undergoing the process of enforced improvement, they might be sufficiently numerous to find among themselves encouragement, sympathy and support, amid the rigours of their schooling; and, on returning might exert the influence of organised communities, able to introduce and establish wholesome reforms" (386). In short, American slavery was the Hegelian "cunning of reason" for the elevation of Africans onto the pedestal of the "good," Christian, bourgeois modernity. That was Blyden's passion, one commonplace in the modernization paradigm.

Did Blyden's views as expressed in his most important work, *Christianity, Islam, and the Negro Race,* change as he entered the twentieth century, with the establishment of European colonial rule in Africa? In a collected work of one article and three addresses written and delivered between 1901 and 1903 and published in 1905 under the title *West Africa before Europe,* he writes,

It was imagined throughout the nineteenth century by many of the best friends of the African, even among those who were most strenuous in their efforts to deliver him from physical bondage, that he had in his native home no social organization of his own, that he was destitute of any religious ideas and entirely without any foundation of morality. Therefore, it was said, "Let us give him a religion to save his soul and a morality to save his body."[26]

He objects to such characterization of the African in Africa. "But a deeper knowledge of the [African] man and of his country—a scientific study of the subject—is showing that Africa did not need this benevolent interference. The creeds formulated in Europe are not indispensable to Africa's spiritual development." He adds, "No nation or race has a monopoly of the channels which lead to the sources of divine grace or spiritual knowledge." He further states that the "Ten Commandments and the Golden Rule are indispensable to the usefulness, happiness, and prosperity of Africans as every other race of men, and these are observed in every African community untouched by European civilisation, and observed with a strictness and efficiency not always found even in European communities" (132–33). It is as if Africans were following the Old and New Testaments without ever knowing about them. This point nullifies any need on the part of Europe to introduce Christianity in Africa. It makes missionary work superfluous. But then he always thought that the introduction of Christianity into Africa would be a great force of spiritual improvement. Which view are we to take as the authentic voice of Blyden? These two contradictory views dwell in the same fertile mind with formidable intellectual prowess, one who spent his adult life fighting the race war and defending the dignity of the "African race." Blyden is a brilliant intellect of incurable contradictions.

For Blyden, Europe did not distinguish itself as a land of religious piety. "Europe was never distinguished in the past for pious impulses or religious leadership. In the greatest tragedy of human history, Africa was represented as associated with the Divine Sufferer—going to the valley with Jesus. Asia betrayed the God-Man into the hands of Europe—gave him up as sheep to the slaughter. Europe slew Him and plundered His clothes after His death." Europe, who put the "God-Man" to death, has the audacity to bring his teachings to Africa, the land that gave him sanctuary and saved him from early death at the hand of Herod. Later on his way to Golgotha, Africa provided the man who helped him carry his burden, the cross. "Now the racial descendants of these [Roman] soldiers, who are soldiers yet—God's soldiers—the overlords and policemen of humanity, believe, apparently, with an inextinguishable faith that they can carry this Jesus whom they slew into Africa" (148–49). He seems to ignore the fact that the Europe that slew Jesus was not the same Europe that brought Christianity to Africa during the nineteenth century. The only similarity between the two is race, an idea that did not exist at the time of Jesus's death.[27] Blyden froze race and could thus link pagan Rome with nineteenth-century Christian Europe.

Even as we think Blyden has at last cast the European missionary enterprise and the need for African proselytization in doubt, since Africans already have all the spiritual and moral character taught by this religion, he still applauds it. "No one can dispute the nobleness, the greatness, of the missionary enterprise in its aims and purposes, and often in its emissaries and agents. For a hundred years, it has poured out of its best, of men and money, of prayers and tears, but so far with moderate success, and with little prospect of any larger results in the future" (35). Blyden believes that it was good that European missionaries came to Africa; it is just that they have been sloppy in their work of conversion or that Africans did not find their religion that appealing. The question still is: why do Africans need to be Christian if they already were Christians before Christianity, Jewish before Judaism, as he himself says earlier?

In his letter to Booker T. Washington, written on November 28, 1894, Blyden reiterates his belief that the calling of the African is to serve others. "The African spirit is a spirit of service. I do not mean in a degrading sense, but in the highest sense, in which the Son of man came not to be ministered unto but to minister—the sense He took upon Himself the form of a servant—slave in the original." He explains the rationale that the calling of the African is that of service to the world:

> The spirit of service in the black man is born of his spiritual genius. It is his essential characteristic; and how to show you that I connect no servile or unworthy idea with this remark, I hasten to add that I believe that that spirit must lead in civilization before it can become distinctly Christian—the supple, yielding, conciliatory, obedient, gentle, patient, musical spirit that is not full of offensive resistance—how sadly the white man needs it![28]

Blyden believes that blacks should refrain from involving themselves in American politics, as their lot lies in service of others. He reminds Booker T. Washington, "We believe that the interest of both races will be served if the Negro will eschew politics and political aspirations, where every step of the way is hampered and covered with thorns and briars" (207). He states that the "Negro" is "called to higher and nobler work," including the religious.

It is in this light that Blyden, like Booker T., eschews politics in America. He believes that politics is better left with whites. "Let him [the white man] fight the battle of government on the stump, at the polls and in the legislative halls. Our kingdom in America is not of this world." He further notes, "We cannot compete with the Anglo-Saxon. He is so dreadfully determined, so intolerant and self assertive, intent upon carrying his point at all hazards, having good in view of course; but the wheels of his mind and understanding need oiling sadly with the oil of African good nature" (207).

Blyden compares the rugged individualism of the Anglo-Saxon with the tenderness of the African heart. "The Negro is a very different being from what superficial observers of him in the house of his bondage imagine him to be. It is worse than a farce to talk of the savagery of a country where such a man as Livingstone, unprotected and alone, took his little family and lived and died, not only without molestation but tenderly looked after! Think of the devotion shown to Stanley!" (207). Overall, "The Negro is on a different plane, religiously, from the white man. He has a more spiritual nature; and may be the teacher of his master in spiritual matters" (205).

In his famous lecture, "Study and Race," which he delivered to the Young Men's Literary Association of Sierra Leone on May 19, 1893, Blyden restates his view that "the African is called for service": "The Negro was made for service. He will put his peculiar power into vital action for the human race." Furthermore, "No foreign Race need be afraid of us, in spite of the universal oppression and injustice of which we have been victims. They need not dread the development of our personality. It will be free from any tinge of bitterness towards them or any pompous self assertion." Blyden adds, "We were made for that highest of all glory, which is service for Humanity. He that will be chief let him become your servant, said the great Master" (202). He indeed sees glory in suffering: "The glory of the African thus far has been the glory of suffering—the glory of the cross—the glory of the Son of Man—the man of sorrows and acquainted with grief. But the future will have a different story to tell. The Cross precedes the Crown" (203). He sees positive in suffering; he smells the "rose in the cross."[29]

For Blyden, Africans are the only true, authentic Christians. Africans are the only authentic followers of Jesus, his life, works, and teachings. European Christianity, by contrast, must be spurious Christianity, a Christianity not of service to humanity but rather of domination. European Christianity would be incompatible with Jesus's moral philosophy of serving humanity.

According to Blyden, European Christians did not suffer in service rendered to humanity. Instead, they followed in the footsteps of their Roman antecedents, who knew only domination. As such, European Christianity was a Christianized version of the Roman Empire, Roman in content and Christian in form. Those who do not serve others and suffer thereof could not follow in the footsteps of Jesus. But we have this problem: Blyden spent his life pleading for and advocating the introduction of Western civilization in Africa, including, of course, its brands of Christianity. What a monumental contradiction!

Still, we cannot help but ask: Did Blyden envision two distinct kinds of Christianity, one Western and another African? Did he envision the former as a Christianity of domination and the latter as a Christianity of subjection, of service, of suffering? Do the three Ss—service, suffering, and subjection—mark "true" Christianity from the impostor one? Is the latter spurious, superfluous, and pretentious? Was Europe unable to transcend its Roman heritage of oppressing others to become genuinely one with the teachings of Jesus? I see it as follows: Western Christianity is the Christianity that became the hegemonic pillar on which Western history was built from Emperor Constantine in the fourth century to Blyden's own time and beyond. This Christianity justified and rationalized the Crusades, the Inquisition, the extermination of Native Americans, African enslavement, colonialism, Jim Crow, apartheid, and so on. These are obviously all scenes of domination, not of suffering in service to humanity.

Blyden, much like Frederick Douglass, points out that enslaved Africans made a distinction between the teachings and lived experiences of Jesus, and the religion practiced by their Christian masters.[30] While they yearned dearly for the former, they detested the latter. "It is a curious thing that in all the long and weary years of the Negro's bondage in America to white Christians," he writes, "the slaves clung to Christ." They "did not believe in the religion of their white masters." Indeed, "Very few among races alien to the European believe in the genuineness of the Christianity of the white man. For neither in the teaching nor the practice of the lay white man do they see manifested, as a rule, anything of the spirit of Christianity."[31]

He favorably compares the religion and customary morality of Africans regarding Jesus's central teaching—"the law of love"—as opposed to that practiced by white Christians.

> The case is different among the so-called benighted Africans. They can and do in their uninvaded solitudes fulfill the law of love. All fair-minded travellers on this continent are forcibly struck with the decided superiority in morality which characterises the interior natives untouched by civilization, compared with those in the seaports who have come under the influence of so-called Christianity and civilization. It is with the Mohammedans and those who are least affected by the fringe of European civilization that I prefer to associate; these, it appears to me, possess in their conditions of life more room for vigorous individual and racial growth, and are less compressed into set shapes than any others.[32]

He becomes the advocate of "nativism." What he has firmly and consistently campaigned for, the introduction into Africa of the three Cs—Christianity, commerce, and civilization—he condemns as producing fakes on the African side: people with denationalized minds, without real knowledge or historical projections into the future.

In one of his most profound critiques of Christianity, Blyden produces a remarkable African liberation theology, challenging some of the fundamental tenets and practices of Christendom itself.[33] In *The Three Needs of Liberia*, he calls the topic of religion, "the most important of all subjects."[34] He challenges the very rationale for the existence of the church as a religious institution: "They have organized what they call a church or churches for which there is no authority anywhere in the Bible" (21). He further notes, "The word church, in the sense in which it is now understood, nowhere occurs in the Bible" (22).

Having denied the historical and theological legitimacy of the church in the history of Christianity, Blyden articulates his liberation theology: "When Jesus Christ appeared in the world, He identified Himself with the despised and oppressed. Not in the palace of Caesar or in the court of the High Priest was he born, but with the beast of the field, in a manger, according to the Gospel narrative." Jesus was born "as many an African child is now born." Blyden cites what Jesus said to his disciples: "I am among you as he that serveth." From this, he draws the association between Jesus and the Africans. "Jesus identified himself with Ham not with Japheth. He is emphatically the Saviour of the African, and in the house of bondage Jesus was the comforter and the example to whom he strove to cling" (21). He further declares, "The Christ we worship must be an African. . . . The Christ revealed in the Bible is far more African than anything else. Hence all the pictures drawn by Europeans professing to represent Him are false for us" (32).

Blyden's critique of organized Christianity, especially Western, is so intense, piercing, and passionate that he would go to the extent of foregoing the religion itself if it does not stand for justice for the downtrodden, primarily for Africans.

> We may adopt it as a safe rule that whenever we find that our physical, intellectual, or religious progress is hindered and our life destroyed by what we have been told is the teaching of Christ, we may, I say (and we have the authority of Christ Himself for this) take it as a safe rule that we are *not* following Christ but the tradition of men, which makes the commandment of God *for us* of none effect, and rendering vain all our worship. (6)

Blyden states that class distinction between the rich and poor, especially as found in capitalist societies, is "not Christ's idea, and it is not the African idea. The African idea is the idea of the first Christian church" (20). What Blyden calls the "African idea," which he likens with the teachings of Jesus, is African communalism, the rejection of class distinctions. Sounding very much like Nyerere decades later with his idea of African socialism, Blyden writes, "In Africa, there is only one interest and that is the people's interest. Farming is *communistic*, allied to and guided by a patriarchal head. The land is owned by everybody." He adds, "The men, women and children all work, engage in labor as a duty they owe to themselves and to each other, and all reap equal rewards. That is unto each according to his several ability. Under the African system there can be no absolutely rich man and no absolutely poor man" (19). It is this social system that Blyden calls, the "African idea," one he saw as being in accord with the life experiences of Jesus and his disciples, the first Christians, and the first church.[35]

Blyden, like Frederick Douglass, draws a fundamental distinction between what he calls the "Christianity of Christ" and the Christianity practiced in Europe and America.[36] "I am sure that the Christianity of Christ is an energy that will stimulate all action, all righteousness, all goodness. I am sure that in its presence all things would become brighter and larger, all men would be happier and more free." Based on such reading, Blyden judges Western Christianity: "I am sure that Christianity, as conceived and modified in Europe and America, with its oppressive hierarchy, its caste prejudices and limitations, its pecuniary burdens and exactions, its injurious intermeddling in the harmless and useful customs of alien peoples, is not the Christianity of Christ."[37]

Yet Blyden also declares, "I am not prepared to deny that the religion *professed* in America is the true religion for humanity; but I cannot admit that we have an exemplification of the spirit of that religion, so far as it has affected us." Discussing the relation between religion and politics in America, he states, "American politics flourish under the shadow of the American religion, if it is not the offspring of that religion. Nearly all the decisions of the Supreme Court of that country affecting the Negro have been in diametrical opposition to the Golden Rule; and in their social and industrial relations with us, there is not one of the ten Commandments which has not been violated with impunity." For Blyden, American Christianity was slaveholding Christianity. "Therefore, the religion we were taught in America was the religion of the house of bondage: Its fundamental tenet was, 'Slaves, obey your masters.'"[38]

In *Christianity, Islam, and the Negro Race*, Blyden had written, "American Christianity, though having its roots in Europe, differs from European Christianity in many important respects—in the wide tolerance which pervades it, in the form which it has assumed, and the impression which it leaves on the mind. It is the religion of a democratic people."[39] In Blyden's Christology, it seems that American Christianity would be a Christianity of democratic slavery, that is, a democratic people who upheld the sanctity of African enslavement!

The question now is this: Africans who suffered and served throughout history were not Christian. Yet their suffering and service through enslavement was justified by those who were Christians. If this is so, is Blyden telling us that it is after all possible to be like Jesus, to follow his example, to suffer and serve like him, without ever having heard his name, not to mention his teachings? Were those non-Christian Africans who toiled in the inferno of American slavery natural-born Christians? In American slavery, Christianized and semi-Christianized slaves invoked Jesus, whom they knew as one who suffered to serve humanity. They saw Jesus as being like them. The slaveholder, gun wrapped to his waist, whip in the right hand and Bible in the left, invoked Saint Paul as he whipped his possessions in human form.

Why didn't he cite Jesus? Well, Jesus has no paradigm that justifies slavery. The enslaved knew that; so did the slave holder.[40]

Which Africans did Blyden have in mind when he says the glory of Africans is the glory of service and suffering? Africans dragged by the millions across that ocean of deep sorrow to make America rich, powerful, and conceited; Africans who suffered and served humanity were the true Christians. There were Africans who served and suffered under the Roman yoke before the birth of Jesus. As long as Africans suffer and serve humanity, and in that lies their glory, they may not even need to convert to Christianity, for per Blyden's paradigm, life given to service and suffering is Jesus-like. Africans are natural Christians without needing to be historical Christians. They knew Jesus before Jesus was born; they followed Jesus without even knowing that he ever existed. Why then did Blyden fight so hard to make the European missionary enterprise in Africa successful? One may say that I am making an exaggerated claim, that all Blyden was articulating was that the African resembles Jesus in his suffering and service for humanity. But then he says that the essence of the African lies in the three Ss—service, suffering, and subjection.

At the end of it all, Blyden believes that Africans are the closest to Jesus:

> Jesus is lame. He has been wounded in the house of his friends. We must bind up his wounds. Treading in the footsteps of our immortal countryman we must bear the cross after Jesus. We must strip him of the useless, distorting and obstructive habiliments by which he has been invested by the materialising sons of Japhet. Let Him be lifted up as He really is, that He may be seen, pure and simple, by the African, and He will draw all men unto Him.[41]

For Blyden, Africa's service to humanity is not confined to the material level. It also extends to the spiritual plane. Africa gave sanctuary to the prophets, and to the God that became man, Jesus. Blyden writes in *Christianity, Islam, and the Negro Race*, "When, in his final hours, the Saviour of mankind struggled up the heights of Calvary, under the weight of the Cross, accused by Asia and condemned by Europe, Africa furnished the man to relieve him of his burden."[42] He goes on to say,

> When the Saviour of mankind, born in lowly circumstances, was the persecuted babe of Bethlehem, Africa furnished the refuge for his threatened and helpless infancy. African hands ministered to the comfort of Mary and Joseph while they sojourned as homeless and hunted strangers in that land. In the final hours of the Man of Sorrows, when His disciples had forsaken Him and fled, and only the tears of sympathising women, following in the distance, showed that His sorrows touched any human heart; when Asia, in the person of the Jew, clamoured for His blood, and Europe, in the Roman soldier, was

dragging Him to execution, and afterwards nailed those sinless hands to the cross, and pierced that sacred side—what was the part that Africa took then? She furnished the man to share the burden of the cross with the suffering Redeemer. Simon, the Cyrenian, bore the cross after Jesus. (177)

Elsewhere, Blyden goes even further than this, declaring, "We must make Christ an African."[43]

Not only was Africa the savior of Jesus and the foundational home of Christianity, it also provided safe haven for the followers of the prophet Muhammad. Blyden acknowledges that "it was Abyssinia that afforded shelter to the persecuted Muslims, who, in the early days of Islam, had to fly from Arabia for their lives. When Mohammed found that his few followers were likely to be crushed by the opposition at Mecca, he advised their flight into Abyssinia." As such, "If then, the two principal religions [Christianity and Islam] had not their origin in Africa, yet Africa was the cradle which cherished their helpless infancy." From this, he draws the conclusion regarding Ethiopia's place in world history and in the eyes of God:

Now, what are the lessons to be gathered from the preceding discussion? I conceived that they are: *First*, That Ethiopia have ever been connected with the Divine administration and manifestations, and that that great country and its people are not left out of the beneficent purposes of the Almighty. *Second*, That the Gospel, to be successfully carried into Africa, must be carried by Africans. To "a man of Ethiopia" must be entrusted the message to Ethiopians. (190–91)

He looks to the Bible to find the glory that was Ethiopia: "There is no people, except the Hebrews and other ancient inhabitants of Palestine, more frequently mentioned in the Scriptures of the Old and New Testaments than the Ethiopians; and there is no country more frequently referred to than Ethiopia; and the record of no people, whether in sacred history or ancient secular history, has less of the discreditable than the record of the Ethiopians" (174).

In *The Negro in Ancient History*, Blyden writes about how peaceful the Ethiopian, a word he uses to mean African, race has been throughout history. He states, "One palpable reason may be assigned why the Ethiopian race has continued to exist under the most adverse circumstances, while other races and tribes have perished from the earth; it is this: *They have never been a blood-thirsty or avaricious people.*" To the contrary, "From the beginning of their history to the present time their work has been constructive, except when they have been stimulated to wasting war by the covetous foreigner." The Ethiopians "have built up in Asia, Africa, and America. They have not delighted in despoiling and oppressing others. . . . The Ethiopians, though brave and powerful, were not a fighting people, that is, were not fond of fighting for the sake of humbling and impoverishing other people."[44] Here he makes the case that Africans lived their lives in peace and harmony until the white man showed up on the shores of Atlantic Africa, "stimulating" wars and destruction.

Blyden uses the word "Ethiopia" as synonymous with Africa, a case of profound race identity grafting. As he puts it unambiguously, "It is pretty well established now, however, that by *Ethiopia*, is meant the continent of Africa, and by *Ethiopians*, the great race who inhabit that continent" (130). The biblical Ethiopia was not synonymous with Africa. It had no reference point beyond northeast Africa. As a man born and raised in the most racialized period of modern history, Blyden could not think in any other way. He mentions a specific locale, Abyssinia, and its relations with historical Christianity and Islam. He seems to make a distinction between this Abyssinia and the word "Ethiopia," which he takes as synonymous with the word Africa.

Blyden takes a different reading with regards to Judaism, the parent religion of Christianity and Islam. He states that Judaism had its origins in Africa:

> The great progenitor of the Hebrew race and the founder [of] their religion sought refuge in Africa from the ravages of famine. . . . In Africa, the Hebrew people from three score and ten souls multiplied into millions. In Africa, Moses, the greatest lawgiver the world has ever seen, was born and educated. To this land also resorted the ancient philosophers of Greece and Rome, to gaze upon its wonders and gather inspiration from its arts and sciences. Later on, a greater than Moses and than all the prophets and philosophers, when in infancy, was preserved from death in Africa.[45] (135)

Africa is the hand that rocked the cradle of the Abrahamic religions. Of course, this "Africa" is actually the two oldest nations on the continent, Egypt and Ethiopia. Both are still the oldest Christian nations in Africa, and two of the oldest in the world. In Egypt, Christianity has been a minority religion for centuries, overtaken by Islam. In Ethiopia, Christianity is still the religion of the majority, although Islam is fast catching up. As the champion of race pride, Blyden folds Egypt and Ethiopia into the larger envelope of modernity's caste identity, race. The glory that was Egypt and Ethiopia became the glory of Africa. Blyden uses a modern concept, race, and applies it to reconstruct the premodern history of Christianity.

Within the context of Western bourgeois modernity, Blyden sees Africa as having yet another spiritual role to play in rescuing Europe from its materialized and excessively commoditized civilization:

> Africa may yet prove to be the spiritual conservatory of the world. . . . When the civilised nations, in consequence of their wonderful material development,

shall have had their spiritual perceptions darkened and their spiritual susceptibilities blunted through the agency of a captivating and absorbing materialism, it may be, that they may have to resort to Africa to recover some of the
simple elements of faith. (143)

Like the nineteenth-century pan-Slav nationalists and utopian socialists who
saw Russia as the spiritual saver of a decadent Europe, Blyden sees the future
of Africa as saving Europe from itself.[46] As he puts it, "Europe exhausted
and utterly materialised will again resort to the so-called Dark Continent for
simple faith in the Supreme Being, and again will that grey haired Mother
of Civilization be a refuge for seers that see and prophets who prophesy."[47]

If indeed the essence of the African is encompassed in the three Ss—service, suffering, and subjection—what are we to do with those African cen-
ters of power and domination, those empires and kingdoms that make many
an Afrocentrist smile with pride and even conceit: Pharaonic Egypt, Nubia,
Aksum, Ghana, Mali, Songhay, Zimbabwe, and so on. What of those great
empire builders such as Ramses II, Shaka, Menelik II, Samori Toure, and so
on? Blyden himself expressed his pride and joy when he visited the pyramids
in Egypt, where he claimed possession by inscribing his name along with
that of Liberia. He was making a profound historical statement, one that
links five thousand years of history, where Blyden's Liberia was but a continuation of the glory that was ancient Egypt. Who were the Africans who suffered and served in these many empires? The working classes? That would
make Blyden a socialist.

Perhaps we may not need all this if we were to simply accept the fact
that nationalism is incompatible with consistency. As a "race patriot,"
Blyden navigates through all kinds of ideas contradictory to one another
as long as they promote the main paradigm: black racial nationalism.
Thus, Ramses II with all his might and splendor would be as African as the
enslaved African toiling in the boiling sun of Cuba's sugar plantation. It
is only that Ramses II was nowhere near experiencing Blyden's essence of
the African, the three Ss.[48]

In his depiction of Africans as the spiritual saviors of Europe from its
excessive materialism, Blyden draws parallels between Jews and blacks. He
holds the view that "the primary contribution of Jews and Negroes to world
civilization must be to provide the spiritual element to a world 'immersed in
materialism.'"[49] Africa would be the spiritual savior of a West overburdened
with its materialistic, acquisitive civilization.

In *The Jewish Question*, published in 1898, Blyden declares, "I approach
everything that pertains to the Jews, with feelings of reverence and awe."[50]
For him, "The Jews, as witness to the Supreme Being, are an indispensable
element—if at present a suppressed element—in the spiritual culture and
regeneration of humanity." He goes on to say, "I have for many years—

indeed since my childhood—been an earnest student of the history of God's chosen people. I do not refer to the general teaching which every child brought up in the Christian religion receives in Old Testament history . . . but also to that spiritual teaching outside the books, which comes from contact with living illustrations." He writes about his upbringing with Jewish neighbors in Saint Thomas, whose culture and religion struck him "with an awe and reverence which have followed me all the days of my life" (5).

Blyden sees Jews as comrades-in-suffering of Africans. Nay, Jews, like Africans, belonged to the spiritual race par excellence. He states that he studies the Jewish question from the "African standpoint" and opines that "the history of the African race—their enslavement, persecution, proscription, and sufferings—closely resembles that of the Jews" (7). Blyden delves into the unique spiritual role the Jews play in world history. "Whenever the Jews, or any portion of the Jews, move together on any question relating to religion, the whole of humanity is affected. It shows how closely the spiritual life—that is, the only true life—of the world is connected with their special work and destiny" (8).

Blyden supports Zionism, calling it "that marvellous movement" (7). Although he understands that Zionism is a movement for a Jewish homeland, his view is that Jews can do more leading the world spiritually than politically. Here he is referring to the three Abrahamic faiths—Judaism, Christianity, and Islam:

> I believe that rising Jewish scholars are disposed to recognize that the Jew has a far higher and nobler work to accomplish for humanity than establishing a political power in one corner of the earth. They believe that their race have been qualified by the unspeakable sufferings of ages to be the leaders not in politics but in religion; that to them has been entrusted the spiritual hegemony of mankind; that it is they who are to bring about the practical brotherhood of humanity by establishing, or, rather, propagating, the international religion in whose cult men of all races, climes, and countries will call upon the one Lord under one Name.[51] (8)

The Jew's lot is like that of the Africans, a compendium of infinite suffering:

> Through darkness and storm and weariness of mind and body a passage has been built up for Israel to the gates of light. The mysterious people have suffered and are still capable of suffering. The burning bush has not been consumed and never will be consumed. They have reached the throne of universal sympathy and of complete *rapport* with every section of the human race by their experience and their capabilities of sorrow and suffering. They are the spiritual race and their work is a spiritual work. (8–9)

Blyden points to a "globalization" of the children of Abraham. "The four continents, Europe, Asia, Africa and America, are divided as to religion, between the two sons [of Abraham]; Europe and America to Isaac; Asia and Africa to Ishmael" (17). He locates Abraham himself in Afro-Asia, that is, Egypt, Palestine, and Arabia. He does not respect the great Asian religions of Hinduism and Buddhism, as well as the many indigenous religions and cultures of Native Americans in the Americas.

In *The Significance of Liberia*, written in 1906, Blyden declares of Africa: "There is nothing to be ashamed of in the whole history of the continent or of the race; on the contrary, there is a great deal to be grateful for. It has been said of our Fatherland—it was said as long ago as the days of Aristotle—that she is ever bringing forth something new; new and always helpful; nothing detrimental to the interests of humanity."[52]

He states that he does not intend to bring the glory of ancient Egyptians and Ethiopians to lay claim on the rest of the world: "I have seldom in my writings referred to the connection of the modern Negro with the great races who, in the eastern and northeastern portions of Africa, originated civilization. I mean the Egyptians and Ethiopians. I do not like to refer to this historical fact to strengthen the claims of the Negro upon the respect of the rest of mankind. I rather like to feel that we are men by the grace of God, and that is enough" (2). This approach is quite different from that of Chiekh Anta Diop and the Afrocentric perspective. Blyden seems to reject the golden-age Egyptomania of black nationalists of later generations, including even Senghor. All he wants is to establish the equality of Africans with other people around the world. He does not want to claim African superiority in historical seniority in civilization. Blyden is an advocate of polycentric, multiracial, multicultural cosmopolitanism.

Yet Blyden does not shy away from stating that ancient Egyptians and Ethiopians were indeed black. "The ancient Egyptians and Ethiopians were . . . clearly of the Black race. Whatever modern research, coloured by the prejudices of the day, may say, I would much rather trust Herodotus than the whole tribe of modern commentators on his writings, who arrive at their conclusion with the aid of contemporary inspiration. Herodotus, writing in the simple innocence and candour of an unsophisticated eye-witness, affirms that the Colchians must have descended from the Egyptians because they have black skin and wooly hair." He also cites Homer and his high praise for Ethiopians as being the favorites of the gods (6). Like Frank Snowden and St. Claire Drake decades later, he explains the ancient Greek view of blacks: "in the minds of these noble old Greeks, the black skin and woolly hair, instead of being associated with the meanness and misery of slavery, with ignorance and degradation, were associated with all that is noble in civilization, respectable in learning, delightful in the arts, and splendid in military achievements" (7).

Blyden writes about Africa, which he calls, "the soil of Ham" (8). He reminds us what the world owes to Africa: "In Africa was the beginning or the scene of the preservation of the three great religions to which the best elements of modern civilization are supposed to be due, viz., Judaism, Christianity and Islam. For a great part of their religion then, Europe, Asia and America are largely indebted to our Fatherland." Blyden asks, "But does Europe owe nothing to Africa in her secular or political affairs?" He answers by citing how "enquiring philosophers of Greece and Rome" came to Africa "in search of wisdom." He also cites Africa's military intervention in the struggle between Greece and Troy, to help the Trojans, which in turn helped the rise of Rome (9). From all this, Blyden calls Africa, "the cradle of empires." He asks, "What then, do the inheritors of the strength and wisdom and glory of Rome not owe Africa?" (11).

Blyden writes about how Africa once again may be able to do its work of helping others—this time, the Jews. He supported the British idea of settling Jews in Africa, that is, Uganda. He writes of the Jews, "Begun in Africa, their great work may be finished on this continent." By "great work" of the Jews he is referring to their spiritual role in the development of religion and moral laws. He calls their spiritual labors, the "crowning work for humanity" (12).

Blyden's passionate articulation of the idea that Africa's contribution to humanity lies in her service, suffering, and subjection to others is, in a profound way, an embrace of working class history. He is not embarrassed or ashamed that Africans served humanity; instead, he celebrates it. This aspect of Blyden's philosophy of history is diametrically opposed to the Afrocentric perspective, which is almost exclusively celebratory of the pharaohs of Africa's past. For Blyden, the pharaohs of ancient Egypt do not represent Africa; the toiling masses do. Indeed, when he refers to Egypt, the pharaoh represents oppression, not freedom. Blyden's pharaoh is the Biblical pharaoh, who incurred the wrath of God for refusing God's command, "Let My People Go!"[53] For Blyden, the greatness of Africa of the past lies not in great names such as Ramses II, but rather in those who served him. In all this, one sees how far removed Blyden is from what became the Afrocentric perspective, mostly in America. Yet, Blyden objects to the depiction of Africans as being all the same, as *only* hewers of wood and drawers of water.[54] After all, Blyden knew "Pharaoh" was an African, a "Negro"; and he carried no wood or water.

2

The Critique of Eurocentrism

Whatever others may do for us, there are some things we must do for ourselves.

—Blyden, *Christianity, Islam, and the Negro Race*

Blyden was one of the first black intellectuals to formulate a systematic critique of Eurocentrism long before the term itself came to use. This critique centered on culture, including education. Blyden sees the education of the black Christian in the Western world, unlike that of the Muslim counterpart in Africa, as defective, an example of the "mis-education of the Negro."[1] As he puts it in *Christianity, Islam, and the Negro Race*, "The Negro in Christian lands, however learned in books, cannot be said to have such a thing as self-education. His knowledge, when brought to the test, often fails him. And why? Because he is taught from the beginning to the end of his book-training . . . not to be himself, but somebody else."[2] He declares, "From the lessons he every day receives, the Negro unconsciously imbibes the conviction that to be a great man he must be like the white man. He is not brought up to be the companion, the equal, the comrade of the white man, but his imitator, his ape, his parasite." He further writes, "To be as like the white man as possible—to copy his outward appearance, his peculiarities, his manners, the arrangement of his toilet, that is the aim of the Christian Negro—this is his aspiration. The only virtues which under such circumstances he develops are, of course, the parasitical ones" (44).

Blyden was a vehement critique of the phony imitation of whites by blacks. He writes, "Imitation is not discipleship. . . . A disciple, when freed from leading-strings, may become a producer; an imitator never rises above a mere copyist. With the disciple progress is from within; the imitator grows by accretion from without. The learning acquired by a disciple gives him capacity; that gained by an imitator terminates in itself. The one becomes a capable man; the other is a mere sciolist" (44). He hammers hard on the "incubus of imitation":

One fatal drawback to the Negro in America is the incubus of imitation. He must be an imitator; and imitators see only results—they never learn processes. They come in contact with accomplished facts, without knowing how they were accomplished. They never get within, so as to see how a thing originates or develops. Therefore, when they attempt anything, they are apt to begin at the end, without the insight, patience or experience which teaches that they begin at the beginning. (398–99)

Blyden cites examples from West Africa of the mimicry of Western-influenced Africans. "In the European settlements on the coast there are visible the melancholy effects of the fatal contagion of a mimic or spurious Europeanism. . . . Some who have been to Europe, bring back and diffuse among their people a reverence for some of the customs of that country, of which the more cultivated are trying to get rid" (400).

Blyden provides one of his most brilliant and original perceptions regarding education and the Eurocentric cultural hegemony on the black world in his piece, "The Aims and Methods of a Liberal Education for Africans," included in *Christianity, Islam, and the Negro Race.* "The object of all education is to secure growth and efficiency, to make a man all that his natural gifts will allow him to become; to produce self-respect, a proper appreciation of our own powers and of the powers of other people; to beget a fitness for one's sphere of life and action, and an ability to discharge the duties it imposes." How do black people measure up in this sphere in their long encounter with Western modernity? Blyden answers, "the Negro, notwithstanding his two hundred years' residence with Christian and civilised races, has nowhere received anything like a correct education. . . . We find him everywhere—in the United States, in the West Indies, in South America—largely unable to cope with the responsibilities which devolve upon him" (85). He ponders, "There are many men of book-learning, but few, very few, of any *capability*—even few who have that amount, or that sort, of culture, which produces self-respect, confidence in one's self, and efficiency in work. Now, why is this?" He goes on to provide the reason: "The evil, it is considered, lies in the system and method of European training to which Negroes are, everywhere in Christian lands, subjected, and which everywhere affects them unfavorably. Of a different race, different susceptibility, different bent of character from that of the European, they have been trained under influences in many respects adapted only to the Caucasian race" (87).

In a brilliant analysis of the hegemony of Western culture on the modern black intelligentsia, Blyden writes that these "Christian and so-called civilised Negroes live, for the most part in foreign countries, where they are only passive spectators of the deeds of a foreign race; and where, with other impressions which they receive from without, an element of doubt as to their own capacity and their own destiny is fastened upon them, and inheres in the intellectual and social constitution." He goes on to elaborate the mental universe of such class of people and the processes of their cultural deracination:

> They deprecate their own individuality, and would escape from it if they could. . . . Hence, without the physical or mental aptitude for the enterprises which they are taught to admire and revere, they attempt to copy and imitate them, and share the fate of all copyists and imitators. Bound to move on a lower level, they acquire and retain a practical inferiority, transcribing, very often, the faults rather than the virtues of their models. (87–88)

He explains how modern Western culture has systematically dehumanized people of African origin by turning them into caricatures. Focusing on the English-speaking world, he writes, "In all English-speaking countries the mind of the intelligent Negro child revolts against the description given in elementary books—geography, travels, histories—of the Negro." Blyden calls these "pernicious teachings." In a discourse similar to that of Fanon eight decades later, Blyden writes of the Western-educated black intellectual, "Having embraced, or at least assented, to those errors and falsehoods about himself, he concludes that his only hope of rising in the scale of respectable manhood is to strive after whatever is most unlike himself and most alien to his peculiar tastes."[3] As he is a bad copy of his teacher, "he can never bring any real assistance to the European. He can never attain to that essence of progress which Mr. Herbert Spencer describes as *difference*; and therefore, he never acquires the self-respect or self-reliance of an independent contributor." As such, "He is not an independent help, only a subordinate help; so that the European feels that he owes him no debt, and moves on in contemptuous indifference of the Negro, teaching him to contemn himself" (88). By "independent help" he means help that stands on its own two feet, help of an independently grounded subject. It is help whose help cannot but be respected, accepted, and even needed. "Subordinate help," on the other hand, is help dependent on the one that provides it in the first place. Since Western-educated black intellectuals are but a copy of their white teachers, they do not get respect from those who taught them what they know. Indeed, they do not deserve it. So says Blyden.

Turning to the question of color, Blyden, much like Fanon later, writes, "The standard of all physical and intellectual excellencies in the present civilisation being the white complexion, whatever deviates from that favoured colour is proportionally depreciated, until the black which is the opposite, becomes not only the most unpopular but the most unprofitable colour." Hence "Black men, and especially black women, in such communities, experience the greatest imaginable inconvenience. They never feel at home. In the depth of their being they always feel themselves strangers in the land of their exile, and the only escape from this feeling is to escape from themselves." In such a racialized world, "flippant and eulogistic reference is constantly made to the superior physical and mental characteristics of the Caucasian race, which, by contrast, suggests the inferiority of other races, specially of the race which is the furthest removed from it in appearance." He adds, "It is painful in America to see the efforts which are made by Negroes to secure outward conformity to the appearance of the dominant race. This is by no means surprising; but what is surprising is that, under the circumstances, any Negro has retained a particle of self-respect" (89).

If such is the condition of racist hegemony, which imposed itself with such formidable power of cultural dislocation and self-deprecation among its victims, what does Blyden suggest as the way out? Blyden's reply: the cultivation of an African methodology. "The African must advance by methods of his own. He must possess a power distinct from that of the European. . . . We [Africans] must show that we are able to go alone, to carve out our own way. . . . We must not suppose that the Anglo-Saxon methods are final, that there is nothing for us to find out for our own guidance, and that we have nothing to teach to the world. There is inspiration for us also" (89–90).

What is this African methodology, and how is it to be attained? Blyden's solution is similar to what Cabral called the "return to the source."[4] "We must study our brethren from the interior, who know better than we do the laws of growth for the race. . . . We look too much to foreigners, and are dazzled almost to blindness by their exploit—so as to fancy that they have exhausted the possibilities of humanity" (90). For Blyden, Africans of the interior, far away from the influence of Western hegemony, are the curators of authentic African culture and African personality. They are the ones who know the "laws of growth for the race." The race for modernity is to be one that binds with those who know the "laws of growth of the race." He elaborates this perception:

> Things which have been of great advantage to Europe may work to ruin us; and there is often such a striking resemblance, or such a close connection between the hurtful and the beneficial, that we are not always able to discriminate. . . . So we have reason to apprehend that in our indiscriminate appropriation of European agencies, or methods in our political, educational, and social life, we are often imbibing overdoses of morphine, when we fancy we are only taking Dover's powders! (91)

The key idea here is his critique of "indiscriminate appropriation of European agencies, or methods." Blyden is not against the West. He is the impeccable modernist; as such, he admires Western Christian bourgeois modernity. But he is also the uncompromising and proud black racial nationalist who eschews anything that smacks of black racial self-deprecation. Blyden was the quintessential voice of black racial nationalist modernity.

For the successful implementation of Blyden's project of black racial nationalist modernity, Africans are not to shun the outside world, including the West, and wrap themselves up in their tropical warmth. On the contrary, Africa is to remain open to the outside world. But its door is not to be open too wide for intervention by rude and rowdy crowds. Africa needs to be wary of letting everyone in without question; it ought to discriminate the good and useful from the bad and harmful. Africa should be welcoming outside influences on its own terms: "When we receive impressions from without we must bring from our own consciousness the idea that gives them shape; we must mould them by our own individuality" (92–93). This view is akin to the historical experiences of Ethiopian civilization, one which Donald Levine calls "creative incorporation."[5]

Blyden's critique of Eurocentrism is impressive. In the sphere of educational pedagogy, he came up with a sophisticated academic curriculum for Liberia College. In the study of history, he follows Frederick Harrison's classification of the six historical ages: theocratic, Greek, Roman, medieval, late medieval and early modern, and post-French Revolution. Of these six ages, he picks his choice: "We shall permit [in] our curriculum the unrestricted study of the first four epochs, but especially the second, third and fourth, from which the present civilisation of Western Europe is mainly derived." He wanted to exclude the last two ages: "We can afford to exclude, then, as subjects of study, at least in the earlier college years, the events of the fifth and sixth epochs. It was during the sixth period that the transatlantic slave-trade arose, along with the degradation and proscription of the Negro" (94–95).

Two questions arise. First, Blyden's acceptance of Harrison's six ages is problematic in that it has no place for Africa. As in other standard historical texts of the nineteenth century, Harrison teaches that Africa had no history. For him, the first age, the theocratic, is the age of Asian history, while the remaining five ages are all European. This classification is the same as that of Hegel, for whom history began in the Orient and progresses further only in the European theater.[6] Like Harrison, Hegel excludes Africa from history. Blyden, who has argued that Africa has a history, should have been cautious of uncritically appropriating such a standard Eurocentric academic undertaking.

Second, Blyden's exclusion of the last two periods, which saw the Atlantic enslavement of Africans and the concomitant rise of racist views that depreciate their worth as human beings, is puzzling. His argument is that young minds should not be taught such demeaning pictures of Africans. The problem with his argument is that it focuses on what the Europeans thought and felt about Africans, and not on what Africans thought and felt about themselves. He makes Europeans the subject, Africans the predicate. Moreover, to shun young minds from the history of European racism against Africans is counterproductive. As long as the education given them about racism is conducted in the right way, by teachers who have the interest of Africans at heart and who teach about racism to show its arbitrariness and irrationality, it makes more sense to reach youth at an early stage to teach and prepare them for the struggles ahead.

Furthermore, his choice of the first four ages is based on a Eurocentric understanding. His rationale is that African students need to learn the foundation of Western civilization, which was laid down in the first four stages. Moreover, in these stages, Africans were not dehumanized as in the last two ages. As he puts it, "The instruments of culture which we shall employ in the College will be chiefly by the Classics and Mathematics. By Classics I mean the Greek and Latin Languages and their literature. In those languages there are not, as far as I know, a sentence, a word, or a syllable disparaging to the Negro" (97). One could raise the question, "Why should African students study about European history, anyway?" Blyden's answer is simple: during his time Europe was the pinnacle of human accomplishment. As such, Africans must be able to drink deep at the fountain of this land of civilization that is Europe.

Blyden does not say that African students should study only European history and European classical languages. He includes in the curriculum the study of Arabic and many African languages spoken in the interior of Liberia. "It will be our aim to introduce into our curriculum also the Arabic, and some of the principal native languages—by means of which we may have intelligent intercourse with the millions accessible to us in the interior, and learn more of our country" (101).

In a powerful rebuttal of the Eurocentric knowledge structure that informed the modern education that Africans received, Blyden writes,

> We have young men who are experts in the geography and customs of foreign countries; who can tell all about the proceedings of foreign statesmen in countries thousands of miles away; can talk glibly of London, Berlin, Paris and Washington; know all about Gladstone, Bismarck, Gambetta, and Hayes; but who knows anything about Musahdu, Medina, Kankan, or Segu—only a few hundred miles from here? Who can tell anything about of the policy or doings of Fanfi-doreh, Ibrahima Sissi, or Simoro of Boporu—only a few steps from us? These are hardly known. Now as Negroes, allied in blood and race to these people, this is disgraceful; and as a nation, if we intend to grow and prosper in this country, it is impolitic, it is short-sighted, it is unpatriotic. (101–2)

Blyden is an advocate of concrete universalism, one enriched by the embrace of the myriad of humanity's cultural variations. He states, "culture is one, and the general effects of true culture are the same; but the native capacities of mankind differ, and their word and destiny differ, so that the road by which one man may attain to the highest efficiency, is not that which would conduce to the success of another." It is from such reflection that Blyden decides not to copy verbatim the experiences of other peoples. "The special road which has led to the success and elevation of the Anglo-Saxon is not that which would lead to the success and elevation of the Negro, though we shall resort to the same means of general culture which has enabled the Anglo-Saxon to find out for himself the way in which he ought to go" (96–97). He advocates that Africans should learn and critically appropriate whatever is of universal value, including Christianity. "We will study to cultivate whatsoever things are true, whatsoever things are honest, whatsoever things are just, whatsoever things are pure, whatsoever things are lovely, whatsoever things are of good report" (104).

Black women are part of Blyden's plan for the education of Africans, by combining the best that the West offers alongside Africa's own traditions. He writes, "I cannot see why our sisters should not receive exactly the same general culture as we do. I think that the progress of the country will be more rapid and permanent when the girls receive the same general training as the boys." He adds, "We need not fear that they will be less graceful, less natural, or less womanly; but we may be sure that they will make wiser mothers, more appreciative wives, and more affectionate sisters" (102–3).

Blyden laments the damages done to Africans in their uncritical acceptance of things Western.

> All our traditions and experiences are connected with a foreign race. We have no poetry or philosophy but that of our taskmasters. The songs that live in our ears and are often on our lips are the songs which we heard sung by those who shouted while we groaned and lamented. They sang of their history, which was the history of our degradation. They recited their triumphs, which contained the record of our humiliation. To our great misfortune, we learned their prejudices and their passions, and thought we had their aspirations and their power. (105)

What is to be done, then? His answer: "return to the source." "Now, if we are to make an independent nation—a strong nation—we must listen to the songs of our unsophisticated brethren as they sing of their history, as they tell of their traditions, of the wonderful and mysterious events of their tribal or national life, of the achievements of what we call their superstitions. . . . We shall in this way get back the strength of the race" (105–6).

Blyden suggests that returning to the source requires spatial proximity, to have "the College away from the seaboard—with its constant intercourse with foreign manners and low foreign ideas." That way, "we may have free and uninterrupted intercourse with the intelligent among the tribes of the interior . . . and mingle with our brethren and gather fresh inspiration and fresh living ideas." Reflecting on the agony of rejection of the modern back intelligentsia struggling for recognition in the white world, Blyden writes, "It is the complaint of the intelligent Negro in America that white people pay no attention to his suggestions or his writings; but this is only because he has nothing new to say—nothing that they have not said before him, and that they cannot say better than he can." He adds, "Let us do our own work and we shall be strong and worthy of respect; try to do the work of others, and we shall be weak and contemptible. There is magnetism in original action, in self-trust, which others cannot resist" (106).

He closes this brilliant piece with the following remarks: "How shall we make our 'lives sublime'? Not by imitating others, but by doing well our own part as they did theirs." "We have a great work before us, a work unique in the history of the world." "Let us show ourselves equal to the task" (107). He was a believer in human equality with diversity. "All truth is one. All true religion is true philosophy and all true philosophy is true religion." Included in such truth is the precept that "the conventional morality of Europe cannot be the conventional morality of Africa."[7]

Blyden wrote extensively about the Eurocentric cultural hegemony injurious to Africans and how to overcome it. In "Sierra Leone and Liberia: Their Origin, Work, and Destiny," included in *Christianity, Islam, and the Negro Race*, he states, "In our contact with the Christian world, our teachers have of necessity been Europeans, and they have taught us books too much, and things too little—forms of expression, and very little the importance of thought." He goes on to deplore

> the notion, still common among Negroes—educated Negroes I mean . . . that the most important part of knowledge consists in knowing what other men—foreigners—have said about things, and even about Africa and about themselves. They aspire to be familiar, not with what really is, but with what is printed. Very few among us have got [*sic*] past this step. Hence, some of us are found repeating things against ourselves, which are thoroughly false and injurious to us, and only because we read them in books, or have heard them from foreign teachers. (253)

He complains, "we were trained in books written by foreigners, and *for a foreign race*, not *for us* . . . and from some of these books we learned that the Negro at home was a degraded being—a Heathen, and worse than a Heathen—a fool; and we were taught everything excellent and praiseworthy about foreigners" (254).

Blyden explains the damage such education has done to Africans, especially regarding history. "We have had history written for us, and we have endeavoured to act up to it; whereas, the true order is, that history should be first acted, then written. It is easy to account, then, for the want of genuine life and spontaneous activity in the people." He bemoans the stultifying impact of Eurocentrism on Africans: "It would be a melancholy outlook for Africa, with its vast territories and countless tribes, if its development and prosperity were altogether contingent upon the labour of foreigners, or even upon the genius and life of a few natives, educated on foreign models and in foreign ways of thinking, to be produced and brought upon the stage of action by the machinery of an alien people." But then, as elsewhere in the Blydenian corpus, he contradicts himself when he says right in the next paragraph, "It is a very interesting fact that the main body of the settlers who planted civilisation on these shores in both colonies [Liberia and Sierra Leone] were men deeply imbued with the religious spirit. Like the puritans of America, the Bible was their code of laws, for civil and religious life" (254). We may ask, what is the importance of comparing African American settlers in Liberia and Sierra Leone with that of the Puritans of America if not a case of relying on "foreign models" and "foreign ways of thinking"?

Blyden warns Africans to be cautious of undue imitation, but also of unnecessary rejection: "The great incubus upon our development has been unreasoning imitation. This we must try to avoid. But do not run to the other extreme of avoiding what is foreign simply because it is foreign. There are many good things in foreign customs—many useful things, many precious things, not only conducive and helpful, but indispensable to a healthy Christian growth. These we must find out and cherish." Although what he says here refers to the need for the Africanization of the West African Church, it also applies to his overall pedagogical philosophy. As he warns against both narrow nativism and hollow imitationism, he still would write, "All educated Negroes suffer from a kind of slavery in many ways far more than subversive of the real welfare of the race than the ancient physical fetters. The slavery of mind is far more destructive than that of the body."[8]

Blyden was a firm believer in the capabilities of Africans for improvements, given the "right conditions." "Make them [whites and Africans] equal in culture, and the balance must be in favour of the Negro." He still cautions,

> The Negro mind, perhaps more than that of any other race, needs all the help to be secured from disciplinary agencies. We have been the victims not only of ages of barbarism, but the most advanced of us have been the victims of what is far more pernicious—namely, foreign oppression; and our faults and failings, partly the result of remote influences of the past, but chiefly the result of our immediate antecedents, are often the subject of unappreciative remark by those of our foreign teachers who know us only in exile.[9]

For him, Western modernity has a double-edged relationship with Africans, both in Africa and the diaspora at large. Just as it introduces a "benighted" people to the light of modernity, it also oppresses them.

Blyden finds the method followed by European missionaries in Africa to be defective and racist. It yields few positive results, if any. The missionaries' model, "however useful they might be in Europe, become, when introduced indiscriminately into Africa, artificial, ineffective and absurd" (*Christianity*, 75). The attempt to Europeanize Africans will not only be counterproductive and destructive for Africans but also unproductive for Europeans too. It "will always be a profitless task." Indeed, "the African would then fail of the ability to perform his specific part in the world's work, as a distinct portion of the human race" (76). Both Africans and Europeans would benefit from each other's relations only if they were to maintain their essential and ineradicable distinction. Both would benefit less in their relations if they were alike than if they were essentially different. If one were to be the extended reproduction of the other, the duplicate would be in an inferior position to the original. "To make the African a parasite upon the European would be no gain to mankind." The question is, Blyden relays, "How to elevate the African, or enable him to elevate himself, according to the true Christian standard. Any progress made otherwise must be unreal, unsatisfactory, precarious, transitory" (77).

As a dedicated promoter of an Africanized version of Western modernity, Blyden fought hard against the trend that focused on the negative that came from Europe and ignored its immense uplifting influence. He notes in frustration, "It is unfortunate for the English and other European languages that, in this part of Africa, they have come to the greater portion of the natives associated with profligacy, plunder, and cruelty, and devoid of any connection with spiritual things; while the Arabic is regarded by them as the language of prayer and devotion, of religion and piety, of all that is unworldly and spiritual" (79). Blyden never doubted that Africans had what it takes to achieve modernity without being carbon copies of Europeans. For him, modernity may have begun in Europe, but it is not Europe's private property. Modernity, like Christianity, belongs to all humanity. But it needs to be localized; it needs to be made to fit what he calls the "idiosyncrasies of each race."

Blyden's fundamental belief is that human beings are divided into different and irreducible but equal racial categories. Being that, each race needs to grow in its own way. If all racial groups were to evolve toward a single goal, along the same path, toward a uniformity, that would be an impoverishment, not improvement, of the rich diversity of the human species. Diversity, not unity, is the law of nature, including the law of race. Nay, it would be a violation of the divine law that gave the earth to the three sons of Noah—Ham, Shem, and Japheth. It is from these three sons that Blyden, alongside the religious and racial views of his time, deduces the three racial categories— Caucasoid, Negroid, and Mongoloid. He sees the Ham line leading to the black race, the Japheth line to the European white race, and the Shem line to the Semitic race of Arabs and Jews. But he classifies the latter "race" as a subcategory of the Caucasian race. Hegel, in accord with his time, divided the Caucasian race into two—European and West Asian. The former he subclassified into Germanic, Romanic, and Slavic, in that order of hierarchy. The West Asian branch of the Caucasian race he subdivided into Semitic and the non-Semitic, although Hegel did not use the term "non-Semitic."[10] In this subdivision are included Persians and Turks.[11] But unlike Blyden, Hegel drew the race distinction not from the three sons of Noah but from contemporary science. Blyden was writing decades after Hegel had died, and with more "scientific" material on race than was available to Hegel. Yet the Mongoloid race was not there. It was left without a trace in Blyden's race trance.

Blyden complains that Westerners want to know Africa the land more than African the person. He laments, "While every effort is made to explore and describe the country, very little attempt is made to study the man of Africa" (*Christianity*, 301). Western racism denigrates Africans and elevates Africa. For the Western traveler, Africa's nature is more attractive than African culture, even more than the African people themselves. As Blyden puts it, "Nearly all other modern travellers have regarded the Man of Africa with contempt, in comparison with the natural features—the physical grandeur and material resources—of the country" (304). He goes on to describe the contempt: "The outside world thinks it knows the Man of Africa. Has not the Negro been seen as a labourer in every part of the world? Has he not for centuries been on the plantations in all western hemisphere? Have not numerous travellers written about him, and has he not been minutely described by scientific men, from his skull to his heels?" He shows how this alleged knowing of the African is based on chimera. "Only the Negro will be able to explain the Negro to the rest of mankind" (301). He further states, "the intellectual character and susceptibility of the Negro will probably, for ages yet, elude the grasp and comprehension of the most sagacious European" (303).

Blyden singles out David Livingstone apart from the other Westerners. "Livingstone . . . has come nearer than any other European to understanding the Man of Africa. . . . He of all travellers made the Man an object of his study, and the benefit of the man the ultimate aim of his labours." He "had the first and most important pre-requisite to proficiency in that class of study, viz., sympathy with his subject. He not only loved Africa, but the African." He "has thus become the popular and most trustworthy teacher of the best portion of the Christian world with regard to the African" (303–4). Blyden praises Mary Kingsley the same way he praises Livingstone. She "became the Prophet of Africa to her own people."[12] If we were to single out two "Anglo-Saxons" for whom Blyden had the highest respect, it would be these two, Mary Kingsley and David Livingstone.

In many of his correspondences, Blyden addresses the impact of Eurocentric hegemony on Africans. In his letter to Mary Kingsley, written on May

7, 1900, Blyden writes admirably about the Gold Coast nationalist and law-yer John Mensah Sarbah, author of the 1897 work *Fanti Customary Laws*, fol-lowed by the 1903 book, *Fanti National Constitution*. "While acquiring the English language he [Sarbah] did not forget his own; and his aboriginal parents, both by precept and example, indoctrinated him with Native laws and customs."[13] Africans like Sarbah were few and far between. For Blyden, Sarbah is the role model the African ought to be: Western and African, in symbiosis, founded on African grounding.

Aiming his arrow at the Eurocentric knowledge structure into which Afri-can youth was dragged, Blyden states, much like Fanon and Cabral later, "The Christianized Negro looks away from his Native heath. He is never taught like Antaeus of old to touch the ground—his mother earth—for recuperation. He is under the curse of an insatiable ambition for imitation of foreign ideas and foreign customs." Blyden calls this the "black man's burden," one in which the Western-educated African was made to forget, ignore, or be ashamed of "the rock whence he was hewn and the hole of the pit whence he was digged." Yet, unrepentant Christian that he was, Blyden writes that Africa needs the Gospel, but "a different and wiser gospel, which should be preached by her own sons educated in European learning."[14]

Blyden informed Mary Kingsley of his wish to "establish a Mary Kingsley Scholarship of Arabic, Mandingo or Vey." He also wanted "to raise up a Pro-fessor of West African Languages and Religion." This vision is in accord with Blyden's long-cherished ideal of the need for the development of an inde-pendent African nationality. "Such a chair seems to be absolutely necessary for the healthful development of an independent Negro state in West Africa, with millions of aborigines within its territory, who must be co-operated with and incorporated if the Republic is to have a permanent and useful place on this continent."[15]

Blyden makes one of his most profound reflections about Western-edu-cated black elites in a letter he wrote to Dr. Mojola Agbebi on March 17, 1903. Blyden states, "The European teacher, especially the Anglo-Saxon, hampered by dogmatic creeds, cannot help trying not to Christianise but to Europeanise or Anglicise the native. He brings with him his prejudices, his faith in a natural inequality, and his profound disbelief in any race but his own."[16] He further notes, "The great drawback in the character of the negro who has been subjected to training under the doctrines and formularies of European Christianity is his unwillingness to stand up as an African. He does not like to be odd. He is ashamed of anything that does not conform to the European standard or represent European conceptions. This is the inverte-brate condition to which he has been reduced." Blyden laments,

> God has made him odd, and he will do anything not to appear so. There is no other race on the face of the earth like him—"black skin and wooly hair." In

America, he tries to bleach his skin and straighten his hair. But this cannot alter his destiny. It is fixed. His work and his destiny are peculiar and unique. But, under the foreign training he has received, he is never satisfied unless he thinks he is imitating the white man. Observers, however, know that he is not imitating but only aping. This foreigners know and the uncontaminated native knows.[17]

At the beginning of the letter, Blyden writes,

The African has something to say—a great deal to say to the world; and by the world, I mean the Western world—Europe and America—which it ought to hear, which it would like to hear and which it would be useful to hear. But to say it effectively, he must say it in the language of the West. He must be able to use the terms and employ the methods which the West understands, and he can only know these terms and these methods by being admitted to the white man's culture, which, if it is thorough, will not spoil him but make him more strongly African. Any soil well cultivated, by whatever instrument, whether by foreign plough or native hoe, will bring forth the fruit proper to the soil. You will never get apples or peaches from African soil, however carefully you may cultivate it. The deeper the culture, the less chance for the exotic plant. If it shoot above the ground it will only be to perish without taking firm root or bearing fruit.[18]

Does Blyden mean to say that a deep knowledge of Western culture by Africans makes them less Eurocentric, and that aping and imitation come from a superficial encounter with Western modernity? What is the soil and apples metaphor meant to convey? Does it mean the need for the Africanization of Western modernity? Blyden is making the case that no matter what one imports to Africa from outside, it will not bear fruit as long as it is not grounded on African foundations. And the deeper the cultural foundations of Africa are, the more difficult it becomes for the alien plant to bear fruit. This is in tandem with his repeated insistence that the so-called civilized Negro, educated in the Western ways, cannot be anything but miseducated. That is, he becomes a prisoner of what Blyden calls "spurious Europeanism." As he puts it in his last major work, *African Life and Customs*, "The crux of the educational question, as it affects the African, is that western methods denationalise him. He becomes a slave to foreign ways of life and thought." The irony is that it is to this same class of people that he arrogates the calling and responsibility of bringing the light of civilization to the "dark continent." Blyden may have been aware of the paradox. As he retorts, "And now I come to the question of questions. How may the West African be trained so as to preserve his national identity and race instincts?"[19]

Blyden has a different view regarding Islam in Africa. As opposed to Western culture, which he condemned as denationalizing the African, turning him into a mere caricature, a mimic, a puppet, he sees Islam in Africa as a vigorous, dynamic, and civilizing force.[20] The next chapter covers that topic.

3

Ishmael in Africa

Black Protestant Islamophilia

Islam is the form that Christianity takes in Africa.
                    —Blyden, *West Africa before Europe*

If the divinity of a religion may be inferred from the variety of
races among whom it has been diffused, and the strength of
its hold upon them, then there is no religion that can prefer
greater claims than Islam.
                    —Blyden, *Christianity, Islam, and the Negro Race*

In his philosophy of religion, Blyden refers to how different races gravitate
toward one religion or another: "It is remarkable that the eight distinct religions
of which history gives account all had their origin in Asia, and the three highest
religions—the Jewish, the Christian, the Mohammedan—took their rise among
Semitic peoples." Furthermore, "it is equally remarkable that since Christianity
left the place of its birth it has seemed to be the property exclusively of the European branch of the human family." As Christianity "has become the possession
of the Western Aryan, it has shared the fate of that other great religion which
arose among the Eastern branch of the Indo-European family, viz., Buddhism,
as being for the most part confined to one or two races."[1]
    Blyden compares the Aryan and the Semitic "minds" in their views of
the relation between God and humanity. It is the credit of the "West Aryan
genius . . . to divorce God from His works, and to lay great stress upon
human capability and achievement. Man is an end, not a means. . . . The
more favoured race must dominate and control the less favoured race.
Religion is to be cherished as a means of subserving temporal and material
purposes." In short, "Everything now depends upon man. Everything else is
within his grasp. He may even by searching find God. Material progress is
the end of the human race."[2]

According to Blyden, the Semitic mind is different from that of the Aryan. "The Semitic mind . . . destitute, it has been alleged, of the scientific instinct, looks upon man—every man—as standing in direct relation to God, who has not ceased His communication with His creatures, still speaking to them at times in dreams and visions, and at other times by the ordinary events of life." While the "Greek or Indo-European paid more attention to physical than to moral excellence, to the Shemite, the spirit, the mind of a man, was the great object of development and culture—the inward character rather than the outward form."[3]

For Blyden, "It would seem that the very qualities which render Anglo-Saxons irresistible as conquerors—that unrelenting sternness and uncompromising hardness—disqualify them for the subtle and delicate task of assimilating subject races and winning their confidence and affection."[4] This is in line with his many statements elsewhere where he compares the rugged masculinity of the Anglo-Saxon with the soft femininity of the African, or by extension, the nonwhite world at large, including the Semitic. Such a racialized trope was also once entertained by negritude thinkers, including Léopold Sédar Senghor.[5] Blyden was an uncompromising Islamophile. This is all the more remarkable given that he was a Protestant minister. I call his attitude toward Islam "black Protestant Islamophilia."

Blyden wrote extensively on the positive role Islam played in Africa in many of his writings and lectures, the most detailed account of which is to be found in *Christianity, Islam, and the Negro Race*. Blyden knew the history of Islam well. He taught himself Arabic so that he could read the Koran and other writings on Islam in the original language. He ended up teaching the language himself. He sees Islam as a religion in friendly relation with the African.[6] He writes, "Mohammed not only loved the Negro, but regarded Africa with peculiar interest and affection. He never spoke of any curse hanging over the country or people. When in the early years of his reform, his followers were persecuted and could not get protection in Arabia, he advised them to seek asylum in Africa." Blyden is referring to Muhammad's followers who went to Christian Aksum (Ethiopia) during the reign of King Armah, who welcomed them and acted as host until they went back to Mecca to join Muhammad. "It was Abyssinia that afforded shelter to the persecuted Muslims, who, in the early days of Islam, had to fly from Arabia for their lives. When Mohammed found that his few followers were likely to be crushed by the opposition at Mecca, he advised their flight into Abyssinia."[7]

Blyden had a very high regard for Islam, which he saw as a major civilizing force in Africa:

Mohammedanism in Africa counts in its ranks the most energetic and enterprising tribes. It claims as adherents the only people who have any form of civil polity or bond of social organization. It has built and occupies the largest cities in the heart of the continent. . . . It produces and controls the most valuable commerce between Africa and Foreign countries; it is daily gaining converts from the ranks of Paganism; and it commands respect among all Africans wherever it is known, even where the people have not submitted to the sway of the Koran.

His laudatory remarks about Islam's civilizing influence upon "Pagan" Africa abound in many of his writings.

No one can travel any distance in the interior of West Africa without being struck with the different aspects of society in different localities, according as the population is Pagan or Mohammedan. Not only is there a difference in the methods of government, but in the general regulations of society, and even in the amusements of the people. The love of noisy terpsichorean performances, so noticeable in Pagan communities, disappears as the people come under the influence of Mohammedanism.

He adds, "When we left a Pagan and entered a Mohammedan community, we at once noticed that we had entered a moral atmosphere widely separated from, and loftier far than, the one we had left. We discovered that the character, feelings, and conditions of the people were profoundly altered and improved" (6–7).

Blyden's views regarding Islam's civilizing influence on Africa echoes that of Hegel's. Hegel writes, "Mohammedanism seems to be the only thing which has brought the negroes at all nearer to culture. The Mohammedans also know better than the Europeans how to penetrate the interior of the country."[8] Blyden writes that "the Koran . . . is in advance of the Shamanism or Fetichism of the African tribes who accept it" and that "Islam as a creed is an enormous advance not only on all idolatries, but on all systems of purely human origin" (7–8).

For Blyden, Islam's "uplifting" influence on Africans was not limited to religion. It was also found in the sphere of forming larger political and cultural communities brought together by a shared common faith. "The Koran is, in its measure, an important educator. It exerts among a primitive people a wonderful influence. It has furnished to the adherents of its teaching in Africa a ground of union which has contributed vastly to their progress. . . . They are united by a common religious sentiment, by a common antagonism to Paganism" (8).

Blyden sees progress brought about by Islam in the coming together of people with different tongues now sharing the common language of the religion of Islam, Arabic (8). He says that for Muslim Africans, "Mohammedans of Negroland," as he calls them, the struggle for the ascendancy of Islam is their prime concern in life. They see it, and Blyden concurs, as "a struggle between light and darkness, between knowledge and ignorance, between good and evil" (11).

Blyden makes a cogent comparison between Christian "Negroes" and their Muslim counterparts. He bases his comparison on his "exceptional advantages for observation and comparison in the United States, the West Indies, South America, Egypt, Syria, West and Central Africa." Based on such extensive, observational knowledge, he comments,

> Wherever the Negro is found in Christian lands, his leading trait is not docil-ity, as has been often alleged, but servility. He is slow and unprogressive. Indi-viduals here and there may be found of extraordinary intelligence, enterprise, and energy, but there is no Christian community of Negroes anywhere which is self-reliant and independent. Haiti and Liberia, so-called Negro Republics, are merely struggling for existence, and hold their own by the tolerance of the civilised powers. On the other hand, there are numerous Negro Moham-medan communities and states in Africa which are self-reliant, productive, independent, and dominant, supporting, without the countenance or patron-age of the parent country, Arabia, whence they derived them, their political, literary, and ecclesiastical institutions. (12)

Blyden cites five reasons for the differences between the impact of Chris-tianity and Islam on Africans. These distinctions have to do with "the differ-ence in the conditions under which the systems came to those of the Negro race who embraced the one or the other." The first reason is that "Moham-medanism found its Negro converts at home in a state of freedom and inde-pendence of the teachers who brought it to them. When it was offered to them they were at liberty to choose for themselves." The African converts became "Muslims from choice and conviction, and [brought] all the manli-ness of their former condition to the maintenance and support of their new creed." Moreover, "When the religion [Islam] was first introduced it found the people possessing all the elements and enjoying all the privileges of an untrammeled manhood. . . . Their local institutions were not destroyed by the Arab influence introduced. They only assumed new forms, and adapted themselves to the new teachings." As a result, Islam in Africa was Africanized. "In all thriving Mohammedan communities, in West and Central Africa, it may be noticed that the Arab superstructure has been superimposed on a permanent indigenous substructure; so what really took place, when the Arab met the Negro in his own home, was a healthy amalgamation, and not an absorption or an undue repression" (13–14).

Blyden expounds on the theme of the Africanization of Islam: "The Ori-ental aspect of Islam has become largely modified in Negroland, not, as is too generally supposed, by a degrading compromise with the Pagan super-stitions, but by shaping many of its traditional customs to suit the milder and more conciliatory disposition of the Negro." Moreover, the "absence of political pressure has permitted native peculiarities to manifest themselves, and to take an effective part in the work of assimilating the new elements" (14).

He now reflects on the African reception of Christianity as compared with that of Islam. "Christianity, on the other hand, came to the Negro as a slave, or at least as a subject race in a foreign land. Along with the Christian teaching, he and his children received lessons of their utter and permanent inferiority and subordination to their instructors, to whom they stood in the relation of chattels." In the land of their exile, the "religion of Jesus was embraced by them as the only source of consolation in their deep disasters. In their abject miseries, keen anguish, and hopeless sufferings they seized upon it as promising a country." Christianity "found them down-trodden, oppressed, scorned; it soothed their suffering, subdued their hearts." It "directed their aspirations to an heavenly and eternal citizenship; it put new songs in their mouths—those melodies inimitable to the rest of the world." Hence "owing to the physical, mental, and social pressure under which the African received these influences of Christianity, their development was necessarily partial and one-sided, cramped and abnormal." Such a situation could not lead anywhere but utter dependence on the oppressor and lack of self-esteem. "All tendencies to independent individuality were repressed and destroyed. . . . All avenues to intellectual improvement were closed against them, and they were doomed to perpetual ignorance" (14–15).

Contrast this with the advantages enjoyed by Africans who embraced Islam: "Mohammedanism and learning to the Muslim Negro were coeval. No sooner was he converted than he was taught to read, and the importance of knowledge was impressed upon him. The Christian Negro came in contact with mental and physical proscription and the religion of Christ, contemporaneously." Blyden further writes,

> If the Mohammedan Negro had at any time to choose between the Koran and the sword, when he chose the former, he was allowed to wield the latter as the equal of any other Muslim; but no amount of allegiance to the Gospel relieved the Christian Negro from the degradation of wearing the chain which he received with it. . . . Everywhere in Christian lands he plays, at the present moment, the part of the slave, ape or puppet. (15–16)

Unlike Muslim Africans who received Islam on their own land and on their own terms, Africans who received Christianity in the Americas were slaves, and those they received it from were their masters. Blyden writes,

> The Gospel of Christ was travestied and diluted before it came to him to suit the "peculiar institution" by which millions of human beings were converted

into "chattels." The highest men in the South, magistrates, legislators, professors of religion, preachers of the Gospel, governors of states, gentlemen of property and standing, all united in upholding a system which every Negro felt was wrong. Yet these were the men from whom he got his religion, and whom he was obligated to regard as guides. Under such teaching and discipline, is it to be wondered at that his morality is awry—that his sense of the "dignity of human nature" is superficial—that his standard of family and social life is low and defective? (37–38)

There is a problem with Blyden's methodology. He compares Africans in the land of their enslavement in the Americas who came in contact with the Christianity of their slaveholders with that of Africans who came in contact with and embraced Islam in their own countries as free people in Africa. He should have compared the conditions of Africans enslaved in foreign lands as such, and how they came to the knowledge of the religion of their masters: enslaved Africans in the Americas and their contact with Christianity, compared with enslaved Africans in Arabia or other Muslim lands and their contact with Islam. This would have been a commensurate comparison. It is surprising that he hardly talks about slavery in Muslim Africa or about the enslavement of Africans in the Muslim world at large. Had he done so, he may have had a more reasonable comparison to make.[9]

Another problem with Blyden regarding Africans in the lands of their exile in the Americas is his silence about Islam in the Americas. It is strange that as capable a scholar as he was, he said little, if anything, about the African Muslim presence in the Americas during slavery. Had he taken up this issue, he could perhaps have reflected on the relation between enslaved Muslim Africans in the Americas and their Christian slaveholders.[10]

Blyden still could have made even a stronger case by comparing the coming of Christianity and Islam in Africa, where they found Africans at home and free, for example, in North Africa, Ethiopia, West Africa, the Swahili coast of eastern Africa, and the Horn of Africa. There he could have seen how Christianity was Africanized (the best example being Ethiopia) just as was Islam. It was this Ethiopia that became the rallying ground of anticolonial Pan-Africanist protest during the Italian fascist occupation of 1935–41.

The second reason for the superiority of Islam over Christianity in their respective impact on Africans is the difference in the symbolic and artistic representation of divinity in the two religions. Unlike in the Christian encounter with Africa, "Negro Mohammedans . . . have not been trained under the depressing influence of Aryan art." That is, Islam, in line with Judaism, forbids the artistic depiction of divinity. "The Second Commandment, with Mussulmans as with Jews, is construed literally into the prohibition of all representations of living creatures of all kinds; not merely in sacred places but everywhere." He remarks that the "early Christian Fathers believed that painting and sculpture were forbidden by the Scriptures, and that they were therefore wicked arts" (16–17).

How does the artistic depiction of divinity or its prohibition affect the racial reception of the religion? Blyden writes quite persuasively, "No one can deny the great aesthetic and moral advantages which have accrued to the Caucasian race from Christian art, through all of its stages of development, from the Good Shepherd of the Catacombs to the Transfiguration of Raphael, from rough mosaics of the inexpressible delicacy and beauty of Giotto and Fra Angelico." After such appreciation of Western Christian art, he comes to his main concern, the impact of such art upon Africans:

> But to the Negro all these exquisite representations exhibited only the physical characteristics of a foreign race; and while they tended to quicken the tastes and refine the sensibilities of that race, they had only a depressing influence upon the Negro, who felt that he had neither part nor lot, so far as his physical character was concerned, in those splendid representations. To him the painting and sculpture of Europe as instruments of education, have been worse than failures. They have really raised barriers in the way of his normal development. They have set before him models for imitation; and his very effort to conform to the canons of taste thus practically suggested, has impaired, if not destroyed, his self-respect, and made him the weakling and creeper which he appears in Christian lands.

By contrast, "The Mohammedan Negro, who is not familiar with such representation, sees God in the great men of his country. . . . The Christian Negro, abnormal in his development, pictures God and all beings remarkable for their moral and intellectual qualities with the physical characteristics of Europeans" (17). Blyden praises Islam's prohibition of artistic representation, which makes it a religion that helps transcend race distinctions. "This prohibition [of making images] has not been without its advantages to the Negro convert to Islam. His Arab teacher, having no pictures by which to aid his instruction, was obliged to confine him to the book. In this way, his thinking and reasoning powers were developed rather by what he read and heard than by what he saw." Furthermore, "among the first lessons he learned was, that a man of his own race, a Negro, assisted at the birth of the religion he was invited to accept; and, in his subsequent training, his imagination never for one moment endowed the great men whom he heard or read with physical attributes essentially different from his own" (374).

In contrast with Islam's prohibition of artistic representation of the deity, Christianity, especially that of Europe, is one of pictorial-racial Christianity, that is, God is represented as white. This impacts white children differently from black children. White children seeing religious pictures say, "I, too, am white!" Black children ask themselves, "What part or lot have I in this?" (375).

The third difference between the two religions in their impact on Africans relates to the existence of negative portrayals of Africans. The "popular literature of the Christian world since the discovery of America, or, at least for the last two hundred years, has been anti-Negro." By contrast, the "Mohammedan Negro has felt nothing of the withering power of caste. There is nothing in his colour or race to debar him from the highest privileges, social or political, to which any other Muslim can attain. The slave who becomes a Mohammedan is free" (18). Blyden gives the example of Bilal, "whom Mohammed in obedience to a dream, appointed the first Muezzin, or Crier." By contrast, in the Western world "it has been the fashion for more than two hundred years to caricature the African, to ridicule his personal peculiarities, and to impress him with a sense of perpetual and hopeless inferiority." Moreover, "Christian literature has nothing to show on behalf of the Negro comparable to Mohammedan literature; and there is nothing in Mohammedan literature corresponding to the Negro— or 'nigger'" (19–20). Blyden cites Ibn Batoutah, who, "though a Mohammedan, experienced no greater respect among the Muslims of Negroland on account of his colour, than a Negro in the same position would have received. He complains of the cool and haughty bearing of a certain Negro prince towards himself and a number of European and Arab traders who appeared in the royal presence" (21).[11]

The fourth "very important element which has given the Mohammedan Negro the advantage over his Christian brother is the more complete sympathy which has always existed between him and his foreign teacher" (22). How was this possible? Blyden writes, "Long prior to the rise of Islam . . . the Arab merchant had been in communication with the interior of Africa, and had opened the way for the Arab missionary. When, therefore, the Muslim missionary came as the propagator of a higher religion than any that had been known, he did not enter the country as a stranger." Moreover the "political and social institutions of the Arabs had already been tried and found suitable to the wants and tastes of the Negro tribes." Arabs and Africans have had "protracted intercommunication" between them. As a result, they developed, in due time, "similar tastes." As such, "it was not difficult for the Arabs to conform to a great extent to the social and domestic customs of the Africans" (23).

The fifth difference has to do with missionary work performed by the teachers of the two religions. The manner in which Muslim missionaries taught religion in Africa was quite different from that of Western Christians. The "Muslim missionary often brought to the aid of his preaching the influence of social and domestic relationships." In this, "the Arab missionaries often entered into the bonds of wedlock with the daughters of Negroland; and by their teaching, by their intelligence, by their intermarriages with the natives, by the trade and generosity of their merchants, they enlisted so many interests and such deep sympathies, that they rapidly took abiding root in the country." Thus, "Some of the brightest names in the annals not only of Islamitic but of pre-Islamitic literature, are those of the descendants of Arabs and Africans." Arab teachers did not create racial barriers between themselves and Africans; instead they melted in the embrace of Africans, and vice versa. There was more of a symbiosis of blood and mutual respect between Arab missionaries and Africans than there ever was between European missionaries and Africans. "The sympathy, therefore, between the Arab missionary and the African is more complete than that between the European and the Negro." Unlike the Arabs, Europeans were considered stand-offish. The "European seldom or never gets over the feeling of distance, if not of repulsion, which he experiences on first seeing the Negro. . . . Therefore, very often in spite of himself, he stands off from his African convert, even when, under his training, he has made considerable advance in civilisation and the arts" (23–24).

Furthermore, the "Arab missionary . . . often of the same complexion as his hearer . . . takes up his abode in Negroland, often for life, and, mingling his blood with that of the inhabitants, succeeds, in the most natural manner, in engrafting Mohammedan religion and learning upon the ignorance and simplicity of the people" (25). Blyden further notes, "the Pagan village possessing a Mussulman teacher is always found to be in advance of its neighbours in all elements of civilisation. The people pay great deference to him. He instructs their children, and professes to be the medium between them and Heaven, either for securing a supply of their necessities, or for warding off or removing calamities" (202).

The distinctions between the Arab and European missionaries in their relation with Africans have an important impact on the African converts to the respective religions. Referring to the African convert to the Christianity of European missionaries, Blyden writes, "The African convert, under such practical teaching, looking upon his instructor as superior to himself or at least *apart* from himself, not only in spiritual and temporal knowledge, but in every other respect—acquires a very low opinion of himself, learns to depreciate and deprecate his own personal characteristics, and loses that 'sense of the dignity of human nature' which observant travelers have noticed in the Mohammedan Negro" (24–25). By contrast, the "African Mohammedans, as far as we have observed, are tolerant and accessible, anxious for light and improvement from any quarter. They are willing to have Christian Schools in their towns, to have the Christian Scriptures circulated among them, and to share with Christians the work of reclaiming the Pagans" (28).

Despite his euphoric Islamophilia, Blyden believed in the superiority of the Christian religion. He provides one of his most revealing discursive statements on the hierarchy of religions: Christianity, Islam, "Paganism," in that descending order. "We entertain the deliberate conviction—gathered not from reading at home, but from travels among the people—that, whatever it may be in other lands, in Africa the work of Islam is preliminary and prepa- ratory. Just as Ishmael came before Isaac in the history of the great Semitic families, so here the descendant of Ishmael has come before the illustrious descendant of Isaac" (28). By "the illustrious descendant of Isaac" Blyden is referring to Jesus. What he is saying here is that Islam in Africa prepares the path for the coming of what Hegel calls the "consummate," "absolute" reli- gion, by clearing the road blocks put up by "Paganism" and "superstition."[12] The "consummate" religion is, of course, Christianity, especially Protestant- ism. Here Blyden comes across as a black Hegelian.

Although Blyden was Protestant, he was an avid admirer of Roman Catholicism. He saw it as the religion that allows black people room to move around and up, including overthrowing the yoke of oppression in the land of their enslavement. He writes, "the Negro race owes a deep debt of gratitude to the Roman Catholic Church. The only Christian Negroes who have had the power successfully to throw off oppression, and maintain their position as freemen, were Roman Catholic Negroes—the Haitians; and the greatest Negro the Christian world has yet produced was a Roman Catho- lic—Toussaint Louverture" (46).

He sees Catholicism and Protestantism as being very different in their attitude toward blacks. "At Rome, the names of Negroes, males and females, who have been distinguished for piety and good works are found in the cal- endar under the designation of 'saints.'" Protestantism, by contrast, "has no Negro saints." He further condemns the very religion he follows, "In what Protestant university would a Negro professor be tolerated? The most distin- guished Negro produced by a Protestant country, of whom we have read, was Benjamin Banneker; and the only literary recognition he ever received was an appreciative letter from Thomas Jefferson, the reputed infidel" (46–47).

Blyden draws other examples in praise of Catholicism in relation to black people as compared with Protestantism. Thus the "Portuguese his- torian, Borros, says that Negroes are, in his opinion, preferable to Swiss soldiers, whose reputation for bravery has generally stood high." Then he asks, "When and where has there ever been a Negro general in a Protestant army?" Unlike in Catholicism, "The Negro, under Protestant rule, is kept in a state of such tutelage and irresponsibility as can scarcely fail to make him constantly dependent and useless whenever, thrown upon himself, he has to meet an emergency" (47).

Blyden identifies four positive aspects about Roman Catholicism: First, "the Romish Church presents an uncompromising front in the warfare against infidelity in all its forms. Evolution, Agnosticism and Positivism find no place within its fold." Second, it "has always been and is now a protesting power—a conservative force—against the onslaughts of Socialism—against those attacks upon constituted authority which are now perplexing true patriots and statesmen in Europe and America." Third, it "sets its face, especially in America, against the freeness and facility of divorce. It respects the integrity of the family. . . . It exercises a watchful care over childhood. Catholics are wiser than Protestants as to the children of the Church." Last, and this is very critical for his race project, "the Roman Catholic Church respects races. It holds to the belief that those words of St. Paul, which declare that 'God hath made of one all nations of men to dwell upon the face of earth,' are words of inspiration." Roman Catholics "recognise in their calendar Negro saints, and have in their cathedrals the statues and representations of holy men of the African race. In Roman Catholic countries Negroes have always had a fair chance" (258).

Blyden expresses his negative view of the Western Christian impact on black people. "The Christian world, trained for the last three hundred years to look upon the Negro as made for the service of the superior races, finds it difficult to shake off the notion of his absolute and permanent inferiority. Distrust, coldness or indifference, are the feelings with which, generally speaking, any efforts on his part to advance are regarded by the enlightened races" (54). He goes on to lament,

> The Negro came into contact with Christianity as a slave and a follower at a distance. He came into contact with Mohammedanism as a man, and often as a leader. Whatever men of other races may do, can the Negro turn contemptuously upon a religion in which he has a part, and listen without protest to the statement of those who, while bringing him Christianity, tell him that his past has been "blank and hopeless?" (265–66)

Then, Blyden does something of a somersault:

> Whatever, then, the shortcomings of our teachers, they have been the instruments of introducing large numbers of us into the Kingdom of God. The lessons they have taught us, from their uplifting effect upon thousands of the race, we have no doubt contain the elements of imperishable truth, and make their appeal to some deep and inextinguishable consciousness of the soul. While, therefore, we recognize defects—a discrepancy, at times, on their part between precept and practice—we cannot withhold from them the tribute of our respect and gratitude. (53)

After all the lamentations concerning Christian blacks and how they suffer at the hands of Europeans in the land of their exile, Blyden ends up praising the same master-mentors! How so? For Blyden, European master-mentors were the Hegelian "cunning of reason," the only means, although disagreeable and inhumane, through which Africans, hitherto loitering in the darkness of heathenism and superstition, were able to see the light of the Gospel.

Blyden could easily have sat down and had a conversation, heated in agreement or discord, with Hegel, the master of dialectic.

Blyden sees the work of Western missionaries in Africa as being positive and grants them his support. Among his favorite missionaries was David Livingstone. He calls him "that humble missionary" and says that the "results of the labours and sufferings of Livingstone is the light which he has been able to throw upon the subject of the African races at home." He writes regarding Livingstone, "The whole Christian world has been aroused by that humble missionary to the importance of 'healing the open sore of the world,' and penetrating 'the dark continent' with the light of Christianity and civilisation." When it comes to missionary work in Africa, Blyden applauds equally Catholic and Protestant missionaries, although he has such negative views about the impact of Protestantism on blacks. "Catholics and Protestants—Christians of every name and nationality—are vying with each other in endeavours to promote the work of African regeneration" (55).

Blyden knew the history of early Christianity well. He knew that the religion had its theological foundations in Africa. He identified three "primitive Christian churches" in Africa: the Greek-speaking, Latin-speaking, and Geez-speaking (he did not identify the last one by language). "The two most wonderful and productive of all the primitive Christian Churches were both located in Africa, namely, the Greek-speaking Church in North-eastern Africa, and the Latin-speaking Church in North-western Africa. The African Tertullian Latinised the theological and ecclesiastical language of the west." He explains the third African church as follows:

> The case has been far different with the third African Church—the Abyssinian or Ethiopian. Founded by a native, it took hold of the inhabitants of the country, and struck its roots deep into the soil. And we have had very recent illustrations of the vigour and activity of that Church. Only last year the Abyssinian monarch told certain Catholic and Protestant missionaries, who sought to establish themselves in this territory, that he did not want either of them, because the Ethiopians were already Christians.[13] (189)

Of the three churches, the Abyssinian (Ethiopian) Church is the least recognized when African churches are mentioned. Blyden writes, "It is a curious fact that historians, in speaking of the African Church, seldom meant by that phrase the Abyssinian Church, which is far more entitled to that description than any other. Some mean the Church of North-eastern Africa—the Church of Clement of Alexandria, and Origen; others mean the Church of North-western Africa—the Church of Tertullian and Cyprian" (188).

Given the fact that Africa, far from being an outsider to Christianity, was actually its founding home, the grounding for both the Latin Catholic

Church and the Greek and Geez Orthodox Churches, it would be safe to say that the Western missionary enterprise in Africa was not an introduction of a new religion to Africa but rather its reintroduction. The only Christianity that Africa played no role in was Protestantism. And Blyden was Protestant!

Although Blyden wrote extensively regarding the depth of cultural denationalization of Western-trained blacks and how they were unable to stand on their own, feeling ashamed of themselves and their race, it was to this very people in the American diaspora that he turned to for his "civilizing mission" in Africa. The next two chapters cover Blyden's ideology of the civilizing mission of African Americans.

4

The African American
"Civilizing Mission"

Civilisation has its advantages and disadvantages, its privileges
and its burdens; the White man's Burden and the Black man's
Burden.

—Blyden, *West Africa before Europe*

Blyden is a modernist.[1] He is an ardent believer in that typical ideology of
nineteenth-century liberalism, one he calls "the law of progress."[2] As he
puts it, "There is no such thing as standing still in life. The law is either forward or backward; if there is no conscious movement forward, there is an
unconscious movement backward."[3] Based on such a belief, he sees Africa
as a backward continent. He tirelessly advocates the need for Africans to rise
above and beyond their material and spiritual degradation. He writes in *A
Voice from Bleeding Africa on Behalf of Her Exiled Children*:

> The man who desires to do good in his day and generation; who wishes to keep
> up with his times, and leave marks behind him of his having lived; must stand
> hard by the railroad track of Improvement; and when the whistle is sounded
> for the moving of the train, he must, without delay, jump into first vehicle that
> presents itself; otherwise, if he stop to argue with others as tardy as himself,
> on the propriety or impropriety of taking this or that car, he will certainly lose
> his chance, and the probability is will always be left in the rear by those more
> prompt and energetic than himself.[4]

He called on black people to jump on the "railroad track of Improvement,"
to be counted among the great nations of the world. For this to materialize,
he advocated the idea of the diasporic African American civilizing mission
of Africa.[5]

Blyden was neither the first nor the last person to hold firm the idea of
the African American civilizing mission of Africa. Alexander Crummell,

Martin Delany, and even Marcus Garvey, among others, thought that they had the moral responsibility and the racial calling to help uplift Africa out of what they perceived as its entanglement in savagery and barbarism. That way, the black race would find the much needed respectability it so lacked, yet so much desired. The whole discourse of "uplifting" Africa, and the need for the African American or black diaspora civilizing mission to carry out this heavy uplifting, is a remarkable example of the extent to which the Hegelian Eurocentric developmentalist paradigm was appropriated by some of the most talented black Atlantic thinkers of the nineteenth and twentieth centuries.[6]

Blyden's ideology of the African American civilizing mission to Africa is based in part on his positive appraisal of the "training" of black people in Western ways in the house of their bondage in America. As he puts it, the black person's "residence in America has conferred upon him numerous advantages. It has quickened him in the direction of progress. It has predisposed him in favour of civilisation, and given him a knowledge of revealed truth in its highest and purest form."[7] Elsewhere, he juxtaposes the positive with the negative: "It can not be denied that some very important advantages have accrued to the black man from his deportation to this land [America], but it has been at the expense of his manhood."[8]

Blyden's trenchant advocacy of the civilizing mission of African Americans is based on two fundamental views he firmly holds: (1) what he calls the black "burden of existence in America" and (2) the notion of Africa as the "dark continent," calling African Americans to uplift it through the blessings of Christianity and civilization.

The Black "Burden of Existence in America"

In *Liberia: Past, Present, and Future*, Blyden writes, "Black men of refinement and energy of character will feel more sensitively than ever the burden of existence in America." This "burden of existence in America" represses the development of "true and perfect manhood," causing men to "limp through life with crippled energies, always in the rear of their superiors in number."[9] In a biting indictment against the American slaveholders, he writes how they "debar him [the slave] from all means by which men are improved and elevated above the level of the brute; and, imposing upon him the ponderous weight of barbarous despotism, they expect him to exhibit the same intellectual and moral greatness with other men."[10]

In *The African Problem, and the Method of Its Solution*, a published discourse delivered on January 19, 1890, in Washington, DC, commemorating the seventy-third anniversary of the American Colonization Society, Blyden identifies three phases of the "Negro problem" in America.[11] The "first phase of the Negro problem was solved at Appomattox, after the battle of the warrior, with confused noise and garments rolled in blood." The second phase is the "education of freedmen" by the state and private philanthropy. The third and last phase is "Emigration." In the third phase, "the Negro, freed in body and in mind, shall bid farewell to these scenes of his bondage and discipline and betake himself to the land of his fathers, the scene of larger opportunities and loftier achievements."[12]

Blyden compared the African encounter with Western modernity with that of other "peoples of color" around the world. "Africans were not doomed to share the fate of some other darker races that have come in contact with the aggressive European. Europe was diverted to the Western Hemisphere. The energies of that conquering race, it was decreed, should be spent in building up a home for themselves on this side. Africa followed in chains." He cited the "opinion of an African chief that the man who discovered America ought to have been imprisoned for having uncovered one people for destruction [Native Americans] and opened a field for the oppression and suffering of another."[13] Unlike the views of the unidentified African chief, Blyden accepted both the African in chains and the Native American genocide as caused by divine providence.[14]

Blyden untiringly reminds African Americans about their hopeless situation in America. "It ought to be clear to every thinking and impartial mind, that there can never occur in this country [America] an equality, social or political, between whites and blacks. The whites have for a long time had the advantage. All the affairs of the country are in their hands. . . . Having always had the lead, they have acquired an ascendancy they will ever maintain." Blacks in America "are the weaker class overshadowed and depressed by the stronger. They are the feeble oak dwarfed by the overspreadings of a large tree, having not the advantage of rain, and sunshine, and fertilizing dews."[15] He puts it categorically: "I give it as my most serious conviction, that there will be no real prosperity among the African in this land, no proper respect shown them by the dominant race, so long as they persist, as a mass, in ignoring the claims of Africa upon them. All their efforts at self-elevation here which shall leave Africa out of the question, will be as 'sowing in the wind.'"[16] The honor African Americans aspire after is to be attained only in the land of their ancestors. And their families from Africa are calling for them to come home.

Blyden has a close knowledge of the condition of black existence in America. Writing at the heels of the American Civil War, he says, "We greatly fear that should the blacks continue to dwell there, the intercourse between them and their white brethren, instead of being an intercourse of peace, and friendship, and righteousness, will be one of avarice and political injustice on the one hand, and of heart-burnings, jealousies, and discontent on the other." For him, the black struggle for equality in America was too much of a burden to carry, with too few benefits to come out of it, if any. In black American life, "half the time and energy which will be spent" in the "struggle against caste," time which could be better devoted instead to "the building up of a home and nationality of their own," which "would produce results immeasurably more useful and satisfactory." He said to those African Americans who opted to stay in America, "better is a lowly home, among your own people, than the most brilliant residence among strangers."[17]

Blyden saw black existence in America as "unnatural."[18] America, the land of degradation, defamation, and dehumanization of African Americans, could not also be the land of their regeneration. America was built on the foundation of profound contempt for Africans. In a powerful critique of white liberalism, Blyden writes, "But among the phenomena in the relations of the white man to the Negro in the house of bondage none has been more curious than this: the white man, under a keen sense of the wrongs done to the Negro, will work for him, will suffer for him, will fight for him, will even die for him, but he cannot get rid of his secret contempt for him" (*Christianity*, 152–53).[19]

In America, the black existential condition is such that "development is denied him; he cannot expand. He fills his belly with theories and dogmas which to him are like the dry, hard husk. He cannot digest them, and they afford him no nourishment. Nearly everything he produces comes from the memory, very little flows fresh from the heart" (170). Rather, "Fascinated by the present, he cannot conceive anything else, and harasses himself with the ever-recurring and ever-unsatisfying and unsatisfactory task of imitating imitators" (169). Blyden further notes, "In the United States, notwithstanding the great progress made in the direction of liberal ideas, the Negro is still a stranger. The rights and privileges accorded by constitutional law, offer him no security against the decrees of private or social intolerance." Indeed, "the Negro child is excommunicated before he is born" (398).

Blyden believes that black people in America were so overwhelmed with powers beyond their ability to overcome that they were bound to bend under the heavy weight of being reduced to insignificance. He writes, "It is our earnest belief that a real independent moral growth, productive of strength of character and self-reliance, is impossible to natures in contact with beings greatly superior to themselves." He further noted, "a powerful, massive character—though it be nearly perfect—may positively injure those within the circle of its influence by giving them a bent in a direction opposite to their own natural tendencies, so as to make it extremely difficult, if not impossible, for them to shake themselves free" (399).

Blyden states, "the educated Negro, in the United States, in the enjoyment of the advantages of culture, has come in contact, throughout the period of his training, with influences which warp him in the direction of self-deprecation, even more powerfully than the books which he reads, or the teachers to whom he listens" (400). It matters not much if a black person was bright or creative, intelligent or inquisitive. He simply could not escape the dungeon of imitation as long as he stays in the country of his enslavement. "The Negro of the most powerful intellect must work by the pattern before him, and reproduce only what he has seen with his bodily eyes. The ideal faculty has not fair play, or any play at all. He is bound to endless imitation. If any original image is formed in his mind, it must be banished, or it is crowded out by the pressure of the actual. There is neither time nor opportunity to work it out" (401–2). Yet despite all the critical reflections on the black predicament in America, he would still write, "But the Negro's residence in America, in spite of all drawbacks, has been of incalculable advantage to him; nor has it been without peculiar benefits to the dominant race. The discussions which have arisen in consequence of his presence there have taught numerous wholesome lessons to the ruling class. Human rights have been better understood, and have been placed upon a firmer footing than ever before" (403–4).

According to Blyden, the suffering of African Americans was a lesson of moral challenge to their historical oppressors. The "presence of the Negro in the Western world is still necessary to teach other lessons equally important in the direction of Christ-likeness, to the hard and conquering Anglo-Saxon; to impress upon him the truth of the essential sociability and solidarity of humanity." He retorts, "After this survey of the European in Africa, and the African in America, it is difficult to escape the conclusion forced upon Bishop Haven, after visiting Liberia, that the solution of Africa in America, is America in Africa; and further, that the solution of Africa in Africa, is Africa in America" (404–5). It was this idea that the American Colonization Society was working hard to realize, an idea that Blyden never wavered in his support in principle, although not always for the people running the organization, or even more important, for the people sent to Liberia.

The fundamental question then is this: how is it possible that the very people Blyden condemns as having been indoctrinated in "spurious Europeanism" be the ones who would be the agents of the African American civilizing mission to Africa? Blyden is frustratingly self-contradictory. Yet this contradiction is easy to explain: it is a tension between race and religion, the espousal for Western Christian modernity and the rejection of the horror of its racism.

Blyden maintains the view that the African American had no way out of his predicament in America other than either submit to the racial insult and subordination there or emigrate to Africa to attain his freedom. "The exiled Negro, then, has a home in Africa. Africa is his, if he will. . . . He is entitled to a whole continent by his constitution and antecedents. . . . And he is going to Africa." If he were to remain in America instead, "he is hampered both in mind and body. He can conceive of no radiance, no beauty, no inspiration."

If he "has made up his mind to remain in America, he has also made up his mind to surrender his race integrity; for he sees no chance of its preservation." By contrast, "in Africa, he casts off his trammels. His wings develop, and he soars into an atmosphere of exhaustless truth for him" (144–45).

Blyden saw Africa as being held on permanent reserve for exiled African Americans to come back and possess it. Africa "is his by creation and inheritance." Africa is the "field for the physical, moral, and spiritual development of the Negro, where he will live under the influence of his freshest inspirations . . . with the simple shield of faith in God and in his race, and with the sword of the spirit of progress" (167).

If black people were to expect respect from those who kept them in bondage, they might as well be living in fancy. Those who revolt against their condition in America succeed in their protest by leaving America for Africa.

> For the Negro pure and simple, there is no country but Africa, and in America his deeper instincts tell him so. He will never be understood, nor will he ever understand his European guide and teacher, as long as he remains in the countries of his exile. He is often misled by the overflowing and ceaseless generosity of white men into a belief that his benefactors are getting nearer to the idea of practical oneness and brotherhood with him. (152)

How to overcome the American "burden of existence," that is the question. "Abandoning the disappointing and fretful illusions which harass them [African Americans] in the land of their birth, they will look abroad for some scene of untrammeled growth." In this, "Africa will, without doubt, be the final home and field of operation for thousands, if not, millions, of them."[20] Blyden's solution to the "burden of existence in America" was to leave America's burdens at its shores and head east. Africa was the solution. Blyden called on those who had suffered in America to carry out the African American civilizing mission to uplift their benighted brethren in the land of their ancestors.

For Blyden, African American emigration to Africa fulfilled two main objectives: the attainment of untrammeled freedom of African Americans who ventured to and resided in Africa, and the spiritual and material progress of "indigenous" Africans. Together, they would bring forth the healthy development of the black race.

Thou Shalt Uplift Africa! The Civilizing Mission of African Americans

Blyden holds the firm conviction that black people in America would never get the respect they so desired and the recognition they so much aspired for, as long as they stayed in America. He notes that the white man in America had no reason to see black people as worthy of respect.

Africa, the "gray-haired parent," is calling for African Americans. Are they not heeding her call? Blyden warns, "If you turn away from the work to which Providence evidently calls you, with the selfish hope of elevating yourselves in this country [America], beware lest the calamities to those who neglect to honor their parents."[21] For him, Africa was the land "adopted to us—given to us by Providence—peculiarly ours, to the exclusion of alien races."[22] Those who groan under the inferno of the American "peculiar institution" have a peculiar land kept for them by God, Africa.

Blyden makes it clear that he does not advocate that African Americans be driven out of America against their will:

> It is not that we wish the blacks to be forced, by any legal enactments, out of the country of their birth against their will; for we honestly believe that centuries of toil, and suffering, and bloodshed, entitle them to respectable and honorable residence in that land; and we believe that, amidst all the political and social rapacity, of which they may be the objects, they will bear themselves with the most exemplary forbearance and moderation.[23]

He also states, "We do not ask that all the coloured people should leave the United States and go to Africa. If such a result were possible it is not, for the present, at least desirable; certainly it is not indispensable. For the work to be accomplished much less than one-tenth of the six millions will be necessary."[24] Blyden was well aware that there were African Americans who did not care about Africa at all. "I freely admit the fact, to which attention has been recently called, that there are many Afro-Americans who have no more to do with Africa than with Iceland, but this does not destroy the truth that there are millions whose life is bound up with that continent. It is to them that the message comes from their brethren across the deep, 'Come over and help us.'" Indeed, "The inspiration of the race is in the race."[25]

Blyden holds the belief that the civilizing mission of African Americans was divinely ordained, as was their bondage. It was "as if in fulfillment of a Divine plan, some are beginning to return to their fatherland [Africa] from the house of their bitter pilgrimage, laden with the blessings of Christianity and civilization, and are successfully introducing them among their benighted brethren." He reminded African Americans, "You were brought away by the permission of Providence, doubtless, that you might be prepared and fitted to return and instruct your brethren."[26]

As a Protestant minister, Blyden saw God as the author of all things in the universe. He has plans for every people, and they are carried out. Blyden says God speaks to human beings in two ways: "one is by his word and the other by his providence." He remarks that God did not send a Moses to the descendants of Africans in America, but he sent his providence. And how do we know of God's providence regarding the descendants of Africans in

America? Blyden provides four arguments in support of such view. First, providence began "by suffering them to be brought here [America] and placed in circumstances where they could receive a training fitting for the work of civilizing and evangelizing the land whence they were torn, and by preserving them under the severest trials and afflictions." Second, it continued "by allowing them, notwithstanding all the services they have rendered to this country, to be treated as strangers and aliens, so as to cause them to have anguish of spirit, as was the case with the Jews of Egypt, and to make them long for some refuge from their social and civil deprivations." Third, it helped "by bearing a portion of them across the tempestuous seas back to Africa, by preserving them through the process of acclimation, and by establishing them in the land, despite the attempts of misguided men to drive them away." And fourth, God provided for them "by keeping their fatherland in reserve for them in their absence."[27]

This is perhaps the most complete account of Blyden's philosophy of providence pertaining to Africans. If one does not believe in Protestant theology, the whole argument would be a heap of nonsense. To see Africa as a land in reserve without an expiration date, waiting for its enslaved descendants in America to come back, to claim and rescue it from its material and moral degradation by the elevating influences of Christianity, commerce, and civilization—this is Blyden's paradigm of the African American civilizing mission. This paradigm is a discourse of the three Rs: reclaim, rescue, and rehabilitate. African Americans reclaim Africa as their own "natural" abode; rescue it from itself, as it has been stuck in the insurmountable cycles of poverty, ignorance, and superstition; and rehabilitate it through the hard labor of civilized uplifting!

For Blyden, one of the ways God preserved Africans in America was through slavery. "Slavery would seem to be a strange school in which to preserve a people; but God has a way of salting as well as purifying by fire."[28] Regarding the transatlantic slave trade, Blyden states,

> But there are two other facts, not, perhaps, generally known, to which I would like to call attention. The first is, that, notwithstanding the thousands and millions who, by violence and plunder, have been taken from Africa, she is as populous to-day as she ever was; and the other is, that Africa has never lost the better classes of her people. As a rule, those who were exported—nearly all the forty millions who have been brought away—belonged to the servile and criminal classes. Only here and there, by the accidents of war, or the misfortunes of politics was a leading African brought away.[29]

As I argued in chapter 1, the elitism evident in this passage clashes head on with Blyden's view regarding the African American civilizing mission in Africa. Who, after all, were these African Americans called on to "civilize" Africa but those who were sweating and bleeding under the inferno of American slavery? How can one enslaved productive class elevate another free productive class? Blyden's answer would be that the enslaved producing class from America has been trained under the close supervision of the agents of Christian bourgeois modernity, while those in Africa were lost in the darkness of material and spiritual degradation. Such view is what informs in part Blyden's call for the African American civilizing mission.

In *Liberia's Offering* Blyden appeals to African Americans: "A call is to-day made upon you from your benighted brethren. Are you prepared to spurn it?"[30] He adds, "There lies the land of your fathers, in its natural beauty and glory—a country well-watered everywhere as the garden of the Lord—a country of hill and valleys, of rivers and brooks, of fields and plains." But this land of beauty was brooding in "spiritual desolation" (26). He pleads, "I entreat you, by all the blessings you have enjoyed, by all the blessings you now enjoy, by all the blessings you hope to enjoy, remember Africa" (28). The "blessings" that African Americans supposedly enjoyed is their close encounter with Western Christian bourgeois modernity, even if it was not on equal footing with whites.

Blyden reminds African Americans of their historic task:

> Have you, O ye children of Africa! No tear to shed, no sympathy to bestow, no effort to put forth for your gray-haired parent in sorrow and affliction; for your brethren who have not, as you have, enjoyed the blessings of civilization and Christianity? Are you ashamed of Africa because she has been plundered and rifled by wicked men? Do you turn your backs upon your mother because she is not high among the nations? Are you neglecting her with the hope of elevating yourselves in this country?

He lends support to his appeal by invoking providence: "You were brought by the permission of Providence, doubtless, that you might be prepared and fitted to return and instruct your brethren. If you turn away from the work to which Providence evidently calls you, with the selfish hope of elevating yourselves in this country, beware lest the calamities come upon you which are threatened to those who neglect to honor their parents" (26–27).

Blyden made one of his most passionate appeals in favor of the emigration of African Americans to Africa in his discourse, "The Call of Providence to the Descendants of Africa in America," given at various northern cities in the United States during the summer of 1862 and published in *Liberia's Offering*. It begins with a guilty indictment against African Americans:

> All other people feel a pride in their ancestral land, and do every thing in their power to create for it, if it has not already, an honorable name. But many of the descendants of Africa, on the contrary, speak disparagingly of their country;

are ashamed to acknowledge any connection with that land, and would turn indignantly upon any who would bid them go up and take possession of the land of their fathers. (67)

He goes on scolding the attitudes of African Americans toward Africa. "It is a sad feature in the residence of Africans in this country [America], that it has begotten in them a forgetfulness of Africa—a want of sympathy with her in her moral and intellectual desolation, and a clinging to the land which for centuries has been the scene of their thralldom" (68). He cites Tocqueville who, in *Democracy in America*, talks about the psychological affliction of blacks in America who try all they can to imitate white society to gain respect and acceptance, but in vain.

Blyden says, "We have been dragged into depths of degradation. We have been taught a cringing servility. We have been drilled into contentment with most undignified circumstances. Our inner sensibilities have been blunted" (68). He sees black oppression in America as the "emasculation" of black manhood; indeed, he sees it is a form of total castration. He appeals to black America to heed the call of Africa:

> It is theirs [African Americans] to betake themselves to injured Africa, and bless those outraged shores, and quite those distracted families with the blessings of Christianity and civilization. It is theirs to bear with them to that land the arts and industry and peace, and counteract the influence of those horrid abominations which an inhuman avarice has introduced—to roll back the appalling cloud of ignorance and superstition which overspreads the land, and to rear on those shores an asylum of liberty for the down-trodden sons of Africa wherever found. This is the work to which Providence is obviously calling the black men of this country. (70)

Even as he was pleading with his African American audience about the providential calling for them to return to the land of their ancestors, Blyden was also reminding them that they will never achieve equality with white people in America. He refers to free blacks in the northern part of the United States as an example of what blacks will be like after the end of slavery. He says, "there is an extreme likelihood that such are forever to be the exploits which he is destined to achieve in this country [America] until he merges his African peculiarities in the Caucasian" (80). It was with such powerful words that he impresses on African Americans their hopeless situation in America and their calling and duty to go and help uplift the land of their ancestors, Africa.

For Blyden, just as America has proven to be antithetical to the all-rounded development of the black race, Africa provides its exact opposite: it is the land in which the black race can blossom materially and spiritually.

There one finds black power, African power. He declares, "We need some African power, some great center of the race where our physical, pecuniary, and intellectual strength may be collected. We need some spot whence such an influence may go forth in behalf of the race as shall be felt by the nations. We are now so scattered and divided that we can do nothing" (74). Blyden's invocation of "African Power" is reinvoked in Stockley Carmichael's call of "Black Power" a century later.[31]

Blyden calls for the establishment of an African nationality, which he sees as the indispensable foundation for the uplifting of the downtrodden African race. But he sees the formation of this African nationality to be the work not of indigenous Africans in Africa but of their descendants in the Americas who have come back to reclaim Africa. It is them he calls to action. "An African nationality is our great need, and God tells us by his providence that he has set the land before us, and bids us go up and possess it" (*Liberia's Offering*, 75). He puts so much value on the principle of nationality, declaring emphatically, "An African nationality is the great desire of my soul. I believe nationality to be an ordinance of nature; and no people can rise to an influential position among the nations without a distinct and efficient nationality. Cosmopolitan-ism has never effected any thing, and never will, perhaps till the millennium" (v). "Nationality is an ordinance of Nature. The heart of every true negro yearns after a distinct and separate nationality" (76). Blyden's political phi-losophy is one of strong advocacy for the establishment of a distinct, efficient, and separate African nationality. Herein lies his African nationalism.

Blyden's call for the establishment of a distinct, efficient, and separate African nationality has to do with the urgent need he felt for the uplifting of the African race. "We shall never receive the respect of other races until we establish a powerful nationality. We should not content ourselves with living among other races, simply by their permission or their endurance, as Africans live in this country [America]." A "well-established African nation-ality is the most direct and efficient means of securing respectability and independence for the African race" (90). The building of "negro states," the establishment and maintaining of institutions, the administration of laws, the building and preservation of churches, the creation of legislation, and the development of shipping lines, and so on are tasks Blyden lists that need to be carried out for the success of the principle of nationality (75–76).

It is in the context of the black yearning for nationality that Blyden judges Liberia's role. "Impoverished, feeble, and alone, Liberia is striving to estab-lish and build up such a nationality in the home of the race." By "home of the race," he means Africa. "Liberia with outstretched arms, earnestly invites all to come." Liberia's invitation is extended to the entire black diaspora, including those "from the Canadas, from the East and West Indies, from South-America, from everywhere." The call is made, "to come and take part with us in our great work" (76). Liberia becomes the modern version of the Ethiopia of old: "Ethiopia stretches its hands unto God!" Blyden would perhaps have said, "Liberia stretches its hands unto an African Modernity!"

Liberia

Liberia had a special place in Blyden's philosophy of black racial national-ism, including his advocacy of the African American civilizing mission. In *Liberia's Offering* he writes, "My heart is in Liberia, and longs for the welfare of Africa." And in *The Significance of Liberia*, he declares, "I am thankful that I am a Liberian. . . . I am proud also that I am an African."[32] He saw Liberia as "a center whence is beginning to radiate to different points of that land the light of Christianity." There are "fifteen thousand civilized and Christianized Africans striving to accomplish the twofold work of establishing and main-taining an independent nationality, and of introducing the Gospel among untold millions of unevangelized, and barbarous men." Liberia is the light that shines over the darkness that is Africa. "Liberia has resisted the influ-ences of heathenism. She has stood her ground against the encroachment of superstition."[33]

According to Blyden, those "fifteen thousand civilized and Christianized" African Americans brought material and moral improvements in Liberia. Their efforts made possible "the triumphs of love over hatred; the triumphs of peace over war; the triumphs of humanity over barbarism and outrage; the triumphs of Christianity over heathenism." Liberia was testimony to the "efforts to civilize and Christianize that dark land."[34] "By their exertions a free and independent nation of colored men, Republican in its politics, and Protestant in its religion, has been established on these long-neglected shores." This was Liberia, a nation Blyden cited with pride as having been recognized by the most powerful nations in the world, including the United States, Great Britain, France, Prussia, and Belgium. He writes that without Liberia, and its neighbor republic Sierra Leone,

> There would be no Christian colonies, standing, like a "chain of light," along this benighted shore, and spreading their civilizing and recovering influences upon the surrounding degradation and barbarism. There would be no "lone star," rising amid the stillness of silence of the awful gloom, and gradually dissi-pating, by its gentle rays, the moral dimness. There would be no such cheering signs of the dawn of a better day, and of the termination of the horrible night which has so long sat brooding upon this land; but superstition, ignorance and vice would still be holding undisturbed sway, and reigning, in all their tyranni-cal and debasing influences, over the mind of men.[35]

Blyden calls the part of Africa untouched by Christian Western civilization "moral desert," "moral night," and "moral and intellectual chaos."[36] Africa was the land that "has lain so long under the cheerless gloom of ignorance," that "should not be left any longer without the influence of Christian civilization." He calls on African Americans "for a far more glorious work to save extensive tracts of country from barbarism and continued degradation than to amass for themselves the means of individual comfort and aggrandizement." In an unabashed expression of sheer arrogance toward Africa, Blyden writes, "Liberia appeals to all African patriots and Christians—to all lovers of order and refinement—to lovers of industry and enterprise—of peace, comfort, and happiness—to those who having felt the power of the Gospel in opening up to them life and immortality, are desirous that their benighted kindred should share in the same blessings."[37] His view of Africa is similar to that of Hegel, who called Africa the land "wrapped in the dark mantle of night."[38]

In *Liberia's Offering* Blyden pays homage to the African American pioneers in the making of Liberia:

> The declaration of the Independence of Liberia, the establishment of the first Republican government on the Western Shores of Africa, did not, it is true, solve any intricate problem in the history of nations. It did not shed any new light upon mankind with reference to the science of government. It was not the result of the elaboration of any novel principle in politics. But it poured new vigor into the poor, dying existence of the African all over the world. It opened a door of hope for a race long the doomed victims of oppression. It animated colored men every where to fresh endeavors to *prove* themselves men. (135)

He goes on to register his vehement objection to those who dare critique the "founding fathers" of Liberia. "We have noticed of late a growing tendency among some juvenile members of the community to depreciate the labors of our fathers, the pioneers of Liberia" (136). He sees this "juvenile" offense to the founding fathers as a "violation of the command, recorded in broad and solemn characters on the pages of God's Holy Book." Blyden regrets this much: "We regret it because it is doing great injustice to the heroic men who for years have struggled, in sickness and in health, in joy and in sorrow, to maintain themselves on these shores." He goes on to express the trials and tribulations of these "heroic" men. "They have voluntarily expatriated themselves from the land of their birth; forsook the endearing scenes and associations of childhood; severed themselves from the comforts and conveniences of an advanced state of society; denied themselves the enjoyment of health, the pleasure of civilized and enlightened influences, and gave themselves up to a living death on these barbarous shores" (137). What is this that we read here in Blyden? It looks like the African American "pioneers" of Liberia were far from suffering the "burden of existence" in America. Instead, they had the good life: The "comforts and conveniences of an advanced state of society," "the enjoyment of health," as well as "the pleasure of civilized and enlightened influences." Yet they left all these modern, "civilized" amenities to come to Liberia and "gave themselves up to a living death on these barbarous shores." It has been established in this book that consistency was not one of the virtues of Blyden. But the statement here goes well beyond problem of inconsistency. It rather shows the extent to which Blyden had internalized the dominant paradigm of his time about America as the land of "civilization" and Africa as the land of "savagery" and "barbarism."

Blyden ponders why the pioneers paid such a high price in coming to Liberia. "And for what purpose?" He answers,

> That they might found a home not for themselves, for they knew they would not live to enjoy it, but for us their posterity. Foreign means indeed! It is true they were poor men. They had no gold and silver to lavish out upon improvements; but mark their superior self-abnegation and heroism, *they gave themselves*. And what could foreign learning and foreign wealth have done without their groans, and sweat, and blood? Yes, they suffered keenly, and bore up heroically under their sufferings for us. Their work consisted in patient endurance—a task far more difficult than active exertion. (137)

After explaining what troubles the pioneers of Liberia had gone through, Blyden calls for their appreciation, not their depreciation:

> Let us not, then, depreciate their sacrifices and toils, but rather let us endeavor to qualify ourselves to carry on, by labor and well directed effort, what they have begun in intense suffering and endurance. And if we are wise to detect any faults or deficiencies in any of their doings, let us not boastingly expatiate upon them, but rather let us, taking the mantle of charity, hasten to spread it over them, lest, while we luxuriate and delight ourselves with ideas of our own superiority to them, there come over the land a physical barrenness, a mental and moral blight, because we have not accorded the reverence due to our fathers. (137–38)

Although Blyden objected to the lack of respect and appreciation of the pioneers of Liberia by the younger generation, he did not advocate a wholesome embrace of them either:

> We are not by any means, however, asserting that it is incumbent upon us to entertain such unquestioning deference to the opinions and actions of our fathers as to reenact their errors, and proceed, right or wrong, in the beaten track; but we are for interring with their bones the ill they may have done, encouraging the vitality of their virtuous deeds, and immortalizing their exemplary conduct. Let us emulate their noble actions. Let us not be content to live

and die without doing something to ameliorate the condition of our down-
trodden race. Oh! let us not be drones in the great hive of humanity. (138)

Blyden believed that black people in America had no chance of making it there. Instead, they would remain a despised race groaning under a
despicable, degrading, deplorable, and dehumanized existence. If their life
in America was such, then it makes sense for them to seek new land. But if
their life in America was not what Blyden said it was, that they could indeed
make a decent living in America, surrounded with and benefiting from an
enlightened and civilized lifestyle, then the only rationale for their immigra-
tion to Africa (including Liberia) would be driven by a messianic zeal: to
sacrifice themselves on the shores of "forbidding" Africa to fulfill the higher
calling of the race for modernity, that is, black modernity.

The same "mulattoes" he was to vilify in his later years were among the
pioneers who supposedly brought light to a hitherto benighted land. They
were selfless heroes who sacrificed their comfortable life in America on the
altar of "living death" on the "barbarous shores" of Africa. Both mulatto and
darker-skinned African Americans heeded to the calling of the race for African modernity. Moreover, and this is even more telling, Blyden repeatedly
stated that mulattoes die in Africa at a much higher rate than "pure blooded
Negroes" like himself. This was one of his "arguments" for excluding them
from coming to Africa. If they were dying at higher rate than people who
look like himself, they were, per his own logic, paying a higher sacrifice for
the work of the race than the "pure Negroes." Blyden therefore should have
praised them more for their bravery of paying the ultimate sacrifice. Yet his
attitude toward, and relationship with, them was full of bitter indictments,
accusations, and harsh name callings.

In addition, if mulattoes were more likely to have a better access to the
luxuries of American life, which was indeed the case, then his earlier statements of African Americans leaving a "civilized" life in America for the "living death" in Africa applies to them more than the darker-skinned ones. In
that case, the very fact that they were coming to Africa itself, per Blyden's
view of it being a "living death," should be seen as noble and admirable.
They did not deserve the vilification and dehumanization he espoused during the last three decades of his life.

In his *Inaugural Address*, delivered at the inauguration of Liberia College
at Monrovia on January 23, 1862, Blyden declares, "This is an auspicious
day for Liberia, and for West Africa. The first College Edifice erected on
this benighted shore has been completed; and we, descendants of Africa,
are assembled to inaugurate it." Bringing providence into the train of his
thought, he reflects on that day as one in which the descendants of Africa,
"having escaped the fiery ordeal of oppression and slavery, and having
returned to their ancestral home, are laying the foundations of intellectual

empire, upon the very soil whence their fathers were torn, in their igno-rance and degradation. Strange and mysterious providence." He boasts, "We are here isolated from the civilized world, and surrounded by a benighted people, with whom we are closely identified."[39]

Blyden continues, "As a race we have been quite unfortunate. We have no pleasant antecedents—nothing in the past to inspire us. All behind us is dark and gloomy and repulsive. All our agreeable associations are connected with the Future. When other people speak of glorious reminiscences and recollections, we must speak of glorious hopes and expectations. Let us then strive to achieve a glorious future." He closes his address with this reflection: "The first College in West Africa is founded. . . . We have this Institution as the precursor of incalculable blessings to this benighted land—as the har-binger of a bright and happy future for science, literature and art, and for all the noblest interests of the African race."[40] Seven years after the deliv-ery of his inaugural address, Blyden provides in *The Negro in Ancient History* examples of the great accomplishments of the black race in the distant past, when Europe was still enthralled in wilderness. In this, Blyden anticipated a century earlier Chiekh Anta Diop's views regarding ancient Egyptians.[41]

In his travelogue, *From West Africa to Palestine*, Blyden describes how he felt when he saw the Great Pyramids at Giza, in Egypt. "Feelings came over me far different from those which I have felt when looking at the mighty works [of] European genius." The pyramids, he says, were "built by that branch of the descendants of Noah, the enterprising sons of Ham, from which I am descended" (105). He "engraved [on the pyramid], not far from a name dated 1685, the word Liberia, with my name and the date—July 11, 1866—immediately under it" (112). He calls Egypt the "land of my 'father's sepul-chers'" (128). As Egypt was the pride of Africa's glorious past, Liberia was to be the "hope" of Africa's bright future. He refers to ancient Egypt as a nation that "sent civilisation into Greece," including the training of "the teachers of the fathers of poetry, history, and mathematics—Homer, Herodotus, and Euclid" (105). He relies on the authority of the Bible as testimony of what the descendants of Ham built, while the descendants of Japheth and Shem remain blank spaces in the annals of the biblical narrative (106).

In *The African Problem, and the Method of Its Solution*, Blyden makes the case that ancient Egyptians and Ethiopians were descendants of Ham. They were black, and they created the origin of civilization, at whose feet the Greeks sat to learn. Furthermore, he sees the Egyptian Sphinx as the symbolic repre-sentation of Africa.[42] And in *The Liberian Scholar*, he says, "The instruments of culture are not the monopoly of any one race or nation. For this culture, Greece sat the feet of Egypt. Socrates, Plato, Pythagoras, Aristotle, all drank at the Egyptian fountain, and Egypt is in Africa. Rome got it from Greece, and the rest of Europe from Greece and Rome."[43] In all these references and others, Blyden held high the historical accomplishments of the black race. From these citations, we find not a "Negro" past that was "dark and gloomy and repulsive" but rather one that was bright, shiny, and attractive. It could well be that Blyden was referring to the African diaspora in the Americas, not Africans in Africa, when he declared that the past of the "Negro" race was "dark and gloomy and repulsive."

In his piece, *Our Origin, Dangers, and Duties,* an annual address to the mayor and Common Council of the City of Monrovia, delivered on July 26, 1865, Blyden provides one of his most powerful rationales for the existence of Liberia and its historic task of bringing to fruition the African American civilizing mission. He boasts, "We are laying of the foundations of empire on this coast." He includes the calling of Liberians to include "developing a stronger attachment to the cause of race, and a more determined zeal for the up building of an African nationality" (5–6). He acknowledges that the development of a true national character takes time. "National character is a thing of slow formation. Nations advance by minute and inappreciable gradations. They seldom reach solidity and greatness by rapid transition. Like children, they require the training of arbitrary rules and the restraints of arbitrary regulations before they are fitted for the freedom and guidance of principles" (13).

Blyden delves in depth about the people who made Liberia. He calls them "a peculiar people," products of the American "peculiar institution." "They were those who themselves or whose ancestors had been, in the providence of God, suffered to be carried away from heathenism into slavery among a civilized and Christian people; and who, from the degradation necessarily attached to all countries to those in any way related to slaves, could not rise" (7–8).

African existence in America was unbearable. Africans were languishing under the "force of circumstances over which they had no control," and it "kept them down-hopelessly down." It was then that they "saw clearly that to remain in that land and contend against what they could have no reasonable hope of overcoming, would be no more that 'beating the air.'" They decided to part company with the land of their birth. "They left the land of their birth, forsook the scenes of associations of their childhood, and came, with hearts heavy and distressed, to this far-off and barbarous shore—*forced,* by irresistible circumstances, from the native country in their poverty and ignorance, to seek a home where to be of African descent would involve no disgrace" (8).

Black people had it bad in America. "We have been so cruelly oppressed, that we have, in great measure, lost our self-respect. Almost any little untoward event will scare us into the belief that we cannot succeed in our undertaking on this coast." This view, Blyden says, needs to be shaken off. Blacks should unload the weight of their past and start anew. "But we must endeavor to shake off the influence of the past. We must have faith in the negro race"

(34). In other words, "we must cultivate *pride* of race" (33). The Liberian experiment was such a test case of African race respectability. What was at stake in the Liberian experiment was not "only the highest welfare of the few thousands who now compose the Republic, but the character of a whole race is implicated in what we are doing" (35). Blyden saw Liberia as the germ of the new Africa. "We have the germ of an African empire. . . . The tribes in the distant interior are waiting for us." American Liberians expanded the frontiers of civilization, where "the wilderness and the solitary place shall be glad for us; until the whole land becomes the garden of the Lord. The light intrusted to us will be passed on from tribe to tribe, until we encircle the land in a glorious blaze" (42).

In *Liberia: Past, Present, and Future*, Blyden writes about Liberia's role in carrying out the African American civilizing mission in Africa. Liberia "has poured new vigor into the poor, dying existence of the African all over the world."

> It has opened a door of hope for a race the long-doomed victims of oppression. It has animated colored men everywhere to fresh endeavors to prove themselves men. It has given the example of a portion of this despised race, far away in the midst of heathenism and barbarism, under the most unfavorable circumstances, assuming the responsibilities and coming forward into the rank of nations; and it has demonstrated that, notwithstanding the oppression of ages, the energies of the race have not been entirely emasculated, but are still sufficient to establish and to maintain a nationality.[44]

Here, as elsewhere in many of his writings and discourses, Blyden sees Africa as a "dark continent" in want of the light of civilization. Whether the light comes from "civilized Negroes" from America or European colonialists, he welcomes them both. He sees more harm done to Africa when left to its own fate than to see it fall under the "civilizing" influences of advanced colonizers, be they black or white.

Deeply engrossed in his civilizing-mission paradigm, Blyden writes of two institutions—Liberia College and Syrian Protestant College—as agents of Africa's regeneration. "May they be happily alike in successful efforts to roll away the cloud of darkness, prejudice, and selfishness now enveloping the millions of minds upon which it will be their part, either directly or indirectly, to operate." The founding of these two colleges, "almost simultaneously, is the pledge given by God of better days for these Eastern countries; that all the coarser passions and brutal instincts and superstitions of the people shall disappear amid the increasing and abounding light of knowledge and love." These two colleges were "conceived by American philanthropy, founded by American benevolence, and fostered by American and English Christians." Theirs were "the natural and genuine products of an advancing civilization, and an impressive illustration of the spirit and power of a pure Christianity."[45]

In *Christianity, Islam, and the Negro Race*, Blyden writes, "No agency has yet been tried for Africa's regeneration which promises so much and is capable of so much for the permanent welfare of the people as the method of the American Colonization Society in the establishment of Liberia." He adds, "The United States, then, have furnished Africa with the most effective instrument of unlimited progress and development in the Republic of Liberia." It was this society behind the Liberian experiment that Blyden supported wholeheartedly. Indeed, he made America the source and agency for the "uplifting" of Africa. "If Christians in America will trust to the healing and restorative power of Nature, and will help the thousands to migrate to Africa, and then, under the influence of the earth and sky and sea of the ancestral home, will further assist them with elementary schools and plain Gospel preaching, and with tools for mechanical and agricultural work, Africa will soon lift up her head."[46]

In *The African Problem, and the Method of Its Solution*, Blyden calls the American Colonization Society "more than a *colonization* society, more than an emigration society. It might with equal propriety and perhaps with greater accuracy be called the African *Repatriation* Society; or since the idea of planting towns and introducing extensive cultivation of the soil included in its work, it might be called the African Repatriation and Colonization Society." In praise of the authorities of the American Colonization Society, he writes,

> They have always recognized the inscrutable providence by which the African was brought to these shores. They have always taught that he was brought hither to be trained out of his sense of irresponsibility to a knowledge of his place as a factor in the great work of humanity; and that after having been thus trained he could find his proper sphere of action only in the land of his origin to make a way for himself. They have believed that it has not been given to the white man to fix the intellectual or spiritual status of this race.[47]

The view of Africans as "irresponsible" and in need of training under the authority of the white man—and once trained to discipline and hard labor in bondage in America be sent back to Africa to elevate their racial brethren, still brooding under the dark cloud of ignorance and superstition—and that all this is in accord with divine providence, is irredeemably racist.[48]

In *The Significance of Liberia*, Blyden again pours boundless praise for the American Colonization Society:

> I do not believe that in the history of any philanthropic movement can more examples be presented of magnificent purpose, of elevated and fervent devotion, of exalted liberality, of brilliant and convincing oratory, than are presented

in the history of the American Colonisation Society. And as time rolls on and Liberia arrives at and develops her own African life, exhibiting the strength and beauty and force of genuine African character, the American citizen, however exalted his position, will be proud to look upon her as one of the chief glories of American history.[49]

Blyden writes of Liberia, "this Republic as a sovereign and independent State, possessed of the English language—that greatest of human instruments for obtaining general culture and diffusing information—it is impossible to calculate the extent and depth of the influence she might wield in behalf of Africa and the African race." Liberia "is the offspring not only of American philanthropy, but of American prayer. Liberia is the child of many prayers."[50]

For Blyden, no matter how much help and support Liberia may get from abroad, primarily from the United States, the work of race and nation respectability is to be done by Liberians themselves, and by extension Africans. As he puts it in *Christianity, Islam, and the Negro Race*, "The friends of Liberians abroad cannot help them to national or racial expression. They must fight their own battles and achieve their own victories, if they are not to be overawed, depressed and overcome, not so much by the merits and virtues as by the vices and failings of foreigners, whose literature they read and whose commodities they purchase" (426). Yet Blyden calls for outside help for Liberia, mostly from African Americans. He laments, as he scolds those who did not heed to Africa's call for help, "Shall Liberia, for the want of a generous and far-sighted sympathy, be compelled to linger in the unhealthy regions of the coast, circumscribed in the field of her operations, and paralysed by physical and moral malaria, while thousands of possible agents of an effective work, within and beyond her borders, wander uselessly" (432). Blyden describes the people of Liberia of American origin and their role in the "civilizing mission" of Africa in the following paragraph:

> They recognise the necessity—the prime necessity—of the moral and religious emotions. Their minds are strengthened and expanded by the wide and glorious prospects which their independent nationality and the vast continent on which they live with its teeming millions of their blood relations open before them; and they stretch out their hands to the United States for the return of their exiled brethren, to increase their civilised and Christian force. (427)

In a remarkable twist of the famous biblical adage, "Ethiopia stretches its Hands unto God!" Blyden in this quote renders America the God of modernity from whom little, poor Liberia invokes help! Biblical Ethiopia was transcended by Liberia, a product of African American invention, with the generous support of the American Colonization Society, as well as the

United States government, and private individuals who believed African Americans have no place in white America.

Blyden refers to "the British Colony of Sierra Leone and the American Colony of Liberia" as "one in origin, not only as respects the philanthropic purpose that gave them birth, but as to the materials of the first settlement. Both were planted by Negroes who, having passed through the baptism of slavery on American soil, brought with them as spoils from the land of their captivity the elements of Anglo-American civilisation." And they "receive the same name. *Freetown* is the Saxon for the idea of which *Liberia* is the Latin" (232). These "two countries may be said to represent the true principle or method by which civilisation is to be introduced into Africa" (275). One such element of civilization was the possession of the English language. "Next to the Christian religion, the most important element of strength and prosperity in Liberia, is her possession of the English language. This gives her an advantage with the outside world. It is the language in which knowledge, secular and religious, is most abundantly diffused" (417).

Blyden sees African American colonization of Liberia as different from other cases of colonization in history. "The struggles of the early Liberian colonists against the ignorant opposition of their own people, stimulated by slave-traders, have a species of pathos and romance to which the struggles of the colonists in America offer nothing similar. The battles of the African pilgrims were not for empire over an alien race; not for power or dazzling wealth; but for room in the land to which they had a hereditary right" (411–12). Furthermore, "The work of Liberia, as I have said, is different and nobler. . . . Our work is moral and intellectual as well as physical. We have to work upon the *people,* as well as upon the *land*—upon *mind* as well as upon *matter*."[51] By "we" Blyden means blacks like himself who came to Liberia from America. By "the people" he means the indigenous people of Liberia. True to his conviction of the African American civilizing mission, he makes the former the teacher, the latter the student; the former the leader, the latter the follower.

Blyden writes, "Our prosperity depends as much upon the wholesome and elevating influence we exert upon the native population, as upon the progress we make in agriculture, commerce, and manufacture." He further notes, "We believe that no policy can be more suicidal in Liberia than that which would keep aloof from the native around us. We believe that our life and strength will be to elevate and incorporate them among us as speedily as possible."[52] The idea of elevating and incorporating the indigenous peoples of Liberia and bringing them up close to the status of the emigrant population is the same discourse as the European colonial mantra of civilizing missions, be it through assimilation, association, or so-called indirect rule.[53]

Blyden challenges those who saw a distinction between the settlers from America and the indigenous population in Liberia. "No candid person who has read the laws of Liberia, or who has visited that country, can affirm or believe such a thing."[54] He argues his case by comparing America with Liberia. In America "persons from all parts of Europe assimilate, but what great difficulty the Negro, the Chinese, and the Indian experience! . . . The Negro, the Indian, and the Chinese, who do not belong to the same family, repel each other, and are repelled by the European." This contrasts with the situation in Liberia. "But the case with Americo-Liberians and the aborigines is quite different. We are all descendants of Africa. In Liberia there are found persons of almost every tribe in West Africa, from Senegal to Congo. And not only do we and the natives belong to the same race, but we are also of the same family." In Liberia "the aborigines are not a race alien from the colonists. We are part of them."[55] He believes there could be no oppressive relationship between people who belong to the same race, although this is something his erudite knowledge of history should have cautioned him against. He knows well the antagonistic relationship between the English and the Irish in the British Isles, despite both belonging to the Caucasian race.

Blyden states, "The two people [Americo-Liberians and the indigenous people] are no more to be kept from assimilating and blending than water can be kept from mingling with its kindred elements." He explains the kind of assimilation he has in mind: "The policy of Liberia is to diffuse among them [the indigenous people] as rapidly as possible the principles of Christianity and civilization, to prepare them to take an active part in the duties of the nationality which we are endeavoring to erect."[56]

Two points stand out in this citation. First, Blyden makes the assimilation one-way. He even reserves the word "Liberians" to the Americo-Liberians, referring to the rest of the population as "aborigines." He sees Americo-Liberians as the center of the diffusion of civilization, and the indigenous people as the recipients. The former offers the blessings of civilization, the latter receives them with adoration. Second, he denies as slander the description of a separation between the Americo-Liberians and the "aborigines." He himself writes extensively, especially in his letters, about such separation but puts the blame on the mixed-race African American settlers, the mulattoes.

Blyden declares triumphantly that the "Negro emigrant has arrived from America, and, slender though his facilities have been, has produced these wonderful revolutions." He cites the clearing of forests, developments of modern habitations, in short the "civilizing" influences on the "natives," enabling them to be "lifted into manhood." Liberia "is a fact, an aggressive and progressive fact, with a great deal in its past and everything in its future that is inspiring and uplifting."[57]

Blyden bemoans the slow progress of civilization introduced to Liberia by African American colonists. "In these days of 'scramble for Africa' and contempt for paper rights, men laugh at our pretense to control a coast of four hundred miles on which not a single government craft appears." He states,

"Africa is to be elevated and civilized by Africans—not merely because of the physical adaptation, but on account of the mental idiosyncrasy of Africans; not only on account of the colour of the Negro, but because of his psychological possibilities and susceptibilities." By "Africans," he does not mean the indigenous Africans, but rather African Americans who have migrated to Liberia. Blyden calls the indigenous people of Grand Bassa County, who fought the Americo-Liberian colonists, "aboriginal savages."[58]

In *The Liberian Scholar*, a published address delivered on February 21, 1900, in Monrovia, Blyden calls those who have gathered for the occasion "Africans" who are "all members of the great Hamitic family." And they had a great task before them. He calls Liberia "not only a *youthful* nation, only fifty years old, but a *new* nation, with a new work, a peculiar work, and a difficult work before it. There is no other community in the world which has before it exactly the work we have to do."[59]

Liberia was a "sovereign and independent nation." As for those who made her, Blyden writes, "We do not belong to what is called the Imperial race, but we do have in our peculiar position a certain amount of Imperial work to do." By "we" he means Americo-Liberians like himself. How was this nonimperial imperialism or nonracial imperialism going to be carried out? He writes, "With the instincts and destiny of one race, we are forced by the conditions of the popular civilisation, we are forced to study the methods, and to use, in many respects, the instruments of another race; for this popular civilisation, which presses upon us from every direction, if we know not how to deal with it, and how to demean ourselves toward it, will engulf us, as it has engulfed others alien to it."[60] By "popular civilisation" he means the Western civilization of his time, which was becoming global through the colonial occupation of people "alien to it." Blyden's message was simple: either we adopt and adjust ourselves to this civilization on our terms, or we perish.

Blyden says of the Americo-Liberians, including himself, "We are here, on the margin of an immense continent, 'flesh of the flesh and bone of the bone' of the millions who inhabit it, with whom, as far as our influence extends, we are to co-operate, and with whom, in some directions, we are to guide." He is not blind to the fact that although "flesh of the flesh" as far as race affinity was concerned, the people he belongs to were different from that of the indigenous population. "But although we are, in a sense, indigenous to the soil, we are not, as a rule, to 'the manner born.'" He goes on to say,

> Another land gave us birth. Our forefathers, by the hand of violence, and also, we must believe, by a Providential hand, were carried into exile beyond the sea. There for generations, we acquired habits and ideas alien to Africa; and, on returning to the Fatherland from chattel bondage, without experience,

without training, without the power of recognising the laws of race written in our hearts, which were obscured and almost obliterated in the land of exile, we have been fighting to introduce laws which, in many respects, are in conflict with the existing racial and climatic conditions.[61]

He cites the two hands that rock the cradle of the African predicament in modern times: the hand of violence by men and the providential hand of God. How did these two hands relate with each other? How did they interact? Was the hand of God a hand of violence too? If not, how was the fate of millions of people of African origin in the Americas decided by such contradictory forces as violence and peace, assuming that the hand of God is the hand of peace? If not, does the hand of God complement the hand of violence? We must reiterate that the hand of violence was actually two hands of violence, one African, another Western. African captives that were to sweat in the inferno of American slavery were torn from their home by the violence of African hands, only to be delivered to the violence of white men who came across looking for their human cargo. These two modes of violence complemented each other.[62]

As Blyden confirms in *The Liberian Scholar*, if American colonists were to succeed in their "peculiar work" in Liberia, they needed to adapt. "What we need is applicability to our surroundings. There is much that is superfluous in the foreign ideas we have imbibed, much that is deficient, much that is injurious. Hence the necessity of the means of thorough culture at home, to produce, not the European Scholar, not the American Scholar, but the Liberian Scholar."[63] And the task before the Liberian scholar is to "study and comprehend the ways of God in Africa." It is to "study from a scientific standpoint" the social life of the indigenous peoples of Liberia (47).

Blyden sees Liberia as duplicating the American experience. "The Liberian Republic is founded on the model of the great American republic, in which our fathers served their apprenticeship" (46). It is strange that Blyden would call slavery apprenticeship. Even as the Liberian scholar is supposed to bring Western modernity to the "native," Blyden believes there is much for the former to learn from the latter. "There is much in what we call their [indigenous people of Liberia] crudeness and their superstitions that is *educative*. There is much in their government, in their religion, in their social customs, which we must study and understand, and take advantage of, in order to live in this country" (47–48). Still, he saw the colonist more as leader than partner. As he declares emphatically, "We must not be content to sit down on the margin of this continent, fold our arms in a corner, protected and scorned. We are to be guides, redeemers, and benefactors, with a 'Forward Movement' upon whatever is dark and chaotic and obstructive before us" (59). The "dark, and chaotic, and obstructive" is the Africa of the "aborigines." As such, "The true policy of Liberia lies in opening roads to the interior, in establishing and fostering alliance with the great tribes around us, in teaching them how to utilize the resources of their country, to suppress their belligerent proclivities, and cultivate the arts of agriculture and commercial industry" (51–52).

Blyden reflects on the relation between the American colonists and the indigenous people. "The aboriginal man is a constant and ever-recurring quantity, the colonist is an uncertain and ever-receding quantity. . . . If we were Anglo-Saxons . . . we should solve it by simply exterminating the aborigines; but that should not save us, we should disappear all the same" (49). He calls for "a great work to be done in Africa by the Africans in independent co-operation with the agencies of Western civilisation" (56–57). Liberia is the vanguard in this "great work." He cautions that the "tendency among us, a tendency which, considering our antecedents, is natural enough, is to initiate things which are sources of strength to Europe and America, but which for us are often sources of disaster, of shame, of death" (51). He further notes, "We are here, a new nation, to unfold a new bud in the garden of nationalities" (57). This new bud is to bring forth something new out of Africa. "The world would gain nothing by having the European reproduced in Africa, even if it were possible to achieve so monstrous a result" (58).

Blyden compares the impulse of the European to come to Africa with that of the African American. "No natural impulses bring the European thither—artificial or economical causes move him to emigrate. The Negro is drawn to Africa by the necessities of his nature."[64] This argument, that African-descended people in the Americas are drawn to Africa by the very nature of their racial constitution, while non-Africans that are drawn to Africa do so due to artificial causes, is a central aspect of Blyden's philosophy of black racial nationalism. As a geoenvironmental determinist, he can see no one thriving in Africa but the African. And, conversely, the African outside Africa is doomed to fail because he is outside his natural domain. These questions remain: If Africa is defined by its geography, and the African as the embodiment of such geography, what is Africa's geography? Does Africa have a geography or geographies? If Africa is defined by hot temperature, is not that what we have in the Caribbean? Why is it that blacks in the Caribbean, living among other black people in a natural setting that resembles "Africa," do not thrive per Blyden's paradigm? What is the nature of Caribbean blacks that necessarily pulls them toward Africa?

Blyden states of the African American, "By the nature of things, he can never enjoy this complete emancipation in the United States. When the Negro begins to feel the need of wider scope for the full expansion of the inherent energies of his mind, he will seek refuge in his Fatherland, for entrance into which Liberia is the most promising door."[65] The question is, What is the "nature of things"? Blyden believes Africa to be the natural abode of black people. If so, what is the natural abode of Europeans?

Europe, obviously. But then we have a problem. Europeans are already in America. They dragged Africans with them. If Africans were fit to work in America as slaves, how come they were unfit to live in America as citizens? Blyden does not raise this point in his voluminous writings. Moreover, if Europe is the natural abode of white people, and if they are already in America, how come they can stay in America but not the black people? Blyden may say he is not concerned about the whereabouts of white people. But the point is that America, which is unfit for blacks, should have also been unfit for whites. Both are immigrants; only the way they came to America and the work they did differ. Blyden does not say America belongs to no one but Native Americans. He believes, and accepts, that America was a country for white people. If white outsiders to America can stay in America, why not black outsiders? Blyden's geoenvironmental racial determinism cannot stand; it crumbles by the weight of its burdensome inconsistency.

Blyden explains the African American colonists in Liberia in as clear a language as possible:

> These will be among redeemers of Africa. If they suffer, they will suffer devotedly, and if they die, they will die well. And what is death for the redemption of a people? History is full of examples of men who have scarified themselves for the advancement of a great cause—for the good of their country. Every man who dies for Africa—if it is necessary to die—adds to Africa a new element of salvation, and hastens the day of her redemption. . . . Spectators weep and wonder; but the sufferers themselves accept the pain in the joy of doing redemptive work.[66]

One can not help but wonder why African American colonists in Liberia, supposedly driven toward Africa by the necessities of their "nature," find the work of "redeeming" Africa that painful?

Blyden says that the Africa "redeemed" by African American colonists is not to be the replica of America. African Americans returning to their "home" in Africa should not make an America out of Africa.

> The nation now being reared in Africa by the returning of exiles from this country will not be a reproduction of the American. The restoration of the Negro to the land of his fathers will be the restoration of a race to its original integrity, to itself; and working by itself, for itself and from itself. It will discover the methods of its own development, and they will not be the same as the Anglo-Saxon methods.[67]

How do African Americans, who have been away from their "home" for centuries, manage to filter out "Anglo-Saxon methods"; rediscover their long forgotten ethnic, religious, and regional identities in Africa; and bring themselves back to their "original integrity"? Has not centuries of oppression under slavery erased this integrity significantly?[68]

Blyden reminds the African Americans who made Liberia their home not to forget whence they came from. "The duty of the African returning from America is, as it was of the Hebrew, to remember the American Egypt as the house of bondage, and the training he received there, except in its material and industrial aspects, as the training adopted to slaves."[69] Yet we wonder how great this supposed training in "material and industrial aspects" was. Most of the enslaved were sweating in the backbreaking agricultural plantations or mines or, in the case of household work, with no fixed time schedule. It behooves one to believe that enslaved Africans were better trained in America under the dictatorship of the whip than as free people before their forced relocation from Africa.

In *The Three Needs of Liberia*, a lecture delivered and published in 1908, a mere four years before his death, Blyden delivers what could be taken as a testament, a confession, of his take on what the struggle for Liberia had come to: "Liberia is called by foreigners an experiment. It is indeed an experiment, an unprecedented experiment. Nothing of the kind has ever happened before in the world's history." He reflects on this "unprecedented experiment":

> A group of returned exiles—refugees from the house of bondage—settled along a few hundred miles of the coast of their Fatherland, attempting to rule millions of people, their own kith and kin, on a foreign system in which they themselves have been imperfectly trained, while knowing very little of the facts of the history of the people they assume to rule, either social, economic or religious, and taking for granted that the religious and social theories they have brought from across the sea must be adapted to all the needs of their unexpatriated brethren.[70]

He explains Liberia: "Liberia is a little bit of South Carolina, of Georgia, of Virginia—that is to say—of the ostracised, suppressed, depressed elements of those States—tacked on to West Africa—a most incongruous combination, with no reasonable prospect of success; and further complicated by additions from other sources. We take a little bit from England, a little bit from France, a little bit from Germany, and try to compromise with all." He admits candidly, "We have no definite plan, no dominating race conception, with really nothing to help us from behind—the scene whence we came—and nothing to guide us from before the goal to which we are tending or should tend." Sounding resigned to the reality of the failures of the Liberian "experiment," he expresses his belief that it was a wonder that Liberia should last so long. "We are severed from the parent stock—the aborigines—who are the root, branch, and flower of Africa and of any Negro State in Africa" (1–2).

Blyden states how "unnatural" Liberia is, severed as it is from the laws of evolution, cut off from its "aboriginal" roots. "Away from them [indigenous people] we are cut off from the evolutionary process by which men and nations normally grow. And as evolution is the law of life, we can have neither real permanent life nor vigorous or continuous growth. Without the aborigines in our domestic, social, religious, and political life, there is nothing before this State but death." He goes on to register what Liberia would be like without the aborigines. "Take away the aborigines from our *industrial* life, where should we be? Where would be our farms? Where would be the tillers of our soil, our instruments of movement, of travel, of commercial enterprise. Who would work our canoes, our boats, carry our hammocks, load our ships and land our cargoes from abroad?" (1–2). He opines, "No people can take root in any country where they cannot do these things for themselves" (2–3). He calls aborigines "the life and back bone of the country" (27).

This passage is as remarkable for its lucidity and honesty, as it is shocking for its revelation. In none of the contributions to the welfare of Liberia is there one instance that Blyden cites other than a rigid class distinction where the Americo-Liberians are the elite ruling over the indigenous people, who do all the manual and menial work, from the household to the public arena. No wonder Blyden, the indefatigable advocate of aborigine upliftment, felt so hopeless about the future of Liberia. Yet Blyden still denies that there is such class distinction in Liberia: "We have been striving to produce the independently rich man, with its opposite, the abjectly poor, but we have everywhere egregiously failed" (19). He has in mind the class distinctions of mature capitalist societies in Europe and America. Yet from what he himself registers regarding the division of labor between Americo-Liberians and the indigenous people, it cannot be seen in any way other than class distinction, with the added element of distinctions of origin: those who migrated from America on the one hand and the aborigines on the other.

As for his statement, "No people can take root in any country where they cannot do these things for themselves," this is not quite true. We have numerous examples where colonizers have triumphed and prospered by turning the indigenous people into their manual workers, while they enjoyed the benefits of leisurely lifestyles. South Africa, Australia, United Sates, and Canada are all examples for such an outcome. After all, Liberia still exists a century after Blyden's death!

Articulating a sophisticated elucidation of the racial nationalist imagination that is the driving soul of his political philosophy, Blyden writes, "We can take our proper place in Africa and in the world only by obeying the laws of the Fatherland. Our progress will come by connection with the parent stock. The question, therefore, which we should try to study and answer is, What are the underlying principles of African life, not American life, but *African* life?" Blyden values freedom above all. And he recognizes the right to such freedom by everyone. "But no nation can have this freedom of life, and make this contribution, which no other nation can make, without connection with its past, of which it must carefully preserve the traditions, if it is to understand the present and have an intelligent and inspiring hope of the future" (3).

In a heart-wrenching, melancholic rendition of the tragedies of black existence in America, Blyden writes, "But we have no past across the sea of which we can be proud or to which we can look for inspiration. America to which our fathers were carried by violence, where we lived and still live by sufferance as unwelcome strangers, is not the rock whence we were hewn. Our residence there was and is transitional, like that of the Hebrews in Egypt, or Babylon looking to an exodus" (3–4). His calling the centuries-old existence of African-descended peoples in America "transitional" testifies, perhaps more deeply than any other rendition, the precariousness of black life in America, the feeling of homelessness. It captures the depth of despair that black life entails for the lack of recognition by the larger society in which it is embedded by force and deception. Blyden is referring to racism, that indelible embodiment of American civilization.

Blyden explains the "three needs of Liberia" as emancipation, illumination, and harmonization. He reflects on emancipation: "First, then, we need Emancipation. When the first Negro emigrants for Liberia left the United States in the good ship *Elizabeth* in 1820, they escaped *physical* bondage. And when Abraham Lincoln in 1863 proclaimed freedom for the Negroes throughout the United States, he delivered them from material shackles which hampered and degraded the body." What Blyden opts for is total emancipation, body and spirit, physical and mental.

> The body was set free, but the soul remained in bondage. Therefore, the intellectual, social and religious freedom of the American ex-slave has yet to be achieved. When our fathers came across the Atlantic they brought with them the social, industrial, and religious trammels that bound them to the intellectual and material "flesh-pots" of America. Those trammels they transmitted to us. They could not help themselves. The mere passage across the sea did not change their mental condition. (5)

With a straight, unabashed, and honest rendition of the life and times of the African American settlers in Liberia, Blyden continues, "And now, we, their descendants, call ourselves Americo-Liberians or Afro-Americans, that is to say, Africans with the prejudices and predilections, the bias and aspirations of white men." Such ideals, "altogether unattainable, are nevertheless, the burden, the stumbling block and the opprobrium of this nation" (5–6). In sum, "the Liberians need to be Emancipated from the social, industrial and religious theories which they brought with them from America" (25).

For Blyden, Liberia ought to be an African state. He has no intention of compromising on that. Yet, as we saw in this work, he also sees Liberia as proud of its Anglo-Saxon heritage, especially the English language. Here too, in the *Three Needs of Liberia*, Blyden declares categorically that in spite of all the problems Liberians may have faced, they are "superior to their brethren in the British colonies." They have "a priceless jewel, an inestimable spoil . . . the *English language*. They have it not as a foreign tongue, but as a vernacular, as their mother tongue." With this "priceless jewel" in their possession, if they put their house in order, "their usefulness to Africa and the African race would be multiplied beyond calculation" (11–12). Blyden is without doubt the most devoted Anglophile of modern African intellectuals. He never wavers from this stand, remarkable in that he is too much, and too often, given to inconsistencies and even self-contradictions. He praises no language as highly as the language of Shakespeare. Needless to say, for all his struggles to convince the Americo-Liberians to link up with the "aborigines," nowhere does he recommend any of the African languages in Liberia, or Africa at large, with such a distinct prestige and accolade as the one he bestows on English. Yet he is a fierce advocate of African nationalism. But, of course, in English!

Blyden would still claim that "Liberia is, then, a first and foremost a Negro State. That is its basis and that must be its superstructure. All efforts to de-Negroise it will prove abortive. To have a little bit of South Carolina, of Georgia, of Virginia as component element of the State is not progress. We do not want the same thing in Africa we left in America. Progress is difference." He replied to those who wanted to reproduce America in Liberia by saying, "it is better to be censored or even ridiculed for being yourself than applauded for trying to be somebody else" (27–28).

Blyden repeats his call upon the Americo-Liberians to embrace their indigenous kith and kin of the interior. "We do not advance permanently in any department of our life because we have no settled creed as to what African life should be and no fixed hopes of the future. And we have not this creed nor these hopes because we are building upon the sand of exploded theories in Europe instead of upon the rock of indigenous knowledge and experience" (16). Here Blyden is invoking the fundamental and critical need for the Americo-Liberians to link up with the indigenous people of the interior, who are the custodians of "indigenous knowledge and experience." He states in this regard, "We shall know and understand our surroundings; we shall coalesce with the aborigines like kindred drops of water, and going in with them, incorporating and being incorporated by them, we shall form one great, strong, populous, prosperous African State under the name and style, if we prefer it, of the *Republic of Liberia*" (34). He further notes, "It is wisdom to study our surroundings and get light on the subject. The race in its integrity is in the interior. . . . We are but a fragment of it; and without the rock whence we were hewn we are but vanishing fragments" (29). By "our surroundings," he means the indigenous people of Liberia from whom, as per his repeated charges, the Americo-Liberians have shut themselves off.

He sums up the three needs of Liberia: "To summarize then our needs in one sentence: they are, Emancipation from many things we have been taught; Illumination as to many things we have not been taught; Harmonization with our surroundings as a result of this Freedom and Light" (34). He explains illumination as "enlightenment as to the laws governing the true life of the African in Africa. Our people know very little of the laws which regulate and fix the course and destiny of this life" (26). Illumination is the need to know "the laws of African life. We must learn to occupy the standpoint of our aboriginal brother, and to believe that in his place there is no man under the sun better than or equal to him" (31). The "we," "us," and "our" in the references by Blyden mean the Americo-Liberians; they are his target. His aim is to change their ways away from the ways of Europe and America, and toward the African way of their racial kin and kith of the interior. Blyden was battling against formidable foes in Liberia, backed by the power and prestige of the West, primarily America.

Yet he would write, in the thick of his unapologetic Anglophilia,

> I believe in the good intentions of England. No one who has watched for forty years, as I have done, the course and results of British administration in West Africa, but must acknowledge that with all its drawbacks, with all its want of continuity, its often incomplete plans of magnificent purpose, its unfinished excellences, it is a real blessing to Africa and the Africans. To say this is almost an impertinent platitude. I apologise if apology is necessary. But I can assure Liberians that the present attitude of Great Britain in and towards Liberia, if intelligently and loyally appreciated, cannot fail to promote the future material welfare and moral progress not only of the Republic but of untold millions in Africa and out of it (35).[71]

In short, he believes that British colonialism is in the best interests of Africa. All one needs to understand this is to "intelligently and loyally appreciate" it. And Edward Wilmot Blyden did exactly that: he became an intelligent and loyal appreciator of the virtues of Anglophone colonial civilization in Africa. The British did not ignore Blyden's intelligence or his loyalty to the cause of Pax Britannica. He became a paid loyal "citizen" of the empire where "the sun never sets!" To ponder over and reflect how Blyden's ideas germinated in Africa a century after his death is beyond the scope of this work. Suffice to say that Liberia was to be no way forward for Africa. It became instead a small and relatively insignificant place in West Africa. In the late 1980s it descended into civil war. Blyden would never recover if he saw the "gate of the hope of Africa" disintegrate. Per Blyden's race paradigm, he would have pointed a finger at the culprit of that madness: a mulatto by the name of Charles Taylor. He, Blyden would say, dragged the land of hope, tailor-made as a showcase of black race pride, into the abyss.[72]

Blyden's firm belief in the civilizing mission for Africa led him to welcome with open arms the European colonization of the continent. In *The African Problem, and the Method of Its Solution*, published in 1890, he writes, "Africa was completely shut up until the time arrived for the emancipation of her children in the Western world." He credits Mungo Park's expeditions in West Africa, and others, such as Stanley's and Livingstone's in eastern Africa, to have been instruments for the "opening up" of Africa to the outside world.[73] He even cites the "King of the Belgians who has expended fortunes recently in opening the Congo and in introducing the appliances of civilization." Blyden calls on African Americans to join this "scramble for Africa."[74] To call King Leopold II the agent civilization in the Congo shows the extent Blyden would go in support of the introduction of Western modernity in Africa, no matter the cost.

Blyden sees Africa as a "dark continent" contested by two outside civilizing influences: an old, premodern, universalistic creed, Islam, with its Arabic language and script; and a young, dynamic, modern material civilization of Western Christian bourgeois modernity.[75] English and Arabic were contesting for the "possession" of the African, with English tilting the balance in its favor.[76] In *The Problems Before Liberia*, written three years before his death, Blyden reiterates his civilizing mission mantra, this time using the language of Rudyard Kipling's imperialist manifesto, the "White Man's Burden." "The Liberian system of government is European, and we need European help to avoid its snares and pitfalls; without such help and guidance we are continually falling into holes and ditches. We have *nolens volens* taken up the White Man's Burden and we need his aid to enable us to bear it with dignity and success."[77]

Blyden's great error of judgment, one built in the structure of his paradigm, is to see the agency of Africa's "uplifting" to come from without, not within. Although he sees the black diaspora in the Americas as the extension of Africa, he does not suggest that indigenous Africans should lead, with the black diaspora following. With him, it is the other way around. This is all the more paradoxical for someone like Blyden, who believes in geoenvironmental determinism as regards the racial distinctions among human beings. The African American Blyden calls on to carry out the civilizing mission of Africa is the pure-blooded "Negro," not the mixed-race mulatto. The next chapter addresses this topic.

5

The "Mulatto" Nemesis

The law of God for each race is written on the tablets of their hearts, and no theories will ever obliterate the deep impression, or neutralise its influence upon their action; and in the process of their growth they will find or force a way for themselves.

—Blyden, *Christianity, Islam, and the Negro Race*

Blyden sees race as a concrete, material reality determined by the natural conditions of the human existence. Racism, on the other hand, is for him a sociohistorical construct. He writes in *Christianity, Islam, and the Negro Race,* "Hereditary qualities are fundamental, not to be created or replaced by human agencies, but to be assisted and improved. Nature determines the *kind* of tree, environments determine the *quality* and *quantity* of the fruit."[1] He accepts the racial distinctions of his time as matter of fact. Although he sees racial classification as natural, he objects to the racist hierarchical gradation. His is a case of nonhierarchical racialism.[2]

Blyden continues, "The Negro of the ordinary traveler or missionary—and perhaps of two-thirds of the Christian world—is a purely fictitious being, constructed out of the traditions of slave-traders and slave-holders, who have circulated all sorts of absurd stories, and also out of prejudices inherited from ancestors, who were taught to regard the Negro as a legitimate object of traffic." He calls history as his witness. There "is not a single mental or moral deficiency now existing among Africans . . . to which we cannot find a parallel in the past history of Europe, and even after the people had been brought under the influence of a nominal Christianity" (68–69). In these citations, Blyden alludes to the idea of the racist social construction of the "Negro."

Comparing and contrasting Europeans with Africans, Blyden writes, "But to our mind it is not a question between the two races of inferiority or superiority. There is no absolute or essential superiority on the one side, no absolute or essential inferiority on the other side. It is a question of difference of endowment and difference of destiny." He goes on to declare,

No amount of training or culture will make the Negro a European; on the other hand, no lack of training or deficiency of culture will make the European a Negro. The two races are not moving in the same groove, with an immeasurable distance between them, but on parallel lines. They will never *meet* in the plane of their activities so as to coincide in capacity or performance. They are not *identical*, as some think, but *unequal*; they are *distinct* but *equal*; an idea that is in no way incompatible with the Scripture truth that God hath made of one blood all nations of men. (317)

He seems to admit that "Negroes" are indeed lacking in some way compared to Europeans, as he identifies the former as one with "lack of training or deficiency of culture," while the latter is depicted as the opposite. For Blyden, Africans and Europeans are *essentially* different from each other.

The mistake which Europeans often make in considering questions of Negro improvement and the future of Africa, is in supposing that the Negro is the European in embryo—in the undeveloped stage—and that when, bye-and-by, he shall enjoy the advantages of civilisation and culture, he will become like the European; in other words, that the Negro is on the same line of progress, in the same groove, with the European, but infinitely in the rear. (316)

Blyden does not want to leave race distinctions in their frozen state, where one race does not reach out and touch another. On the contrary, he writes: "In the music of the universe each [race] shall give a different sound, but necessary to the grand symphony. There are several sounds not yet brought out, and the feeblest of all is that hitherto produced by the Negro; but only he can furnish it. And when he does furnish it in its fullness and perfection, it will be welcomed with delight by the world." And "when the African shall come forward with his peculiar gift, he will fill a place never before occupied." The human race, which consists of many races, is like a grand symphony with several sounds joining to make the music, and "each race is endowed with peculiar talents" (318).

One of the most important sources for understanding Blyden's idea of race is his famous lecture, "Study and Race," which he delivered to the Young Men's Literary Association of Sierra Leone on May 19, 1893, and later published in *Black Spokesman*. There, Blyden critiques those who opted for transcending the idea of race. He writes, "It is sad to think that there are some Africans, especially among those who have enjoyed the advantages of foreign training, who are blind enough to the radical facts of humanity as to say, 'Let us do away with the sentiment of Race. Let us do away with our African personality and be lost, if possible, in another Race.'" He sees this as being "as wise or philosophical as to say, let us do away with gravitation, with heat and cold and sunshine and rain" (200–201).

He states that those who opt for transcending racial categories end up being swallowed in another race. "Of course the other Race in which these persons would be absorbed is the dominant Race, before which, in cringing self-surrender and ignoble self-suppression, they lie in prostate admiration." Race, Blyden says, is embedded in *"the whole course of nature."* Admonishing those who wanted to go beyond or deny race as a legitimate category of classification, he remarks, "Preach this doctrine [of transcending race] as much as you like, no one will do it, for no one *can* do it." To attempt to do away with race is tantamount to "do away with your personality." And that entails "doing away with yourself." He told his audience, "Your place has been assigned you in the Universe as Africans, and there is no room for you as anything else" (201). For Blyden, both science and Christianity uphold the idea of race. He sees race not a social construct but rather as one ordained in nature itself. Race is also of divine inspiration. As such, race is of double construction: divine and natural. But then, since the natural is created by the divine, we can say that Blyden sees race as being of singular construction: God created race!

Blyden advises his audience that "the duty of every man, every race is to contend for its individuality—to keep and develop it. Never mind the teachings of those who tell you to abandon that which you cannot abandon. If their theory were carried out, it would, with all the reckless cruelty of mere theory, blot out all the varieties of mankind, destroy all difference, sacrifice nationalities and reduce the human Race to the formless protoplasm from which we are told we came." He adds, "Honour and love your Race. Be yourself, as God intended you to be or he would not have made you thus. We cannot improve upon his plan. If you are not yourself, if you surrender your personality, you have nothing left to give the world" (201).

Blyden believes the racial peculiarities of each race are ordained by God. The "racial peculiarities are God given. For his own glory they are and were created. To neglect them, suppress them, or get rid of them is to get rid of the cord which binds us to the Creator." It is "God's intention for you that you should be different from all the rest of mankind—that he placed you here to reveal a phase of His character not given to others to reveal; our duty is to find out what it is." Furthermore, "Race is the cord that binds humanity to the creator" (202). He cites the authorities of God and science in defense of the rationality of the race classification. If science were to prove that race does not exist, he would still have God as his ultimate proof for the validity of the idea of race. He would have no theory, no argument, and almost no material to write on had he ever believed that race does not exist. Blyden wants to keep the idea of race, but without racism. He cannot envision that race exists only in a racist social structure. That is, it is not the existence of races that leads to racism but the other way around. Blyden was a man of his time. And his time was one where the idea of race was a conventional prejudice. Grounded in his idea of race, Blyden says of the African race, "It is a great Race—great in its vitality, in its powers of endurance and its prospect of perpetuity." The African race "has passed through the fiery furnace of centuries of indigenous barbarism and foreign slavery and yet it remains unconsumed" (200).

In *The African Problem, and the Method of Its Solution,* Blyden makes a distinction between color and race. Color is a "superficial accident." Race, on the other hand, "lies deeper than color." Race is "the outcome of not only climate, but of generations subjected to environments which have formed the mental and moral constitution." He further states that the differences between the white race and the black race is "not a question then of purely reason. It is a question also of instinct. *Races feel; observers theorize.*" Because the races are distinct but equal, the work that awaits the exiled African American when he ventures back to Africa will not be the reproduction of America in Africa; it shall not be the Americanization of Africa. "The work to be done beyond the seas [Africa] is not to be a reproduction of what we see in this country [America]. It requires, therefore, distinct race perception and entire race devotion" (22). "Distinct race perception" constitutes the race paradigm; the "race devotion" spells out its race project.

Such race paradigm and project "is not to be the healing up of an old sore, but the unfolding of a new bud, an evolution; the development of a new side of God's character and a new phase of humanity." Furthermore, "Each race sees from its own standpoint a different side of the Almighty" (22). This makes all races equal. Because God manifests himself in the racial varieties of human beings and because God is in a way embedded in the human variations, "slavery of any kind is an outrage. It spoils the image of God as it strives to express itself through the individual or the race" (23). Still, in the same speech we are citing here, Blyden would say of the Hebrews of old, which he likens with Africans in exiled bondage in the Americas, "Slavery would seem to be a strange school in which to preserve a people; but God has a way of salting as well as purifying by fire" (9). Overall, he believes that "the whole of mankind is a vast representation of the Deity. Therefore we cannot extinguish any race either by conflict or amalgamation without serious responsibility" (23).

Blyden's view is to preserve the distinct races in their original and undiluted condition. God is in the races, not above or beside them. God is transcendental in many ways, but race is not one of them. To amalgamate or exterminate race distinctions diminishes God's multiracial manifestations. Blyden comes full circle about race and agrees with race theorists who have said that racial groups are of God's will. It is as if the divine mandate says, "Thou Shall not mix races!"[3] As an example of how each race manifests the many sides of the deity, Blyden cites the Hebrews. "Only one race has furnished the prophets of humanity—the Hebrew race; and before they were

qualified to do this they had to go down to the depths of servile degradation."[4] Yet in *The Significance of Liberia*, Blyden writes, "Divine inspiration is
confined to no race."[5]

Blyden is a vehement opponent of race mixing. In part due to this objection, there is no group of people he detests as much as the mulatto. He
hates them all, and mulattoes of Liberia the most. He blames them for
almost everything that goes wrong in Liberia, including the troubles in his
personal life. This hatred comes out more in his many correspondences,
including those to the American Colonization Society.[6] Hollis Lynch, the
editor of *Selected Letters of Edward Wilmot Blyden*, says the "first uncompliment-
ary reference to mulattoes I have found in Blyden's private letters" is in a
letter he wrote to Alexander Crummell on April 14, 1866.[7] Let us now turn
to Blyden's private correspondence, where his views regarding mulattoes are
expressed the most.

In a letter written on July 20, 1871, to William Coppinger, secretary of
the American Colonization Society from 1864 to 1892, Blyden relates to
him that Liberia is "the only gateway to Africa." It is the site of the "great
African nationality—the home of millions in America." This home "is not
to be on the narrow strip of coast now called Liberia." Instead he holds "it
up continually as an axiom that there can never be any proper or healthful development of national life on that coast without the aborigines. This
you must inculcate upon every emigrant whom you send out. They cannot
transplant America to Africa and keep it America still." He adds, "We shall
have America in Africa—but Africanized. To have vitality and growth it must
be Africanized."[8] The plan for Liberia to be the site of a "thriving population composed of a fusion of American blacks with the aborigines" is a
critical part of Blyden's political and intellectual project. It is from this vantage point that almost all he wrote against mulattoes is derived from, including his accusation that they have become obstacles to the healthy fusion of
American blacks and the indigenous peoples of Liberia. He charges that
instead they created a caste system, reproducing America in Africa.

In a letter written on October 19, 1874, to William Coppinger, Blyden
writes about "a conspiracy against the Negro race" that has been going on
at Liberia College. He says that he was the right candidate to be president
of the college and writes about the support he had from many professors to
that effect. "If you see proper, I should be glad if you would use your influence to have me appointed, or some other Negro who can appreciate the
work to be done in this country."

Blyden registers his protest to Coppinger against the mulatto emigration to Liberia in uncensored language: "It will become to you in America
a matter of more and more perplexing concern how far you are to continue to send to this country men whose race affinities are largely with foreign races—who feel that their 'country is the world and their countrymen

all mankind.'" He goes on to say, "By continuing to send such a people to this country [Liberia], you are really doing more damage to Africa than the slave trade did. You are planting here a nest of vipers who hate the country and the race. Do save us from this inundation." To say that few hundred, perhaps few thousand, people of mixed racial background from America have done more damage to *Liberia* than the slave trade had done to *Africa* shows the extent to which Blyden would go to register his vehement opposition to mulattoes.

Blyden vilifies the mulattoes of Liberia. "Nearly all the leading mulattoes who were here when Liberia became independent have died, leaving a rotten but malignant progeny. In the days of slavery you could not help the kind of emigrants you sent out. You were obliged to send such as the south offered, but now you have the power of selection and you should exercise a discrimination." He saw nothing positive for Liberia and Africa at large that could come from mulattoes. "The people of mixed blood never get into thorough sympathy with the work here. . . . They never become thoroughly acclimated. They drag out a feeble existence making slaves, as far as they can, of the natives and ignorant Americans, and *tools* of you in America to carry out their purposes."

Blyden appropriated wholesome Western scientific racism of his time. And he used it to vilify people of racially mixed background. "The progress of ethnological studies and of Comparative Physiology . . . has shown that the ideas of a people depend largely upon blood. If there is blood degeneration, there will be *thought* degeneration. Depend upon it that you will never succeed in building up in this country a Christian state of the mongrels you send hither." Having made his case against not only the desirability of mulattoes coming to Liberia but also of their degeneration due to blood mixing, Blyden pleads with Coppinger to send him only Africans of "pure Negro" blood. "The men, whose acts have commanded respect in the history of Liberia, were men of pure African blood." By contrast, "the men who have done most to corrupt the country by using public moneys—for selfish purposes and exchanging wives as if they were animals, have been half-breeds, and so it will ever be. No mongrel state can succeed. You must do all you can to get the country out of the hands of such men even if we have to begin afresh and take a new start."

Blyden fulminates against what he calls the "mongrel clique" in Liberia. He cites a certain W. H. Lynch, who "says he is of the Mohawk tribe" and "evidently a half-caste Indian." "Now, how in the world are we to get a clear African idea or any persistent effort for the building up of the race when on every hand there are such diverse ethnological sympathies?" In today's language, Blyden may support diversity but not race mixing. Diversity is good as long as each race keeps to its distinction, based on equality. But if diversity were to mean the blending of racial distinctions by mixing blood across racial lines, he would object it most empathically. What he calls "diverse ethnological sympathies" is such blending of race distinctions. Protesting as highly and mightily as he could, Blyden implores that the continued emigration of mulattoes to Liberia would introduce a "war of races into Africa."

Blyden let Coppinger know of his views about mulattoes: "The mulatto, conceived as he was as a general thing in violation of all moral and social laws, has brought to the Negro race nothing but physical degeneracy and mental and moral obliquity." He believes this despite being privy of the fact that in America the distinction between the so-called mulatto and the so-called purebreed Negro was not that important, as both groups were classified as black. He pleads with Coppinger to help save Liberia from the mulattoes: "Now the same principle which led you to seek to deliver the blacks from the rule of a foreign race by which they were overshadowed in America, should lead you to protect them from the pernicious influence of their half-brothers here, who are far worse than foreigners would be." He sees them as a more dangerous foe to Africans than other foreigners, including Europeans.

Blyden not only detests mulattoes; he is also afraid of them. He ends the postscript of this letter to Coppinger: "Now, if you want to have me shot you have only to let it be known here that I have written you such a letter. Remember that of all the elements out here, the Negro is the one who has the keenest interest in the success and safety of the ship; and for this reason I plead for the cause."[9] He wants the letter to be kept secret with Coppinger.

In a letter written on December 17, 1875, to the reverend John C. Lowrie, Blyden accuses mulattoes of "inheriting as they do the worst qualities of each race—the unbridled pride and passion of the one (in the Southern States) and the servile abjectness of the other—taught to hate their fathers and despise their mothers. Africa may well mourn the introduction of such persons." He refers to the objection he faced in America from many black leaders who saw his views as being no different from the proslavery ideologues. Many told him that he "was influenced by mercenary obligations to the [American] Colonization Society."[10] He defends himself from the charge by saying that "on the score of humanity, common sense and Christian principle, men of mixed origin ought not to be abused and ill treated for what they cannot help." Yet they "ought not to be placed in prominent positions" in carrying out the "race work," as had been the case "since the founding of Liberia."[11] He makes his case that he has nothing against people of mixed racial background, which they cannot do anything about. His objection to them is based on what they have done and will continue to do in Liberia if they have positions of power and privilege. His critique of them, he claims, is based not on biology but sociology. Yet, as we saw earlier, Blyden believes in the natural, genetic inferiority of the mulatto, that it is a dying race, that it is biologically unfit to survive and thrive in a tropical region like Africa. Blyden has drunk so deep at the fountain of Western scientific racism that he is unable to throw up this water polluted with the toxic elements of unbridled racism.

In a letter addressed to William Coppinger, written on April 23, 1879, Blyden writes, "The only way to build up a Negro State (in this country) [Liberia] of Christian Negroes and to give the aborigines a fair chance is to keep the mulatto, and all who claim to have foreign blood in the United States. They have done nothing and will do nothing but obstruct and destroy here." He complains that if the mulattoes continue to come to Liberia, "they will be bringing canker worms which will introduce blight and destruction into everything." He reiterates that mulattoes have contempt for the indigenous people of Liberia. He pleads with Coppinger, "For God's sake let them remain in America until at least we get our work here fairly established and the aborigines by seeing their own people at the head of affairs, who will insist upon the fact of our oneness, come to understand that they and the Americo-Liberians are really one people." He puts the blame entirely in the mulatto camp, what he calls "a small moribund clique" of "mongrel elements," for the antagonistic relationship between the Americo-Liberians and the indigenous people. He wants to see both peoples fused as one; the mulattoes, on the other hand, he alleges, want to perpetuate the caste system that they brought from America.

Blyden believes that mulattoes are unfit to survive in a tropical climate like that of West Africa. This was one of his many reasons for his plea to attract "pure blooded Negroes" from America who, he believed, were racially "programmed" to adapt to their "natural" environment. He laments, the "promiscuous arrangement of blacks with mulattoes in the history of Liberia has been a melancholy thing for the blacks."

Mulattoes are not meant for Liberia. "They die. The settlements of Careysburg and Robertsport were mainly by mongrels. They have passed away and Africa is said to be unhealthy because she will not give the same welcome to half-aliens who are sent to her shores, that she does to her own children returning uncontaminated from exile." The "uncontaminated" children of Africa returning from exile are those who have no "white blood" running through their veins. They are the true children of Africa; the mulattoes, by contrast, are "half-alien," and thus half-Negro. Blyden does not want halves; he wants "full blooded Negroes" like himself.

Rejoicing at the emigration of "pure blooded Negroes" from America to Liberia, Blyden tells Coppinger, "Send us Negro men and Negro women from America and in five years you will change the whole aspect of things in Liberia. I said the people you are now sending us have *capacity to suffer.* Yes, both mental and physical capacity—mental because they feel the inspiration of the race urging them to work for the future, and physical because of their adaptation to the climate." With people like these, "you may build up a nation here."[12]

In a letter addressed to J. C. Braman, written on March 27, 1884, Blyden ponders, "has not the time come for the Negro to be assured of freedom in the land of his fathers? Is Liberia to be made a second Hayti [*sic*], through the unprincipled ambition of a mongrel class?" He comes up with a term he calls "true mulattoism" and defines it as follows: "The mulatto in power or out of power is a disorganizer. He has no respect for law or authority when prompted by avarice or ambition, or if he has any project to carry out."[13] He was aware of the color caste in the Caribbean split between light-skinned and dark-skinned people. The colonial establishment, especially after the end of slavery, created a triple color hierarchy—white, mulatto, black—and used the mulatto as a buffer to protect whites from black revolts. When independence came to the Caribbean, it was the mulatto elite that came to power and perpetuated the colonial color caste distinction. Although Blyden did not live to see postcolonial Caribbean, he knew from other colonial experiences of the power and privilege mulattoes had over blacks. It is this specter of the "Caribbeanization" of Liberia, or as his example refers to, the "Haitization" of Liberia, that he was struggling to avoid. If Liberia were to be a second Haiti, that would be a blow not only to all that he was struggling to build in Liberia for so many years, but also to his paradigm of black racial nationalism.

In a letter written on April 13, 1887, to Coppinger, Blyden says, "God is calling me to a different sphere of labour in which my work for Africa's regeneration may be more effective in the future than in the past. . . . I have not left the work of Christ. Once a minister always a minister." He told Coppinger that the mulattoes were the people who made his life miserable. "My sufferings all come from the mongrel element who when it suits their purpose to support me, do so—their main object always being to cripple and destroy my influence and my representation, often using unsuspecting black men to do their wicked acts." He remarks that mulattoes cannot build a black nation on African soil. "The attempt to construct a mongrel nation on this coast will happily be only an attempt—for you can neither beat or cajole Nature. But the attempt to do this is not doing unto others as you would have others do unto you. You compel us to bear besides our own the weakness of other races."

Blyden complains that mulattoes came to Liberia not out of love for Africa but for selfish reasons, that is, to enrich themselves. "Why should such persons be sent here? They make money by hook or by crook with a view of spending it not in the country of their mothers [Africa], which they despise but in that of their fathers [America], who don't thank them but kick them out." Mulattoes were products of white men forcing themselves on black women during and after American slavery. He registers his relentless objection to the export of mulattoes to Liberia. "In sending the mulatto to work with the Negro you put the Negro at a disadvantage in every way.

The mulatto understands the Negro and knows how to take advantage of his peculiarities and weaknesses. The Negro does not understand him—for he is a new and complicated being." He continues with his "analysis" of the mulatto vis-à-vis the "aboriginal Negro":

> But when the mulatto comes to deal with the aboriginal Negro, he feels himself a stranger and at a disadvantage. The aboriginal man does not know him—and therefore wherever he has power his object is to suppress the native. He fears and hates the native, who in the normal possession of his faculties feels towards the mongrel as the white man does. This is the secret of all our troubles with the natives in Liberia. The constant effort of the mongrel element, and they are in every household, is to establish their superiority over the natives and either to displace them or reduce them to subjection.

Blyden believes that the indigenous people of Liberia were on his side. "The feeling among the aborigines . . . is largely in my favour; but this only makes the so-called leaders more determined to help me out of any position of power. They are afraid of native elevation, and this is what Liberia was established to promote—and this is why I support Colonization."[14]

Blyden makes use of the language of scientific racism in a letter addressed to Coppinger, written on October 3, 1887. He refers to President Johnson, who is "the son of a black man and black woman, good hearty Negroes with the genius and spirit of the race." But this Johnson made the mistake of marrying a "quadroon girl. His children are physical dwarfs, puny and sickly with no power to do the work to be done in the country. The great Elijah Johnson has degenerated to a puny mulatto progeny that must die out. Do you wonder at the anxiety of the Southern people to keep their blood pure? Neither Negroes nor whites are benefitted by the mixture."[15] Such was how Blyden appropriated the philosophical anthropology of scientific racism of his time. That he saw no wrong on the part of southern whites in America for practicing Jim Crow in the sphere of race mixing sends a chilling message to anyone who admires the great intellect that Blyden was. He would have had a welcome audience with the Ku Klux Klan, as was the case with his admirer Marcus Garvey.[16]

One point we have to be clear about is this: Blyden advocates race purity and objects to miscegenation not out of any interest to keep white racial purity, but to maintain black purity. His main concern is to have "pure Negroes" who are adapted to carry out the "work of the race." For him, any drop of white blood in the African's veins dilutes that capacity, progressing in its regressive impact as the percentage of that drop increases.

In the October 3 letter, he expresses his concern that people may mistake him for being a prejudiced person. "I sometimes fear that in writing to you I am exposing myself to the suspicion of being prejudiced. But I am no more prejudiced than Moses or David or St. Paul or Washington or Jefferson or the founders of the American Colonization Society, who believed that races had their work and destiny." Mixing providential and biblical arguments with American political history, he thinks he has a firm foundation for enunciating and defending race as a legitimate social category, and he wants to keep it pure. Relying on the biblical account of the division of the earth among the three sons of Noah—Ham, Shem, and Japheth—alongside contemporary scientific racism, Blyden accepts race as legitimate grounds of social classification. His argument that he is no more prejudiced on matters of race than were Washington or Jefferson is curious. We know that both men held Africans in bondage, and both of them were racially prejudiced. Blyden knows that too. So what does he mean when he says he is not prejudiced any more than they were? Moreover, his mixing of biblical figures such as David and Solomon with Washington and Jefferson also miss the mark. He knows the differences between the times in which they lived. Blyden believes that there was no racism against Africans among the ancients, including the people of the Bible.

Blyden continues with his declaration of war against the mulatto. The mulatto is "to white and black an unwelcome intrusion—that both deprecate his existence; and he feels that the black does not treat him as the white man." And when "he comes to Africa where the mass of the continent is in the hands of blacks, he feels himself menaced by his surroundings. He therefore strives, by hook or by crook, by all sorts of humiliations and professions, to get position and influence. When he gets it, his only aim is to keep down Negro talent, to cripple Negro power and to promote the ascendancy of his clique." Citing as proof, he writes, "The first thing the mulatto professors from America attempted was to break up a College with its Negro President and Negro students and the friends of Africa in America helped them to do it."[17]

In a letter addressed to Coppinger written on June 19, 1888, Blyden makes a distinction between the "genuine Negro" and the "spurious Negro." Those "Negroes who are as white as some white men" will "answer well enough in America, where they must all follow the dominant race and must be controlled, but in Africa where a race work is to be done—a work for the Negro race—the black and pure Negro race—the white Negroes will not answer." The distinction between genuine and spurious is this: "There are qualities peculiar to the genuine Negro suited to the work in Africa of which the spurious Negro is destitute, and to put them both together in the track to pull the same political and social vehicle is to introduce hopeless confusion." The "white Negro, having the blood and some of the temperament of the white men, is insubordinate and disloyal, unwilling to be led. He must either rule or ruin. He will wreck the interest of a whole nation to secure predominance." He saw mulatto rule as ruin for Liberia and for the larger issue of the "work of the race." The mulatto does nothing positive for the black race anywhere, be it in the Caribbean, Africa, or America. Its race tendency is to be with the white race to the disadvantage of the black race. The "disorganizing mongrel spirit" is to "pull down the constructive Negro spirit." Blyden cites an example for such a "pulling down" effort of the mulatto in Liberia: "While all Europe is trying to take different parts of Africa, mulattoism in Liberia is doing all it can to alienate from the Republic a most important tribe [the Greboes] and lose a large piece of territory."

Mulattoes, according to Blyden, hate the word "Negro." They resort to all kinds of names to avoid being called by that word. "The mongrel looks upon himself as the man of the colored race in America." A new phrase is thus invented:

> The new phrase is "race-variety." They hate *Negro*. They hate "mulatto" still more; "colored people" would make them a class. They know they are not a race, so they speak of our "race-variety," and try to make genuine black men, who do belong to a great and positive race, come under that stupid, unscientific designation of "race-variety." You see the various shifts to which the mongrel will resort to avoid applying to himself the term *Negro*.

Unrelenting and unrepentant in his belief that miscegenation is the kiss of death that leads to inevitable race extinction, Blyden writes,

> The fact is that there is no possible way for the "race-variety" to be saved. It must die out. If it comes to Africa it will only hasten its annihilation, though in the meanwhile it will have the opportunity of doing uncalculated mischief, while striving to secure at all hazards ascendency and perpetuity for an accidental element of humanity—a "race-variety." There is nothing before it but to die out, let it die out peaceably in America: for its work in Africa is only mischief continually.

Racially mixed people, per Blyden, are "an accidental element of humanity." Those who are ashamed of being called "Negro" are not the ones to guide the Negro to progress. Africans lead themselves, or no one else leads them. This is Blyden's political philosophy of Negro self-determination. In this, mulattoes have no place, as they are not "genuine Negroes." Per Blyden, the rule of the "spurious Negro" anywhere results only in the ruin of the "genuine Negro" everywhere.[18]

In a letter addressed to J. Ormond Wilson, secretary of the American Colonization Society, written on June 26, 1897, Blyden protests that the United States government was sending as its representatives to Africa people who Blyden classifies as mulattoes. "But why should mulattoes be sent to a responsible position in Africa when there are so many Negroes in the U.S.

qualified for the post?"[19] In a follow-up letter to Wilson dated September 17, 1897, he has this to say: "It is better, far better, to send a white man every time than a quasi white" (447). Blyden has many names for mulattoes: mulatto, mongrel, spurious Negro, half-breed, half-alien, half-European, and now quasi white. All this stems from his firm conviction that only "genuine Negroes" can successfully aspire to "understand the value of race integrity and to appreciate race work" (443).

Of all the letters Blyden composed about mulattoes, the one with the most personal resonance is the letter written to the reverend John C. Lowrie on January 15, 1875. In this letter, Blyden reaches deep into his own private life and the afflictions he suffers from the "mongrel element." This time it is about his wife, Sarah Yates, who is of mixed-race background. Blyden was married to Sarah Yates in 1856. She was the niece of B. P. Yates, the then vice president of Liberia. He describes his relation with her in the following harrowing manner:

> I live among an unsympathizing people—and I regret to say an unsympathizing family. . . . My wife seems entirely unimprovable. She is of the mind and temperament of the people around her. Sometimes, pressed as I am on all sides, I feel like making my escape to the interior and never allowing myself to be heard from again. Domestically speaking this has been my life for years. My restlessness and apparent fickleness is largely due to this. I am persecuted outside, but more inside. Uncongenial, incompatible, unsympathetic, my wife makes the burden of my life sore, very sore and heavy.

He further discusses his plight: "In all this community I have but three or four persons who sympathize with me and to whom I am at liberty to communicate my inward sorrows" (183). I do not intend to psychoanalyze Blyden by saying that his hatred for mulattoes may have been an extension of his problems at home with his wife. It may as well be the other way around. That is, his principled stand against mulattoes as the people who ruin whatever he tries to accomplish "for the race" was not healed by the warmth of the love and caring embrace of his wife. She was on the side of his enemies, and that hurt him. That is what he tells us.

In his letter to John E. Bruce, written on Sept. 20, 1896, Blyden expresses elation that African Americans were denied the right to participate in American politics in the aftermath of the end of Reconstruction. "So the Negro has been eliminated from politics—the best thing that could have happened to him in the South" (440). He does not think that African Americans had what it takes to make themselves a political power house in America. He opposes the formation of one large party or organization that brings African Americans together.

In his letter to J. Ormond Wilson, written on September 17, 1897, Blyden states his disapproval of the famous Bishop Turner of the United States, who was doing work for his African Methodist Episcopal (AME) church in Liberia. He charges that Turner "has never brought a black man out with him to aid his work here." By "black man" Blyden means, "pure Negro." He calls on the attention of the officials of the American Colonization Society to send out "Negroes to build up Liberia with white men to assist and guide them." If that were the case, Liberia would have been a "prosperous Negro state." Blyden believes that, unlike the mulatto, the "Negro is drawn hither by his blood and all his instincts" (447). For him, blood is instinct, instinct resides in blood. And the Negro instinct is to live in the "natural" land of the Negro, Africa. There, the Negro lives in harmony with another product of nature, the geographical environment. For Blyden, Africa may as well be called Negroland. In this, he sounds quite Hegelian.[20]

In a letter to Professor John Roach Straton, written on September 8, 1900, Blyden declares what damage race mixing would do to the "genuine Negro." "One drop of foreign blood impairs the integrity and spoils the test." He thinks that a single drop of white blood in the "genuine Negro" has a disintegrating impact on his integrity. He wholeheartedly buys into the "scientific racism" of his time, that race miscegenation leads to degeneration, that is, miscegenation is misgeneration. It is equally bad for the white, as well as the black. He writes against "the notion that the infusion of white blood must be a reinforcement to the Negro." Instead, he sees it as "a reinforcement away from his race instincts and race work." The Negro will "with the same earnestness and fervour as the white man denounce race admixture and will be as busy propping up the fence on his side as the white man is on his." He believes in the American adage good fences make good neighbors, including the fences of race segregation. As opposed to race-conscious black people who strengthen their side of the race fence opposite whites, is the "reinforced Negro," the one who was given white blood transfusion. "The reinforced Negro, on the other hand, wants to solve the race problem by amalgamation, by eliminating the Negro element from his nature, as Mr. Frederick Douglass strove to do."[21]

Blyden's calling Frederick Douglass by name is instructive. In *Christianity, Islam, and the Negro Race*, Blyden has a different take on the same Douglass. "Frederick Douglass, as a Mohammedan, would have been a *waleess*—a saint of the religion, an athlete of the faith; as a Christian, his orthodoxy is suspected, and his very presence is deprecated in a church in the capital of the nation; and further south, his domestic relations would probably earn him a home in the penitentiary."[22] In *The Three Needs of Liberia*, he calls Douglass, "the great Negro leader."[23] So what led Blyden to make such derisive comments about Douglass? It must be that Douglass was a "mulatto," advocating racial integration.

The question is, would Blyden have been mean to Douglass and all the mulattoes had they been Muslim? After all, many of the Muslims Blyden knew and saw in Africa and the Middle East fall into the category of mulatto. How come he did not object to them as much as he did the Christian mulattoes? Was it because Muslim mulattoes' view of their darker brethren was bereft of contempt, which their religion prohibits? In a way, Blyden compares American mulattoes in Africa with Arab mulattoes in Africa. But he never uses the word "mulatto" for Arab-Africans, or Arabs who in every physically describable way look like the racially mixed Americans he so much despised, hated, and feared. As elsewhere, here too, Blyden's views about race are not consistently held up. He welcomes all the possible mixings of blood between Ham and Shem, while he categorically objects to blood mix between Ham and Japheth. Ham and Japheth blood mix puts them both in jeopardy. He was opposed to "the bottomless pit of miscegenation" (*Selected Letters*, 468).

Race for Blyden is of divine providence, as is everything else. God is the one who saw to it that humanity be made up of different races, each with a specific calling. This calling will be unraveled if human beings were to tamper with God's work and start to mix the unmixable, resulting in racial miscegenation. Ham, Shem, and Japheth were to remain eternally distinct until the end of time. He was a racialist in as much as he believed in race purity; he was antiracist in as much he rejected racial hierarchy. Blyden was a multiracial racialist.

In a letter addressed to the editor of the *Charleston News and Courier*, written on March 8, 1909, and marked "*private and confidential*," Blyden states, "I should like to visit the South again and lecture to small assemblies of leading white men privately on the Race question, which I believe the thinking white people of the South understand far better than those of the North." With such a bone-chilling beginning, he delves into the race question in America. "Permit me to say that on the general race issues I am entirely with the Democratic party." After expressing his solidarity with the white South, he writes of his old nemesis: "But after the War the political difficulties were complicated or intensified by the mixed race, whom the unscrupulous and mercenary white invaders from the North utilized to aggrandize themselves at the expense of the South." Blyden's calling the Union army "mercenary white invaders from the North," the same army in which thousands of African Americans joined, the same army that broke the back of the slaveholding South and ended slavery, is simply beyond belief. In a statement that makes one wonder if Blyden had lost his mind or was sunk deep in senility, we read,

> I have often regretted that some great Negro did not arise and make common cause with the white South to suppress the "carpet-baggers" and their wretched instruments; or that some white men did not bring their ex-slaves around them and explain the situation, showing the futility of the ballot in the hands of the blacks in the white community, and the mischievous

consequences likely to accrue from it, with no advantage to the blacks who, as events have proved, are always left out in the cold, partly through their own indifference to politics and partly through the overweening ambition of their collateral relatives. (487)

No, Blyden had not lost his mind or suffered delusions. His mind was as sharp as it had always been. His take on the American Civil War and its outcome is consistent with his long struggle against the mulatto. Blyden is saying that all that Reconstruction brought African Americans is political power in the hands not of "genuine" blacks but mulattoes, who are not black, but their "collateral relatives." This was Blyden's simple message.

In line with his belief that mulattoes are not "pure" but "spurious," their taking seat at the US Congress does not warrant an iota of black representation. Since what blacks in America got after the Civil War was token representation by mulattoes, it may as well be taken away from them since they did not have the political representation anyway. In a twisted and paranoid "logic," he says, "I do not wonder—indeed I rejoice—that the Negro vote has been suppressed in the South. It is of no earthly use to the people, white or black, most interested in its consequences." He renders his advice to Southern whites as how to remember their past and come to terms with it. "In remembering the past you should lay the blame on the unprincipled alien leaders and their facile instruments and not on the dupes, poor blacks, who would have been unwavering in their loyalty to the whites had they not been misled, many of whom (poor people!) had been sold many times." He did not spare northern missionaries who went to the postbellum South from his rant (488). Blyden, the founding father of "African personality," "Negro race pride," and so on, thought poor enslaved blacks would have preferred to be with their white masters had it not been for the Yankee agitators from the North. This view is precisely what the white South has always claimed: "We know our Negroes. They are law-abiding. They know their place. It is the Godless Northerners who put in their minds wrong ideas like freedom from and equality with whites." The same "outside agitator" model was invoked during the civil rights movement in the fifties and sixties by racist southern white politicians.

Like his acrimony with many of the prominent African American leaders of his time, Blyden took issue with Booker T. Washington too. He accused him of believing that "the black man only needs money, a balance at his bankers, to make him the social equal of the white. I have never seen anywhere in the writings of Washington a gleam of real racial knowledge—anything that showed appreciation of racial conditions and adaptations." He cites Jews as example to make his case. "The Jew is often rich enough, but nowhere in Europe or even in America, does his money give him an unqualified social status" (489).

Blyden pleads with the editor of the *Charleston News and Courier.* "It must not transpire that I had written to you such a letter as this. It would injure everywhere in America the cause of the Negro. If the blacks knew it in their present lack of racial consciousness, they would give me away to their enemies and mine, and the mulattoes would traduce me from one end of the country to the other" (490). One wonders why, if what Blyden thought was the right course to follow, it would somehow be injurious to blacks in America if it were to be public knowledge. If that were what he thought, why did he advance such views? Why was it that he insisted that some of the most important letters he wrote regarding his views about mulattoes be kept secret with the receiver of the letter?

Blyden closes this disturbing letter. "Liberia cannot succeed without the guidance of white statesmanship, European or American. She is lost in the quagmire of hybrid ambition, and unless America interferes will become another Hayti on this continent. Please do all you can to prevent such a dire misfortune from befalling West Africa" (490). To avoid Liberia from becoming another Haiti, which is run by mulattoes, Blyden calls on white America and Europe to the rescue. So much for "Negro" race pride! Yet the irony of history is that America did intervene in Haiti too many times in the twentieth century, and we all know the results of these interventions.

In a letter to J. C. Hemphill, editor of the *Charleston News and Courier*, written on March 21, 1910, Blyden makes a paradigmatic statement regarding the difference between the Anglo-Saxon and the African. "I do not believe that in the order of Providence the African was sent to America to learn how to be Presidents and Rulers on Anglo-Saxon lines. As I often say, the School in which he was sent to America to be trained was abolished by Abraham Lincoln." Then comes the usual Blydenian discourse of race gravity: "Left to himself the Negro naturally gravitates to his place as farmer, mechanic, school teacher, preacher. He hates politics. He was forced into it by selfishness, greed and ambition *not on his part*" (503).

As if he wanted to make certain that he is not misunderstood regarding his stand on the race question in general and that of the American South in particular, Blyden declares, "The utterance of Southern statesmen on the race question have nowhere been falsified" (503). To say that southern white statesmen have never been wrong on the race question shows the extent to which Blyden would go to agree with the views of the most rabid elements of American racism.

How do we judge the totality of Blyden's views on the race question? His views combine extremely opposite points. On the one hand, he accepts essential race differences, but without their hierarchical arrangement of superiority and inferiority. Yet he agrees with the dominant American southern white view of race, which was a celebration of unbridled white superiority. Blyden embraces both views as valid! How a mind as brilliant as Blyden's could ignore the fundamental difference between these two views on race, the equalitarian and the hegemonic, is puzzling.[24]

But then, the answer to our puzzle may not be hard to find. Blyden's extreme aversion of mulattoes and his abhorrence of race miscegenation are so ingrained in his thinking that he prefers to agree with the worst elements of southern white American racism than with the best of the mulatto, or even the views of the "average" black person in America. As he puts it unambiguously, "So far as physical health and vigour are concerned, I would rather take my chance here as a pure Caucasian than as a mongrel. The admixture of the Caucasian and the Negro is not favoured by Providence in inter-tropical Africa, whatever may be the case in America."[25]

We cannot help but wonder at the ironies of Blyden's mulatto phobia. Frederick Douglass, the most famous advocate of the rights of African Americans in the nineteenth century, was of mixed-race parentage. W. E. B. Du Bois, the greatest African American intellectual in American history, was also of mixed-race background. So was Malcolm X, one of the most radical African American political figures. Thurgood Marshall is another example. Diane Nash, the spirit behind the freedom rides of the early 1960s, was also of mixed-race background. And so on. There are many African Americans, both in Blyden's time and later, who fought tooth and nail for the rights of black humanity in America and worldwide. To crown it all, the first black president in American history, Barack Obama, happens to be a "mulatto." Perhaps, in his mulatto phobia, Blyden may reject Obama for his racially mixed background but be doubly euphoric about his father: an authentic, "pure Negro" from Kenya, who also was a Muslim. Blyden would have felt at home in Obama's father's house and even in his mother's house, but not with their union, nor in their offspring.

6

Appraising the Colonial Enterprise

It is not the business of Imperialism to make *men* but create subjects, not to save souls, but to rule bodies.

—Blyden, *West Africa before Europe*

For all his contradictions, inconsistencies, and sometimes outright blunders, one issue Blyden follows through with iron consistency is the belief in the need for Africa to move in the direction of modernity. And the modernity he has in mind is primarily Western. This view makes him support the European colonial enterprise wholeheartedly, assuming that it will bring Africa closer to the degree of civilization attained by the West.

In the collection *West Africa before Europe*, published in 1905, Blyden writes that imperialism is "deficient in spirituality. . . . Its most successful work for aliens must be on its material side. Well regulated police supervision, technical and industrial schools, hospitals and dispensaries, are its proper and more effective instruments for civilizing and building up backward races."[1]

Blyden believes that human nature is "everywhere the same. You will find everywhere the incapable, the indolent, and the lazy! 'The dignity of labour' is, I am afraid, only an ornamental phrase, without meaning in the eras of undignified humanity; and a very large proportion of the human race are unfortunately undignified." Based on such premise, he writes the following unbelievable description of Africans:

Now, as far as the African is concerned, any system that will convert that happy, careless, child of the tropics, sleeping (without even dreaming) his time away, into a wakeful, alert individual, anxious not only to supply his immediate necessities, but to improve his own personal surroundings, and to promote the general improvement of his country—I say, any system which will supply incentives to exertion and thrift, which will convert these paupers, as civilisation would call them, into producers for the mills of Lancashire, and consumers of the products of these mills, is deserving of the most consummate patronage of the political and commercial agencies now interested in Africa. (124–25)

This is the central prejudice of the colonial racist paradigm, the idea of the "lazy native," which Blyden approvingly appropriated.

The "father of African nationalism," the author of the idea of the "African Personality," was pleading with European powers to "help" Africa move in the direction of achieving "development." With a focus on equatorial Africa that "must be for the African or for nobody," as its climate prevents European settlement, Blyden gave his "expert" advice to the European powers: "you must foster the native—not cuddle him—but don't kill him, and teach him how to make the best use of his country. With your superior intelligence and experience, with your large scientific attainments, you must find out ways and means for energizing the industry of the people" (121). He made Africa Europe's foster child.

Blyden continues with his advice. European colonial powers in Africa should beware of spoiling the "natives": "Don't stimulate in them a desire for luxury, for that will defeat the end you have in view. The love of luxury will effeminate them and convert them into ambitious idlers, anxious to exploit the labour of others—always plotting and scheming, not to eat bread by the sweat of their own face but by the sweat of the face of others" (122). We cannot but ask, Did not European rulers in Africa exploit the labor of others, eating their bread not by their own sweat but by that of others, that is, Africans? Blyden does not seem to see it that way. For him, it is "natural" for Europe to have Africa work for its luxury, as Europe had the technical know-how to do so. The place Blyden assigned Africa was to be the producer of raw materials for the European industries. He believes in the theory of comparative advantage; he does not envision, nor see, the wisdom of Africa being an industrial powerhouse. As he puts it, "West Africa and England are mutually dependent upon each other." For example, the "Lancashire manufacturer is indebted to West Africa at once for cheap cotton and for a customer." West Africa is for the Lancashire manufacturer "both farm and shop, plantation and market, and it must also supply the necessary labour" (120).

Thick in his support of the European enterprise in Africa, Blyden states that Britain and France, the two largest colonial powers in Africa, "should, by union and co-operation, impress a wholesome direction upon what must be regarded as the most critical period in the modern history of Africa" (118). A key element in this was the building of railways. Sounding like Cecil John Rhodes, he calls on the cooperative effort on the part of France and Britain for building a railway line from "Algiers to the Cape of Good Hope, the terminus on one side being in French territory, and on the other in English." Such an undertaking "would make for the permanent peace, not only of Africa, but of Europe." Furthermore, the "united interests of England and France would be a guarantee for the easy and successful arbitration in any difficulties arising out of commercial or political rivalries." Moreover, "the railway would furnish facilities for most effective police supervision of the continent, which is almost equally divided between the two nations, France, perhaps, having the larger share" (119).

Blyden is concerned about the damage that could come from the European lack of knowledge of Africa and Africans. His attempt is to make certain that he contributes his share in teaching Europeans about Africa and Africans. "The great peril to Africa lies in the ignorance of African character on the part of those who attempt to exploit the new filed or assert responsibility for the government of the people. This ignorance extended in the past not less to the people than to the resources of the country." He applauds the work of European travelers for "opening" up the "secret" of Africa locked behind the iron door of "isolation" from the "civilized world." He admires the "magnificent labours of the noble band of travelers and explorers." Thanks to their labor, the "Natural History and resources" of West Africa are "getting to be fairly understood and appreciated." Yet "the *man* of the country [Africa] is still an unapproachable mystery to the outside world. He is everywhere *prima facie* a stranger" (134). And it is here that the work of the likes of Blyden comes in: to introduce Africans to Europeans, to plead with the latter not to harm the "children" that are Africans but rather to treat them with compassionate paternalism.

For Africans who struggled to keep their heads up in the face of the massive racist onslaught coming from colonial Europe, Blyden could sometimes be an embarrassment of African dignity. The irony, the paradox about this outstanding intellectual was that few are the people who made the respect of black humanity their lifelong obsession as did Blyden. He wants it both ways: to fight for the racial dignity of the Negro race, while believing that European colonialism would play a critical role in the upliftment of Africa. He believes that without Europe's colonial intrusion into Africa, Africans could not stand with their two feet and demand equality that the white man is bound to respect. For Blyden the black "struggle for recognition" could be won as a recognition of blacks by whites.[2] The white master is the subject that grants recognition to his black bondsman. This was to be the consummation of the famous Hegelian dialectic of the *Phenomenology of Spirit.*

Blyden applauds the positive impact European colonialism would have on Africa. In *West Africa before Europe* he singles out England: "Great Britain has done more to open up Africa and bring its inner secrets to the knowledge of the world than any other nation." He is of the opinion that the main reason for the 1807 British abolition of the Atlantic slave trade was an act of humanitarianism and high moral standing. He does not seem to delve into the possibility that British self-interest, including the demands of the Industrial Revolution for African raw material, could be the main reason for this act. "When it [Great Britain] became thoroughly convinced of the pernicious and immoral character of the system [Atlantic slave trade], it not only did all in its power to destroy it, but subjected itself to great labour and to vast expenditure of treasure, and exhausted the resources of diplomacy, to secure the co-operation of others in the work of the complete annihilation of the nefarious trade" (95). England exerted immense pressure and influence "to make Foreign Powers adopt such views of commerce with Africa as are alone consistent with justice and humanity" (96). This commerce with Africa based supposedly on "justice and humanity," as opposed to the Atlantic slave trade that was unjust and inhumane, is known as "legitimate commerce," which Blyden writes about extensively.

Blyden pours praise for the parliamentary debates and papers in Britain about ending the Atlantic slave trade. He expresses "admiration at the perseverance, the single-mindedness, and the ability with which, in accordance with the spirit of true religion and the dictates of humanity, the various administrations, whether Whig or Tory, in a nobler rivalry than party, emulated each other in carrying out the great and arduous task of extinguishing a gigantic wrong, under whatever flag perpetrated" (96). Yet he knows that it was the same England that was the largest slave-trading nation in the eighteenth century. So does he really believe that the British suddenly saw that the slave trade was wrong and tried to end the trade, and even go a step ahead and send their navy and diplomats to convince other nations to do the same? Whence came this sudden religious and moral awakening?

As an astute student of history, Blyden was aware of the historical context of Britain's "change of mind" regarding the Atlantic slave trade. He writes, "The vigorous efforts of England to root out the iniquitous traffic began soon after she had inaugurated what might be called the era of modern exploration, Mungo Park being in the lead, followed by a long list of energetic travellers, ending with Stanley" (96). This was precisely the time of the Industrial Revolution in England, the time when England was the most powerful military and economic power in the world, when it was the advocate of free trade worldwide.

Blyden laments, "It is a curious fact in the political history of England that after her brilliant, scientific work *in* Africa, and her marvelous philanthropic work *for* Africa—after a vast expenditure of blood and treasure—she should have been content, during a long period of years, with a quiescent if not indifferent attitude towards that great continent" (96–97). His dismay is that right after 1807 England did not march with full speed and force into Africa, bringing to the "benighted" continent the blessings of the three Cs: Christianity, commerce, and civilization.

It was in light of the alleged failure of England to follow through the end of the Atlantic slave trade that Blyden declares, "More has been done for African development and progress during the last decade than during the whole period which elapsed between 1807, when the slave trade was abolished, and 1895, when the present administration came into power" (98).

This is a remarkably revealing, indeed troubling, statement. The period 1807–95 was a time of African sovereignty. West Africa was being incorporated into the capitalist world-system, producing raw materials for the core regions under the label of "legitimate commerce." The year 1895 saw the beginning of the European colonization of Africa, as it was a decade since the Berlin Conference came to an end. To say the decade 1895–1905, when Africans lost their sovereignty and were dragged into colonial subjugation by the weapon of mass destruction of the time, the Maxim gun, did more to Africa's development than the previous period of almost a century shows the extent Blyden would go to support the European colonial cause. His view is simply that Africans on their own could not head toward modernity unless dragged into it by Europeans.

Blyden is not singing praise songs for British colonialism in Africa only. He also does so for the French, German, Portuguese, and even for the Belgian Leopold II's Congo. He identifies Britain, France, and Germany as the "three greatest of the European powers," each "pursuing its own lines" of contribution to the development of Africa. "France has a peculiar work to do for West Africa—a work much needed, and suited to the genius of the Celtic race" (13). Furthermore, "France is doing her part to pacify West Africa, to improve her material condition, and to give an opportunity for permanent progress to the sons of the soil" (14). In this praise for the French, there is no mention of the many African anticolonial struggles against the French. It is as if they never took place. He admires the Germans in Africa: "Germany is in West Africa to stay, and come to give her desirable quota to its development and prosperity" (17). Per Blyden, every European colonial power in Africa has a "quota" to fulfill in carrying out the "civilizing mission." He has gone as far as anyone could in his unbridled support for European colonialism in Africa.

Blyden puts Liberia as a force of enlightenment and progress in Africa alongside the European colonial powers. "The next political agency in West Africa . . . is the Republic of Liberia" (20). Liberia is "a British Colony in everything but the flag." It has the "language, the laws, and the literature of Great Britain." "Liberia, then, is an independent English-African State" (23–24).

Blyden drags providence for the rationalization of European colonialism in Africa. Going against his views expressed decades earlier in *Liberia's Offering* and his critique there of Noah's malediction, he writes, "God shall enlarge Japheth and to him he has given the means for the distribution of the earth's resources in the interest of humanity. In the hands of China, Japan, India or Africa, the resources would not be distributed. And that branch of the Japhetic race which is most prosperous is that branch which is most liberal in its method of distribution, which unfetters commerce and breaks down trade barriers" (24–25).

Blyden is an ardent believer in free trade. In this England has the lead in West Africa. She has "done more than any other nation to create, foster, and develop commerce in that country, and England will, as is justly her due, reap most of its rewards in future." As for Africans, Blyden's view is the same as the European colonialists. "But this work of distribution, of development cannot be pushed without help—without subordinate assistance. And the procuring of this assistance brings up the labour question" (26). He knows that the colonial system was not one in which Europeans and Africans were equal. Rather, the former was deemed the superior, the latter the subordinate. The former guides, the latter follows. The former comes with capital and skills, the latter provides "subordinate assistance" in the form of labor.

Blyden accepts the environmental theory that civilization or the lack of it stems to a large degree from the natural environment. "Civilisation has attained its highest point where nature forces man to work. Certain luxuries in these countries become necessities. The tropical man is in the condition of the wealthy heir. He has everything ready to his hand. No climatic whip urges him on. Why should he work unless he wishes to? The man of the temperate region or the cultured man anywhere has no option; his needs are inexorable and must be supplied" (29). This is in contradiction with his own critique of the correlation between race and civilization discussed earlier. There he shows how within the same Caucasian race there were the civilized and the barbarians, and they changed place over time. There were even Caucasians who never attained to the standard of civilization. What he was showing was that race, which is "natural biological" and hence immutable for millennia, has nothing to do with culture. If this argument holds for race, why shouldn't it hold for the environment, which is just another natural phenomenon? Blyden rejects one form of nature-determinism, race, only to embrace another, environment, as the criterion in the development of civilization. What is ironic is that he believes racial distinctions are derived from the geographical and natural environment, thus coming full circle. In all this, his views are similar to that of Hegel, who also draws racial distinctions from the natural geographical environment.[3]

The praise for colonialism in general, and Pax Britannica in particular, is embedded in Blyden's philosophy. He has no qualms when he says, for example, "All intelligent Africans believe in England, in her high moral purpose, in her strong sense of right and justice. They believe that England will not slumber nor sleep whenever any wrong exists in her dominions until that wrong is redressed."[4] In *The African Society and Miss Mary H. Kingsley*, Blyden writes comparing two subjects of the British Empire, Indians and Africans. "But the tribes of India are very different from the tribes of Africa. . . . Nothing has ever occurred or can ever occur in African history, even remotely resembling the horrors of the Indian Mutiny. We firmly believe that, if we except individual instances, there is not a native from the Gambia to the Rio del Rey capable of forming an opinion, who would not regard the abolition of English Supremacy in West Africa as the most terrible calamity that could visit the land."[5] Obviously, Blyden is hostile to the 1857 Indian uprising against the British Empire. We cannot help but wonder which side Blyden would have taken during the so-called Mau Mau uprising in colonial Kenya. Would he have been a British loyalist or a spokesperson for oppressed Gikuyu?[6]

He seems to ignore or downplay the fact that colonialism is inherently unjust and that the only way to redress this injustice is to quit the colony and let the "natives" be free. He is of the opinion that Africans left to themselves were to amount to nothing in the direction of progress. In this, he whole-heartedly shared the ideology and practice of colonial paternalism. Chief among the practitioners of this colonial paternalism in West Africa was Frederick Lugard, the British governor of northern Nigeria. In *West Africa before Europe* Blyden lauds his "bold and daring policy," as well as his "enlightened rule" (100, 102).

Blyden comes up with two pieces of advice to the European colonial powers that "providence" had bestowed on the responsibility of ruling over Africa: "Two principles, it seems to me, should guide the policy of the Imperial Powers which have taken upon themselves to partition Africa":

> First, to encourage the development of the natives along the lines of their own idiosyncrasies as revealed in their institutions. No people can profit by or be helpful under institutions which are not the outcome of their own character. The sudden and wholesale imposition of European ideas and methods upon the African has been like the investing of David in Saul's armour. He is falling before the Goliath of progress. (101)

The second principle is "to give to the African taken under British rule all the advantages, in their spirit and effect, which as individuals or communities, as rulers or people, they would have enjoyed under native conditions." He adds, "Do not deprive them of rights and advantages which they valued and enjoyed before you came, and which were in accordance with justice and equity, without making it clear to them that you give them their equivalent. The sense of justice is as keen in the African as in any one else" (103). Confident of the validity of his advice, he writes, "I believe that the future of Africa will rest with that Power which will establish its authority upon the basis of the two principles I have just enumerated." He reiterates that his advice is not contrary to what the British colonial administration is trying to do anyway. "I am glad that I have said nothing which will be new to the actual responsible authorities who represent Great Britain. I am only supporting and putting on record the policy which they are now attempting to introduce" (104).

Blyden's praise is not limited to the British colonial system. He is support-ive of the French also. He writes about his meeting with Ernest Roume, the governor of French West Africa (105).[7] He praises the French for their con-struction of roads and railways in West Africa, more so than the British. He cautions, "If England does not keep her eyes open, her aspiring, energetic and far-sighted neighbour will command all the traffic between the Soudan and the Mediterranean, and divert it to the Atlantic through French Guinea and Senegal" (116–17).

In a speech on August 15, 1903, delivered at the banquet prepared in his honor by West Africans living in London, Blyden told his audience,

> Our country [Africa] has been partitioned, in the order, I believe, of Divine Providence, by the European Powers; and I am sure that, in spite of all that has happened, or is now happening, or may yet happen, this partition has been permitted for the ultimate good of the people, and for the benefit of humanity generally. There is no partiality in the Power that makes for righ-teousness. The scales are held in even balance, and the victory is ultimately not with vulgar Might but with Divine Right. The dice of the gods, it is said, are always loaded.[8]

Such is Blyden's theory of the divine right of colonialism!

After dragging providence to rationalize the European colonial occupa-tion of Africa, Blyden reflects on atrocities in the Congo: "We have heard melancholy rumours of the treatment accorded to our people at the Congo by their alien rulers, and we have heard also of the efforts made by indi-viduals in England, in the spirit of their ancestors, to have those grievances Redressed. We are thankful for their efforts, which have brought forth an elaborate defense from the Belgian authorities." The kernel of the Belgian defense is that "the native will not work, and that he should be made to work." Critiquing such defense, he states,

> Such a principle is not only liable to abuse, but it has been over and over again abused, to the detriment of real progress and the permanent interests of humanity. The Spanish discoverers of America carried out this principle until the whole race of Caribs in the West Indies was destroyed. The Hidalgos of Castile laid down a policy which they believed to be the only one possible in dealing with the native races of the newly discovered country. The stories of Columbus, Cortes and Pizarro illustrate human nature when influenced by theories of its own invention, and with unlimited power to carry them out.[9]

In a resignation to the colonial reality, and in support of it, Blyden told his audience that Africans ought to help make light the European burden of ruling Africa by explaining the "benighted" continent to them:

Then as Africans we must sympathise with and assist the powers that be as ordained of God, whom He will hold to as strict accountability for their proceedings. We cannot alter this arrangement, whatever our opinion as to the rudeness and ruggedness of the method by which the human instruments have arrived at it. It is a fact. Let us then, to the best of our ability, assist those to whom had been committed rule over our country. Their task is not an easy one. They are giving direction to a state of things that must largely influence the future.[10]

Such a view reminds us of Hegel's famous line in the *Philosophy of Right*: *"What is rational is actual and what is actual is rational."*[11] In *Lectures on the Philosophy of World History*, Hegel states, regarding wrong done in history, that there is "nothing we can do about it now." Indeed, "we retreat into that selfish complacency which stands on the calmer shore and, from a secure position, smugly looks on at the distant spectacle of confusion and wreckage." The "cunning of reason" is at work in the dark pages of history. Hegel ponders, "But even as we look upon history as an altar on which the happiness of nations, the wisdom of states, and the virtue of individuals are slaughtered, our thoughts inevitably impel us to ask: to whom, or to what ultimate end have these monstrous sacrifices been made?"[12] Although Hegel sees that humans "can be held responsible, for good as well as for evil" and that "only the animal can truly be described as totally innocent," he still chastises what he calls the "litany of lamentations" that "the good and the pious . . . fare badly in the world, while the evil and the wicked prosper."[13]

In "Africa and the Africans" Blyden addresses the question of how to motivate Africans to work in the modern context. Agreeing with the colonial stereotype, he says, "So far as Africa is concerned, the natives have but few wants, they live in a genial climate, they possess a sufficient if not abundant supply of food. Absolute poverty is impossible among them." They "have few motives for working" for themselves (36). In light of this, he advises the colonial powers to be patient and gentle with Africans. "I know that what is called progressive civilization cannot be introduced into Africa without European intervention. But it would be a sad calamity for the Natives, as well as for their exploiters, if they should be consigned to a harsh and inhuman discipline, in order to be taught the advantages of civilization" (37). Blyden welcomes the introduction of Western modernity but cautions against its method of exploitation.

For Blyden, Africans are not called for political or industrial leadership. Their task is to dirty their hands on the land. "The gift of the African does not lie in the direction of political aggrandisement. His sphere is the church, the school, the farm, the workshop. For us the tools are the proper instruments of the man." It is from such a view that Blyden sees the necessity of the European partition of Africa: "This is why our country has been partitioned among the political agencies of the world—the Japhetic Powers—for they can best do the work to be done in the interest of the temporal as a basis for the spiritual advancement of humanity. The African and the Jew are the spiritual races, and to them political ascendancy among the nations of the earth is not promised" (44).

Blyden sees the contradictions in the introduction of Western modernity in West Africa:

> The civilised centres of Sierra Leone, the Gambia, and Liberia, are hardly in touch with the aborigines, as these settlements were founded by Africans foreign to the localities, who, out of touch with the indigenous inhabitants could hardly be welded into one with them. Some of them, owing to the smattering which they received of European culture, thought themselves better and wiser than their aboriginal ancestors—despised the rock whence they were hewn, and the hole of the pit whence they were digged. Hence came weakness, decay, inefficiency and general sterility. (41)

Yet he does not conclude that the introduction of Western modernity into West Africa was bad. To the contrary, he sees it as having contradictory effects:

> In looking at the history of the Natives of the British colonies of West Africa, since their contact with modern civilisation, it must be remarked that there has been among them in certain departments a gradual and steady increase in sound knowledge, or information outside the aboriginal scope, and a relative diminution of ignorance on certain elementary matters. On the other hand, there has been evident a hindrance to the normal and healthy development of the people, growing out of the pressure of an alien civilisation. (40)

Blyden is thus cognizant of the ambiguities and contradictions of the Western modernist impact on Africa. Even as he positively appreciates the role of westernization in Africa, he also is astute enough to see the alienation that comes with it. He suggests that the way out of this contradiction is to be cautions against the wholesale and uncritical adoption of Western ways of life in Africa: "We must all enter earnestly and intelligently upon the study of alien customs brought among us, comparing them with the customs of our fathers, with the view of resisting the one so far as they conflict with our true interests, and strengthening the other so far as they conduce to our permanent welfare—always keeping that great truth in mind that 'the life is more than meat and the body than raiment.'" He further states, "We must strive to cultivate the better sense for Africa which our fathers possessed—a sense of superiority to transient interests and foreign glitter, which for us are derogatory aberrations. We must not barter the sacredness and veneration which hang over and sanctify the tombs of our fathers for the glamour of alien popularity. All is not gold that glitters" (43–44). On the positive side,

Blyden states, "I am glad to be able to say that I have noticed recently among thinking natives a reaction against all this—a feeling that we must get back to the standpoint of our fathers—that, loosed from our ancestral moorings, we are drifting into mistakes and errors fatal to physical and intellectual prosperity" (41). Going back to the "standpoint of our fathers" is a theme Blyden repeatedly stresses; it is akin to Cabral's "return to the source."

These are extremely important passages in Blyden's overall paradigm. Through the zigzags and alleyways of his tortured and tortuous path in the search for Africa's modernity, he consistently holds the view that African modernization must be both modern and African. Per Blyden, Africa ought not wholeheartedly swallow Europe's modernity; it rather must appropriate the good, that which does not clash or undermine its "nationality," and reject that which runs contrary to its identity and welfare. He told the young Africans who were in attendance at his banquet, "You have had access to European culture. You should be the leaders of action, and the leaders of thought among them. My message to you to-night, therefore, is to school yourselves to look upon life from the standpoint of your own nationality. With your study of English history and English institutions unite the study of the institutions and customs of your people" (42).

The question is, how does Africa attain modernity on African grounds? Blyden repeatedly states that Africa cannot achieve modernity without European intervention, including colonial intervention, which he supports on the grounds of both Africa's need for modernity and Africa's inability to achieve it on its own. But how do we know if the modernity Africa appropriates from the West is good or bad? As a case, he advocates the widespread teaching of the English language in Africa. Is that good for Africa, or does it undermine African culture and the ways of the "fathers?"

In the collection, *West Africa before Europe*, he calls Liberia an "independent English-African State in Africa." He further notes, "We would not if we could, and could not if we would, alienate our intellectual allegiance to Great Britain, for that allegiance is a guarantee of political and religious liberty and stimulus to the highest possible human attainment. We consider it to be a great privilege to say: 'We speak the language Shakespeare spake.'"[14]

So we may ask, is speaking the language "Shakespeare spake" in line with the standpoint of the fathers of Africa? I do not want find an issue with everything Blyden says. I am grappling with a broad, deep, fertile mind struggling to keep its balance between racial pride and dignity on the one hand and belief in Africa's "backwardness" and Europe's advanced stage on the other. This tension defines Blyden's project. Herein lies Blyden's race for modernity, for and of the black race. A black African racial modernity is Blyden's political philosophy, his primary life vocation.

Blyden sees Africa in the same way as Henry Morton Stanley: the "Dark Continent." Dark, gloomy, and depressed, Africa needs the uplifting and civilizing influences of both East and West. He writes in *Christianity, Islam, and the Negro Race:*

> It is interesting to see that the religion of Isaac and the religion of Ishmael, both having their root in Abraham, confront each other on this continent [Africa]. Japheth introducing Isaac, and Shem bringing Ishmael, Ham will receive both. The moonlight of the Crescent, and the sunlight of the Cross, will dispel the darkness which has so long covered the land. The "Dark Continent" will no longer be a name of reproach for this vast peninsula, for there shall be no darkness here.[15]

He goes on to say, "Where the light from the Cross ceases to stream upon the gloom, there the beams of the Crescent will give illumination; and as the glorious orb of Christianity rises, the twilight of Islam will be lost in the greater light of the Sun of Righteousness. Thus Isaac and Ishmael will be united, and rejoice together in the faith of their common progenitor—Ibrahim Khalil Allah—Abraham, the Friend of God."[16] As Blyden sees it, the Abrahamic religions brought about spiritually uplifting influences in Africa, a continent content with its conditions of being wrapped up in the "dark mantle of night."[17] He seems to see no redeeming element coming from within Africa that was untouched by either of these Abrahamic religions. It is as if indigenous Africa was sitting with folded arms waiting for the redeemers to come from afar: children of Japheth and children of Shem. If Shem came earlier, it was only to plough the rough African terrain and make it ready for sowing the seed of the "absolute religion."[18] Such a depiction of the spiritual and cultural "scramble for Africa" between Japheth and Shem, with Africa as a silent and motionless "receiver" of the blessings of civilization from both scramblers, is quite unnerving, coming from a man of such prodigious intellect, who also happened to have Africa's interest deep at heart.

Yet Blyden also proves capable of being a critic of European colonialism in Africa. In the appendix of *Christianity, Islam, and the Negro Race,* under the title "The Republic of Liberia," he registers his displeasure about the colonial enterprise in Africa. He notes that although European colonies exist "for a higher purpose, and though under their protection and stimulus the missionary can do an unmolested and even apparently aggressive work, yet, in such colonies, the measure of progress allowed to the natives must be limited, seeing that the power and prestige of the Europeans and the promotion of European interests must be made the first consideration." He further reflects on this point:

> In the European colonies along the coast there may be the evidences of material prosperity, but it proceeds with the heavy and crushing indifference of the car of Juggernaut, and, like the conductors of that ponderous vehicle, it looks

upon the possible destruction of individuals as no serious evil; as possibly for their own good and for the advancement of the cause. There is no recognition, therefore, of the fact that there are hearts that feel, no notice taken of sensibilities that may be rudely lacerated, no effort to nurse the well-spring of a nobler life within. The native is, as a rule, simply the victim of an unsympathetic apparatus of political and commercial machinery.[19]

Blyden has other stories to tell, other judgments to make. In *The Jewish Question*, written in 1898, he states,

The sons of Japheth, in solemn conclave, thirteen years ago, partitioned Africa among themselves; and they are, by methods congenial to them, exploiting and endeavouring to develop it. And everybody knows what is taking place there. We dread the consequences of their work upon that continent. We know how heavy the hand of Japheth is upon the darker races of the earth. We know how incapable he is of preserving even the physical life of the weaker tribes of humanity; and we know his indifference, while pursuing his material enterprises, to the spiritual conditions.[20]

This is not the first time Blyden pours lament against the heavy hand of "Japheth" on the rest of the peoples of the earth.

Blyden makes one of his powerful appraisals of the contradictions of the European intrusion into Africa during his lifetime. He sees some tangible material gains for Africans that came in direct contact with colonial rule. Yet this wealth came at the price of deep spiritual loss. Europe, Blyden believes, has no spiritual contribution to make for the regeneration of Africa. Europe has no soul.

Now Europe in the great work which it believes itself called upon to do in Africa is producing conditions in which it is impossible for "souls" to "grow," and bodies can hardly survive. It is introducing the material results of science; it is removing the pressure of many outward evils, dissipating harmful superstitions, and degrading prejudices. In many places the people are taught to live in better houses than their ancestors had, to wear finer clothes, to read and write and cipher. The physical obstructions, encumbrances, and inconveniences are being removed. (22)

After describing such material advantages, Blyden turns to the realm of the spiritual:

But the value of this vast apparatus, this ponderous machinery, and these relentless appliances of civilization, is neutralized and destroyed by their effect upon the spiritual and even physical vitality of the race. The higher life of man, the moral and religious emotions, which nurse the well spring of a nobler life within, are not thought of, except in the weak attempts of a few self-denying missionaries, who owing to sectarian differences and conflicts, and to numerical insignificance, are helpless to extend the principles they inculcate. Christianity in West Africa has had only two stages—infancy and decrepitude; vigorous manhood it has never had.

Blyden expresses his fear for the future of Africa: "We look forward, therefore, with dismay to the unrestrained predominance of the purely secular agencies of Japhetic rule. Science for all the really higher purposes of humanity is a dead organism of latent forces unless it is taken up by the moral nature, unless it is animated by earnest purpose and inspired by a great spiritual idea. This condition Europe is helpless to produce in Africa" (22). In these few paragraphs, Blyden comes across as someone who is not that thrilled about the advantages of the European colonial occupation of Africa. Instead, he sees colonialism as bringing cultural and spiritual ruin for Africans. And for him, that is too much a price to pay for a few glittering material benefits that may accrue to Africans in their contact with the world of European colonial rule.

In such a context, Blyden compared Europe and its Christian religion with that of Islam:

> The Islamic system, given through Ishmael, upholds the value of the individual, as carrying within him a divine and imperishable life—as being a citizen of another world, impressing upon him that the future is immeasurably better than the present. It offers by its teachings strenuous and effective opposition to the Japhetic influence, which . . . deals only with economical, commercial, and statistical questions, by which man's worth is reckoned at so much productive power in the region of matter, and which take no note of the interior qualities of his nature. Now Islam brings a healthful counteracting influence. (23)

Enter now the Jews, the least discussed but first progenitor of the Abrahamic faiths:

> Now Africa appeals to the Jew—the other son of Abraham, preserved during so many ages, and through so many vicissitudes—to come with his scientific and other culture, gathered by his exile in many lands, and with his special spiritual endowments; to the assistance of Ishmael in the higher work for Africa which Japheth, through a few struggling representatives, is laboring heroically under great disadvantages to carry out. (23)

Blyden's intention is simple: "If what I have here written should have no other effect than to attract the attention of thinking and enlightened Jews to the great continent of Africa—not to its northern and southern extremities only, but to its vast intertropical area—I should feel amply rewarded" (23).

Blyden's appeal to Jews to help Africa was made by him "as an African," and "from the African standpoint." His was both an indictment of the neglect of Africa by Jews, as well as an appeal to Jews to do otherwise:

> The great body of the "Dark Continent" has been apparently overlooked by the Jews. I see nothing in contemporary Jewish writings about Africa, as to its spiritual condition. Even the "Dreamers of the Ghetto," and the great Dreamer himself have no dreams on the subject. There is not, to my knowledge, a single synagogue in West Africa, along three thousand miles of coast, and probably not two dozen representatives of God's chosen people in that whole extent of country—not a Jewish institution of any kind—either for commercial, religious or educational purposes. Have the Jews no witness to bear in inter-tropical Africa? Have they no word of comfort or of help for millions of the descendants of Ham in that land? And if report be true there are thousands of Jacob's descendants hidden there under Ethiopian garb. (16)

The last sentence seems to refer to the Beta Israel of Ethiopia, the so-called black Jews.

Blyden does not simply ask Jews to help Africa. He also reminds them what Africa meant and did for them. Jews are called to attention for the reparations they owe Africa:

> If the world owes an immense debt to the Jews, the Jews as well as the rest of mankind owe an immense debt to Africa; for it was upon that soil that a few nomads from Western Asia settled down, and, in the furnace of affliction, as well as in the house of preservation, grew to be a nation: and as I have just intimated there are remnants of Jews there to-day, who have never left it since Jacob, with seventy souls, entered it from Canaan. (16)

It was to the Jews that Blyden assigns supreme responsibility in tackling head-on the two-headed hydra: Western bourgeois civilization intoxicated with crass materialism and the "barbarous" ways of life of those Africans untouched with the Abrahamic "spirits." He would declare, "The message of the great Zionist movement to the Jews, it seems to me, is to rise from their neutrality and co-operating with or utilizing both their children—Christianity and Islam—work for the saving of mankind—the civilized from a deadening materialism and the barbarous from a stagnant and degrading superstition" (14).[21] Who would but those who know not Blyden feel offended about Christianity and Islam being called the "children" of their Judaic parent? Alas, anti-Semitism is the abuse of parents!

In his last major work, *African Life and Customs*, published in 1908, Blyden provides the most powerful defense of the African social structure in all its aspects—religion, politics, family, marriage, and so on. He even defends polygamy and non-Abrahamic indigenous African religions. "The African

Religion is a matter that affects all classes of the people—men, women, and children. . . . As in all other matters, the [African] Religion is communistic. When this system is recklessly and indiscriminately interfered with, the result is what we are witnessing everywhere in West Africa, as in Uganda—dislocations, degeneracy, death."[22] The man who invested his prodigious intellectual labor advocating the introduction to Africa of the blessings of Western modernity with its three Cs—Christianity, commerce, and civilization—reminds his readers of the outcome of such an introduction, the three Ds: dislocations, degeneracy, and death.[23] Yet at the very time when he seems to be defending the African way of life, including African religion, Blyden embraces as positive the European colonization of Africa. In short, *African Life and Customs* is a work of colonial anthropology, meant to explain the African way of life to the new masters, the Europeans, so that they can rule justly, benevolently, and humanely, and with knowledge of African "manners and customs."[24]

The paradox of Blyden's life is that as he grew older, he defended both the "life and customs" of Africans in the interior and European colonialism in Africa. He became the intermediary, the interlocutor, explaining the "native" to the European master, and the European master to his subject. He thought European colonialism in Africa would last but a short time due in part to the inhospitability of the African environment for large European settlements. Yet in this short period of colonial presence, Africa would have materially benefited from its direct encounter with, and appropriation of, Western Christian bourgeois modernity. Colonialism was the price Africa had to pay for such material improvement. And Blyden was willing to pay the price. It was the Hegelian "cunning of reason" in the African attainment of modernity.

Blyden opted for the due recognition and upholding of Africa's "triple heritage": indigenous religion, Islam, and Western Christianity. In *The Significance of Liberia*, written in 1906, Blyden states,

> Two great indigenous agencies of self-preservation appeal to us—Paganism and Mohammedanism. The word Paganism does not in any sense describe the system, but only expresses the ignorance of the outsider. We cannot afford to neglect it. We should enter its sacred groves, as many a European has done, and study it. Our women should enter them and study the laws affecting their sex. The Japanese, as I have told you, did not expel the religion of their fathers for a foreign religion.[25]

For all his advocacy of the importation of Western modernity to Africa, Blyden is also a conservationist, that is, an advocate for the continued preservation of African cultures, religions, ways of life, and so on. He is not a revolutionary in the sense that he wants to destroy and uproot African social and cultural practices and implant in their place those from the West. Blyden accuses Protestants of cultural vandalism in their own land: "Protestants, in their iconoclastic zeal, destroyed everything which in their Pagan days their fathers reverenced; so that in England and America there are no sacred places. An indiscriminate Vandalism has obliterated all the landmarks of native religion, and the people reverence neither places nor persons." Turning his attention to Africa, Blyden remarks that the missionary has been a destructive force. Such missionary "has substituted for what he has abolished, nothing as good. The sacred spots are gone, and wherever this has happened the natives are less spiritual and less moral; less loyal, less obedient and less amenable to order than anywhere else." In Blyden's view, the "Church is no substitute for the Purroh or Bundo; everywhere in Christian West Africa it is losing its hold upon the people, because there is nothing, either in the building or its associations, to appeal to the deeper feelings of the African." In protest to such Protestant vandalism and destructive behavior in Africa, Blyden proclaims, "The true African, whatever his creed, never wholly abandons his aboriginal faith."[26]

Blyden calls for the "peaceful coexistence" of religions—indigenous religion, Islam, and Christianity—as found in Liberia and, by extension, Africa. Blyden reflects on the first two as follows: "I am satisfied that there are elements in the two systems by which, if adopted into the life of the people of Liberia, instead of dying out, as we are now doing, we should rapidly advance in numerical and material prosperity, in physical vigour and effectiveness, in chastity and sobriety, in pure morals and spirituality."[27]

Blyden prefers Africa as an agrarian continent. He sees no benefits in trotting after the scientific, industrial, and technological lives of the ever-inquisitive white West. Accepting Africa's place in the capitalist world-system as natural, he writes, "Africa will be largely an agricultural country. The people, when assisted by proper impulse from without—and they need this help just as all other races have needed impulse from without—will live largely in contact with nature." Blyden contrasts this Africa, supposedly living in harmony with nature, with Europe:

> The Northern races will take the raw materials from Africa and bring them back in such forms as shall contribute to the comfort and even elegance of life in that country; while the African, in the simplicity and purity of rural enterprises, will be able to cultivate those spiritual elements in humanity which are suppressed, silent and inactive under the pressure and exigencies of material progress. He will find out, not under pressure, but in an entirely normal and natural way, what his work is to be.[28]

Blyden also preferred small towns to big cities. "I do not anticipate for Africa any large and densely crowded cities. For my taste, I cannot say that

I admire these agglomerations of humanity." Rather, "I cherish the feeling that in Africa there will never be any Jerusalem, or Rome, or Athens, or London; but I have a strong notion that the Bethlehems and Nazareths will spring up in various parts of the continent."[29]

According to Blyden, the place of Africans is in Africa. This is good not only for Africans, but the whole world too: "The world needs such a development of the Negro on African soil. He will bring as his contribution the softer aspects of human nature. The harsh and stern fibre of the Caucasian races needs this milder element. The African is the Feminine; and we must not suppose that this is of least importance in the ultimate development of humanity."[30] Blyden's ardent advocacy for the restoration of black manhood to its pride and glory, that is, Blyden's version of racialized black masculinity, is one that is deeply feminized. We may call this Blyden's *feminized masculinity*. To the rugged masculinity of Western modernity is contrasted a feminine African, one not interested in controlling nature but in living in compliance with its laws. Except for Blyden giving this view a positive spin, the idea of a natural, feminine African is at the heart of the racist trope that dominated the Western view of blacks until the 1960s. It is also the central principle of Hegel's Eurocentric construction of world history as regards Africans.[31] In many aspects of his philosophy of history, Blyden passes as a black Hegelian.[32]

Blyden writes that the "political economy of the white man is not our political economy, his moral philosophy is not our moral philosophy, and far less his theology our theology; and whenever he has been successful in forcing these upon us there has been atrophy and death." In a remarkable and quite Marxist-sounding statement, Blyden writes about the paradox of trying to import European capitalism in Africa:

> The object of the great social movement in England is to abolish private ownership and nationalize the land, so that this collective ownership of the means of production and livelihood shall be under the control of the people. Here in Africa where the system of collective ownership is an immemorial custom, we are trying to introduce private ownership. I say we are trying to introduce it, because we have not succeeded and cannot succeed.[33]

In *The Arabic Bible in the Soudan: A Plea for Transliteration*, published in 1910, Blyden categorically declares that Africa's future depends nether on East nor West, nor on any or all of the three Abrahamic faiths.

> Islam or Christianity for Africa is not the only alternative. . . . The ultimate fate of Africa does not depend exclusively upon Jerusalem or Mecca. It may be that from some height yet undiscerned, the river of Salvation may flow through Africa and may quench the thirst of other nations also. It will not be the first

time that Africa has given religion to the outside world. Then will come the
end, when all things shall be delivered up to Jehovah.[34]

Here Blyden makes Africa the witness to the "end of time," the harbinger, in
a way, of the coming of the God-Man of the Christian religion.

Blyden wants Liberia and, by extension, Africa, to clear out that which
has been uncritically borrowed from the outside. In *The Significance of Liberia*,
he states the problem in attempting to accomplish this: "I know it is difficult—with some of us impossible—to escape the prestige of the white man,
which has played so important a part in the history of our exile; and even
here, where we are trying to be ourselves, we feel the pressure of his influence."[35] Granted that "the prestige of the white man" is not easy to push
aside, Blyden declares his intentions for carrying out reforms in Liberia:

> The customs we are combating are not African customs. The framework of our
> society is not hoary, rigid and unelastic with age. We are not assailing a heap of
> time-honoured prejudices and traditional institutions. What we have is all cop-
> ied. We have been looking over the shoulders of foreigners, and copying with-
> out question what they wrote on the slate, knowing neither rhyme nor reason
> for the record. It will not cost us much to rub out the unmeaning scrawl. (34)

In other words, Blyden does not see a backward African culture holding
back Liberia's reforms. The culprit is the uncritical and uncreative appropriation of things Western into Liberia. As he puts it quite unambiguously,
"If we in Liberia continue, in dealing with the aborigines, to conform to the
ordinary missionary methods of suppressing instead of utilising indigenous
institutions, it will only be a question of time when, as a result of national,
physical, intellectual and moral degeneracy, some foreign Power will step
in and take charge, as has happened in Hawaii, Madagascar, the Philippine
Islands, and Uganda" (18). How seriously Blyden took this approach can
be seen when he declares, "There is a thing for the life of the people more
important than the Church, and that is Liberty. 'The Love of Liberty,' runs
our inspiring National motto, 'brought us here'; not love of the Church.
The safety of the people is the highest law" (35).[36] For a Protestant minister to declare such views is quite extraordinary. Protestant Blyden protests
against the benighted practices of his coreligionists who went about bulldoz-
ing African cultures. And he would have no part in it.

Blyden has a very high regard for Japan and its approach to modernity.
For him, Japan is a nation "whose marvellous achievements are still the subject of unqualified eulogy among men of all races." He goes on to identify
what he considers to be the strongest point in Japan's "marvellous achievement": The Japanese selected "those elements which they considered useful for their race and country. . . . They eliminated, by severe persecution,

what was peculiar to Europe" (15). Then, he considers Ethiopia, an African nation whose feat resembled that of Japan: "Abyssinia, like Japan, resisted foreign religious invasion, and like Japan, it has held its own against a formidable European Power, and maintained its independence" (16).

What is extraordinarily remarkable about these statements is that they go straight against any form of support for European colonialism in Africa. For what Japan and Ethiopia (Abyssinia) did first and foremost was to maintain their sovereignty against European invasion, including missionaries. Yet, as we saw in this work, Blyden supports European colonial rule in Africa, especially by the British. Japan and Ethiopia took uncompromising and unconditional stands regarding the inviolability of their sovereignty and independence.[37] If Blyden sees Japan and Ethiopia as his role models for Africa, he should have had no business granting even conditional support for the European colonial enterprise.

Even though Blyden embraced European colonialism in Africa in the name of progress and civilization, he was also of the opinion that it would last a short time. Drawing from his geoenivronmental theory that Africa is inhospitable for the settlement of the European, he saw colonialism as a brief episode in the long history of Africa. In this short time, Africans would benefit from their encounter with a higher civilization. In *The Elements of Permanent Influence*, he writes, "The races now holding power in the world have not always held it; but because by the use, at various times, of unchristian methods they have secured power, which must, owing to its origin and use, be brief, even if it lasts a thousand years."[38] Of course, he did not believe that colonialism would last for a thousand years. Reflecting on his wish for the future of Africa, Blyden writes, "The time will come when the enlightened portion of mankind, freed from the necessity of using the African as a means of promoting their material interests, will be willing to render his due. Meanwhile, it is the work of the African himself to vindicate his race in the world of letters: a republic in which there is no such thing as caste."[39]

Blyden is unique in the history of modern black thought for his remarkable, fertile, evocative, and "dialectical" embrace of hard-nosed consistency, as well as for his tiring and frustrating inconsistencies. Edward Wilmot Blyden was the most prolific representation of the magnificent aspirations, projects, and contradictions of diaspora-derived black racial nationalism.[40]

Epilogue

Post-Blydenian Reflections

The Negro African is not finished before he even gets started.
Let him speak; above all, let him act. Let him bring, like a
leaven, his message to the world in order to help build the Civilization of the Universal.

—Léopold Sédar Senghor, *On African Socialism*

The Africans who led the struggles for independence against European
colonialism in the second half of the twentieth century and who became
the first leaders of postcolonial African states were in the main "philosopher kings." They were politicians who were first-rate intellectuals; they were
intellectuals whose vocation was politics. It was not long, however, before
the leadership of these philosopher kings was abruptly interrupted by the
violent intrusion of the rifle. Kwame Nkrumah, Amilcar Cabral, Julius Nyerere, Jomo Kenyatta, Léopold Sédar Senghor, Augustino Neto, and Nnamdi
Azikiwe, among others, were some of those formidable intellectuals. These
were men of vision in, for, and by Africa. It was a calamity that such men were
removed from their leadership positions by coup d'états, assassinations, or
natural death. It is quite telling and chilling to see that Africa has so far
been unable to come up with leaders of their stature, wisdom, and foresight.
The congruence between state power and the highest level of intellectual-
ism that existed right after the end of colonialism was torn asunder in the
subsequent decades. Those with state power were bereft of wisdom; those
who possessed wisdom were silenced, killed, or exiled by those in power.

The idea that peoples of Africa and African origin are essentially one
people but spread out in many distinctions, directions, and dispositions and
that Africa is the home they reside in or venture back from the diaspora
to claim as theirs is the fundamental message of the Blydenian paradigm
of black racial nationalism. All post-Blydenian black thought rotates around
the axis of this matrix. Modern black thought is Blydenian or not, depend-
ing on whether it accepts this view of the black experience in the context of
the history of the modern world-system.

The tentacles of Blyden's paradigm are spread out in all directions,
intellectually as well as politically. The various shades of pan-Africanism,

including those as diverse as W. E. B. Du Bois and Marcus Garvey, contain Blydenian projects: the unity and "uplifting" of the African race. The radical political economies of Eric Williams, Walter Rodney, and Kwame Nkrumah have Blydenian themes regarding the price Africa and its people paid for the rise and development of modern Western civilization and the resulting exploitation and underdevelopment. The racial nationalism represented by the negritude movement is heavily Blydenian. His critique of Eurocentrism and the concomitant deculturation of "civilized Negroes" is a theme central to Frantz Fanon's masterful anatomy of colonial racism. Blyden's admiration for Islam, with his belief that it is the right religion for Africans, finds echo in the politics of the Nation of Islam in America. Blyden's repeated call for the need to link up with Africans in the interior to regain the strength of the race not yet "polluted" by the Eurocentric air is a theme central to Cabral's call for "return to the source." Blyden's defense of "traditional" African life and customs in his last major work, *African Life and Customs*, is a theme of critical importance in the advocacy of African socialism by Julius Nyerere and Léopold Sédar Senghor. And Blyden's insistence that Africa is the origin of civilization finds powerful echo in the prodigious intellectual productions of Chiekh Anta Diop and the Afrocentric paradigm articulated mostly in America.[1] In short, Blyden's intellectual production was of such grandeur and depth that one can find almost any post-Blydenian position articulated by him earlier. It is not necessarily the case that all these intellectual currents in post-Blydenian black thought claim allegiance to the footsteps of Blyden. It is rather that what these thinkers developed as intellectuals and political leaders are themes to be found in Blyden's voluminous writings. It is in this sense that we can speak of Blyden's legacy. Perhaps it is more appropriate to speak of the legacy of Blydenism.

Perhaps the most paradoxical and ironic twist in the history of post-Blydenian black thought is that Blyden's racial nationalism was hardly picked up by Anglophone intellectuals on both sides of the Atlantic, while it was central, in a way, to the writings among Francophone black intellectuals. And this occurred despite Blyden's infatuation for Anglophone civilization, especially the English language, the language of Shakespeare. It is as if post-Blydenian Francophone black intellectuals declared: shake the spear, shake the spear! Yes, theirs was one of shaking the spear of revolt against the West in line with the Blydenian paradigm of black racial nationalism, negritude. Hollis Lynch points this out phenomenon: "As the most articulate and brilliant vindicator of Negro and African interests in the nineteenth century, Blyden's ideas have contributed greatly to the historical roots of African Nationalism, Pan-African and Negritude, and have been a source of inspiration and pride to modern exponents of these ideologies, as well as to English-speaking New World Negro intellectuals in their continuous quest for dignity and equality for members of their race." Referring to Blyden's influence in West Africa, Lynch states, "In West Africa his influence among nationalists in the first three decades of the twentieth century was direct and pervasive, and was most obvious in their efforts at establishing a British West African Federation, in their search for better and increased educational facilities, and in their attempts to foster pride in African history and culture." Lynch writes, "It was J. E. Casely Hayford who most actively carried on Blyden's work."[2]

As we shall see later in the chapter, Blyden's discourse of black racial nationalism was to find fertile echoing ground in negritude. Lynch notes, "Like that of Pan-Africanism, the modern concept of Negritude as expounded by such writers as Aimé Césaire of Martinique and President Leopold Senghor of Senegal can find respectable historical roots in the writings of Blyden." He further states,

> Indeed, Blyden's pan-Negro ideology rested on Negritude—the affirmation that there was an innate Negro character or "Personality"—characterized by emotion, intuitiveness and empathy with nature; and the rejection, at least partial, of European culture and values. The object of Blyden was the same as that of the more recent exponents of Negritude to create among Negroes, long demoralized in a contemptuous white-dominated world, pride, confidence and a cultural identity by assigning them a special and significant role.[3]

The Colonial Situation

A significant portion of Third World scholarship in the twentieth century has been scholarship of negation and protest. None shows this more clearly than the flamboyant work by the Nigerian scholar Chinweizu, *The West and the Rest of Us: White Predators, Black Slavers, and the African Elite*, which critiques Western views of modernity and how it affected Africa and Africans. Alongside the writings of Anouar Abdel-Malek, mostly his two-volume work, *Social Dialectics*, it has become a classic text of non-Western nationalism.[4]

For Abdel-Malek, the relation between Christian Europe and Islam from the first Crusade until the present has been eleven centuries of "*historical surplus value.*" Expanding his analysis to the larger arena of the "three continents," he states,

> This massive, protracted process of accumulation, this looting in depth of the Three Continents over centuries of domination, has been, one would think, strangely ignored by leading thinkers of the ideology of progress in the West. Theirs was the formulation of "capitalist surplus value"—as if the main thing in the history of mankind was the last stage of the class struggle in class societies, during which the capitalists were to exploit the working classes.[5]

Chinweizu and Abdel-Malek, along with Samir Amin, are three of the most outspoken African voices protesting against the Eurocentrism that undergirds Western modernity. Chinweizu is Nigerian; Abdel-Malek and Amin are from Egypt.[6]

Twentieth-century African thought is essentially a series of confrontations and challenges to the colonial order that existed in Africa. These confrontations mean, in the main, the rejection of Blyden's resignationist acceptance of colonialism as a matter of fact, nay, even as ultimately beneficial to Africa. Yet Blyden's appraisal of colonialism, like his views on the overall impact of the West on Africans, is conflicted: he supports it as the work of providence, as he also cries foul about the destruction of African authenticity, the denigration of African personality, and the dissolution of the African humanistic warmth. In short, there is a Blydenian critique of colonialism, as well as praise for it.

European colonial rule was established in most of Africa and Asia by the beginning of the twentieth century. To explain the modality of the colonial relationship, the French scholar George Balandier coined the term "colonial situation." He writes, "the relations of domination and subordination existing between the colonizing and the colonized societies characterize the colonial situation." He further states, "The two most striking features of a *colonized society* are its *overwhelming numerical superiority*, and its basic subordination." Balandier provides a succinct description of the essential aspects of the colonial situation:

> the domination imposed by a foreign minority, "racially" and culturally distinct, upon a materially inferior autochthonous majority, in the name of a dogmatically asserted racial (or ethnic) and cultural superiority; the bringing into relation of two heterogeneous civilisations, one technologically advanced, economically powerful, swift moving and Christian by origin, the other without complex techniques, economically backward, slow-moving and fundamentally "non-Christian;" the antagonistic nature of the relations between the two societies, owing to the instrumental role to which the subject society is condemned; and the need for the dominant society, if it is to maintain its position, to rely not only upon "force," but also upon a whole range of pseudo-justifications and stereotyped patterns of behaviour, etc.[7]

Kwame Nkrumah, the most prominent pan-Africanist from Africa, has similar views as Balandier regarding colonialism. He had a strong belief that colonialism does not end with mere flag independence for the former colonies. As a Marxist, Nkrumah focuses on the socio-economic aspects of colonialism. He writes, "Neocolonialism, like colonialism, is an attempt to export the social conflicts of the capitalist countries. The temporary success of this policy can be seen in the ever widening gap between the richer and the poorer nations of the world."[8]

Senghor provides his own account of the colonial situation. For Senghor, the colonial situation is marked by two fundamental traits: the racial and cultural sphere and the economic sphere. Of the two, Senghor's analysis focuses on the former. As a philosopher and African spokesperson of negritude, he deals more on the racial and cultural dimensions of the colonial situation than on the economic, social, or political spheres. Like Fanon, Senghor's principal category for understanding the colonial situation is the concept of alienation. "The proletariat of the nineteenth century was estranged from humanity; the colonized people of the twentieth century, the colored peoples, are estranged even more seriously. To economic alienations, others are added: political, social, and cultural. The result is physical and moral suffering, poverty, the uneasy conscience, the latter stemming from a feeling of frustration." As such, "Where colored peoples are concerned, it is accurate to speak of a 'revolt against the west.'" He adds, "In Europe, it is a question of eliminating inequalities arising from the formation of classes. In Africa, it is a question of eliminating inequalities arising from the colonial conquest, from political domination."[9]

Senghor, like Nkrumah, sees colonialism as an attempt to mitigate the social problems of European societies. "It is now a commonplace fact that the European masses' standard of living has been able to rise only at the expense of the standard of living of the masses in Asia and Africa. . . . In a word, the European proletariat has profited from the colonial system; therefore it has never really—I mean, effectively—opposed to it." He reiterates the specificity of the colonial situation: "In fact, the European proletarians are held in dependent status as individuals grouped in a class, not as a race or a people. As for us, we have been colonized, to be sure, as underdeveloped, defenseless individuals, but also as *Negroes* or ArabBerbers—in other words, as people of a different race and different culture." Furthermore, "European conquest and colonization benefited not only the capitalistic bourgeoisie, but also the European middle classes and the proletariat. It permitted the emigration of 'poor whites' to the colonized countries, the conquest of exotic markets, easy sources of raw materials. Consequently, it favoured the industrial development of Europe and a higher living standard for the European masses."[10] What later became the theory of underdevelopment and the North-South schism is outlined by Senghor here clearly.

Colonial racism undergirded the colonial situation. The Tunisian scholar Albert Memmi gives a succinct definition of this colonial racism. "Colonial racism: is built from three major ideological components: one, the gulf between the culture of the colonialist and the colonized; two, the exploitation of these differences for the benefit of the colonialist; three, the use of these supposed differences as standards of absolute fact." Memmi elaborates,

The first component is the least revealing of the colonialist's mental attitude. To search for differences in features between two peoples is not in itself a racist's characteristic, but it has definitive function and takes on a particular meaning in a racist context. The colonialist stresses those things which keep him separate, rather than emphasizing that which might contribute to the foundation of a joint community. In those differences, the colonized is always degraded and the colonialist finds justification for rejecting his subjects.[11]

Memmi highlights the colonialist's project of dehistoricizing the relationship between the colonizer and the colonized, making it appear as if it were built in nature. We saw in this work how Blyden repeatedly reiterates the historicity of the colonial relationship, even though he throws in providence to rationalize it. Memmi, like Blyden minus providence, points to how the colonizer removes the colonial relation "from history, time, and therefore possible evolution." With the colonizer, what "is actually a sociological point becomes labelled as being biological or, preferably, metaphysical. It is attached to the colonized's basic nature. Immediately the colonial relationship between colonized and colonizer, founded on the essential outlook of the two protagonists, becomes a definitive category. It is what it is because they are what they are, and neither one nor the other will ever change."[12]

Memmi points to the racialized totalizing of colonized peoples: "the colonized's depersonalization is what one might call the mark of the plural. The colonized is never characterized in an individual manner; he is entitled only to be drawn in an anonymous collectivity ('They are this.' 'They are all the same.')" In Sartre's words "oppression justifies itself through oppression: the oppressors produce and maintain by force the evils that render the oppressed, in their eyes, more and more like what they would have to be like to deserve their fate."[13] For Memmi, racism entails the naturalization of concrete, historical social relations.

In his poetic protest against Western colonial rule, Aimé Césaire describes the colonial "anonymous collectivity" as a discourse of collective naming, which is one of depersonalization: "niggers-are-all-alike."[14] Enraged at such rush of racist judgment, he declares,

Hear the white world
horribly fatigued by its immense effort
. . .
hear its treacherous victories trumpeting its defeats.[15]

In contrast with the materially saturated West, Césaire sees Africa as innocent.

Not caring to conquer, but playing the game of the world
truly the elder sons of the world.[16]

In what Ali Mazrui cites as an example of what he calls "romantic primitivism," Césaire celebrates the African rejection of the Hegelian developmentalist paradigm:

Those who invented neither gunpowder nor compass,
Those who never vanquished steam or electricity,
Those who explored neither seas nor sky,
But who know in its uttermost corners the landscape of pain,
Those who've known no voyages other than uprootings.[17]

Like Blyden before him, who pours out his pain at the racial insults directed at black humanity, Césaire identifies the contradictions and weaknesses of modern Western civilization. "The fact is that the so-called European civilisation—'Western' civilisation—as it has been shaped by two centuries of bourgeois rule, is incapable of solving the two major problems to which its existence has given rise: the problem of the proletariat and the colonial problem."[18]

Reflecting on the Negritude movement, Arnold points out that "the process of raising the level of black consciousness is a complex one . . . and it must pass through a painful period of recognizing that one has interiorized the racist view of oneself."[19] Negritude was born out of the rejection of colonial racism. It is the paradox of the colonial dialectic that Negritude was created by the very people whom French *mission civilisatrice* created, the so-called évolué.

Invented by the poets Aimé Césaire and Leon Damas, and developed further by the poet-scholar-statesman Léopold Sédar Senghor, negritude began as a movement of Francophone black racial nationalism in the 1930s. It was a revolt of the Francophone black intelligentsia, the évolué, against the French colonial situation. Césaire, Damas, and Senghor all came from French colonial possessions, the first two from the Caribbean island of Martinique, the last from Senegal.

Abiola Irele notes that the "only really significant expression of cultural nationalism associated with Africa—apart from small-scale local movements—is the concept of *Negritude*, which was developed by French-speaking Negro intellectuals."[20] Negritude was a protest discourse of the black educated elite against the alienation of colonial society. It was also a rejection of the negative image of blacks in modern Western discourse. Negritude was black self-portrayal, black self-consciousness, black self-definition. As opposed to the black person, whose burden it was to shake off the racial load, was the white person, who, as "master of the world, never bothered to create a literary ideology around his whiteness."[21]

Negritude falls within the larger rubric of the Blydenian paradigm: black racial nationalism. Like Blyden before them, the negritude intellectuals believe that there is a Negro race essence that distinguishes it from the other races, primarily the Caucasian. It is this essence that they grapple with to bring to the light in their poetic and philosophical imaginations. Their writings are post-Blydenian, but Blydenian in perspective, motivation, and historical project.

Léopold Sédar Senghor

Senghor mentions Blyden in the foreword to Blyden's *Selected Letters*. There he expresses admiration for Blyden as the father of the idea of "African Personality." He also discusses his disagreement with Blyden's antimulatto stance. Still, Senghor incorporates a critical element of the Blydenian strand of black racial nationalism. Valentin Mudimbe brings out the symmetry of views between Blyden and Senghor: "Despite discrepancies due to differences of sociopolitical context, psychological situations, and philosophical references, Senghor, on the whole, pursued Blyden's ambiguous thesis. His pronouncements emphasize the African cultural and historical identity in terms of race and consider this concept to be essential."[22]

Senghor is the preeminent African voice of negritude.[23] In "Black Host," written in 1945, Senghor laments,

> Lord God, forgive white Europe!
> It is true Lord, that for four centuries of enlightenment she threw her foaming, yelping dogs upon my lands.

Referring specifically to France, he writes,

> Yes Lord, forgive France, who hates all occupations, and imposes hers so heavily on me.[24]

In his piece "The Psychology of the African Negro," which he wrote for the Second Congress of Negro Writers and Artists held in 1959 in Rome, Senghor provides one of his most sophisticated presentations of African social ontology.[25] Senghor, very much like Blyden, reflects on the modern Western (Hegelian bourgeois) developmentalist paradigm, whose fundamental idea is the domination of nature:

> Let us consider the European white man confronted with the object, the exterior world, nature, the *Other*. . . . He holds it at a distance; he immobilizes it; he fixes it. Armed with precision instruments, he dissects it with a ruthless analysis. Aroused by powerful determination, he kills the Other and, in a centripetal movement, he finds means by which to use it for practical purposes. He *assimilates* it. Such is the European white man.[26]

How do Africans fare compared with Europeans? Senghor declares that the "Negro is quite different":

> First, the African Negro is by his colour as in the primordial night. He does not see the object; he feels it. . . . It is in his subjectivity, at the end of his sensory organs that he discovers the Other. There he is, stimulated, going centrifugally from subject to object on the waves of the Other. . . . Thus, one sees the African Negro who sympathizes and identifies himself, who dies to himself in order to be reborn to the Other. He is not assimilated; *he assimilates himself* with the Other. He lives with the Other in symbiosis. (50)[27]

Cutting through the racist essentialization of reason as exclusively white European and emotion as black African, Senghor retorts, "Though it may seem paradoxical, the Negro élan, the active abandon of the African Negro towards the object, is animated by *reason*. . . . Negro reason, as it appears here, is not, as one might guess, the discursive reason of Europe, *reason through sight*, but *reason through touch*, sympathetic reason."[28] He adds, "European reason is analytic through utilization; Negro reason is intuitive through participation" (51).

Senghor remarks, "I have often written that emotion was Negroid. I have been wrongly reproached for it. I do not see how one can account otherwise for our characteristics, for this *Negritude*" (51). Senghor explains the African world of lived emotion: "the reflexes of the African Negro are, more than all others, spontaneous, *lived*. Thus, the African Negro reacts more easily to excitements; he espouses naturally the rhythm of the object. This sensual feeling of *rhythm* is one of his specific characteristics" (53). Senghor, in line with Blyden's paradigm of the existence of a "Negro" race essence, distinct from all other races, makes the case here about such Negro-African race essence.

Senghor explains the African world of emotion as follows. He calls African society one "based essentially on human relations, perhaps still more on relations of men and 'gods,' an *animistic* society, by which I mean, a society which is less interested in *earthly nourishment* than in spiritual nourishment." Indeed, what "affects the African Negro is not so much the appearance of an object as its profound reality, its *surrealite*; not so much its form as its meaning." Senghor calls African consciousness of emotion, "the *accession to a superior state of consciousness*" (55).

Senghor calls on the authorities of Jean-Paul Sartre and Albert Einstein to support his testimony to the superiority of emotion. He cites Sartre, who calls emotion the "consciousness of the world." He draws on Einstein, who states, "The finest emotion that we can experience is mystic emotion. There lies the seed of all art and of all real science." "It is precisely the seed of African Negro knowledge and of art, where the *e-motion* is *com-motion*" (55).

Senghor provides a sophisticated understanding of the concept of emotion, which he attributes to Africans. The allegation that Senghor's views of Africans as people of emotion, as opposed to reason (reason being on a higher plane of thought than emotion), and that Senghor's views are similar to those of Arthur Gobineau show a shallow understanding of his work. Senghor does not put "reason" above "emotion"; he does not put white people above Africans. Yet the charge continues. Thus Babacar Camara charges Senghor for appropriating Gobineau regarding the emotion and reason divide between Africans and whites, respectively.[29]

In his protest against the racism of the French colonial situation, Senghor thinks of himself turning racist. In a Blydenian genre of the distinct calling of the African in world history, Senghor remarks, "Our distrust of European values quickly turned into disdain—why hide it—into racism. We thought—and we said—that we Negroes were the salt of the earth, that we were the hearers of an unheard of message—and that no other race could offer but us. Unconsciously, by osmosis and reaction at the same time, we spoke like Hitler and the colonialists, we advocated the virtues of the blood." He further notes,

> Relying on the work of anthropologists, prehistorians, ethnologists—paradoxically white—we proclaimed ourselves, along with Aimé Césaire, the "Eldest sons of the Earth," who dominate the world, up to and including the neolithic period, fertilize the civilizations of the Nile and of the Euphrates before they became the innocent victims of white barbarians, nomads melting out of their Eurasian plateau. I confess it, our pride turned quickly into racism. . . . We then had the sincerity of youth and passion.

Indeed, "in the hours of grave difficulties, in the hours of discouragement and doubt, we only have to think of Pharaonic Egypt to convince ourselves that Africa played a primordial role in the elaboration of civilisation. Africa, cradle of the Negro, indeed of '*Homo Sapiens.*'"[30] Pharaonic Egypt is the catharsis of African cultural nationalism.

It is strange that Senghor would confuse negritude, including his own, with Nazis and colonialism. Negritude was not for racial domination but for racial equality and racial freedom. The use of the category "race" does not make one a racist. Racism is domination based on race as a mark of distinction. Hence the dominated and oppressed race cannot fight racism in any other way than by rallying behind the reason of their oppression, their race.[31] Similarly, women fight sexism by organizing themselves around the cause of their oppression, their gender.

Sartre was familiar with the writings of Negritude intellectuals, including Senghor. In his *Black Orpheus* he saw negritude as the antithesis, the negation, the second stage of the dialectical triad.

> Negritude appears as the weak stage of a dialectical progression: the theoretical and practical affirmation of white supremacy is the thesis; the position of Negritude as antithetical value is the moment of the negativity. But this negative moment is not sufficient in itself and the blacks who employ it well know it; they know that it serves to prepare the way for the synthesis or the realization of the human society without racism. Thus Negritude is dedicated to its own destruction, it is passage and not objective, means and not the ultimate goal.[32]

Senghor shares Sartre's view regarding the dialectic of negritude. After taking negritude as the black racial negation of white racism, establishing thus the racial equality of black and white, Senghor moves on to formulate the "negation of negation," the synthesis. Such synthesis would be the symbiosis of the positive achievements of all races and all cultures. He calls it the "Civilisation of the Universal," which is "a symbiosis of the most fecundating elements of all civilizations."[33] It is the guillotine that cuts off the head of racism. Sounding very much like Blyden, Senghor writes, "Our ultimate task is to bring about a symbiosis of our African Negro, or to be more precise, NegroBerber Values, and European Values. European Values because Europe contributes the principal technical means of the emerging civilization. Indeed, all the values from either side cannot be retained."[34]

In the realm of culture, the positive of each culture is to be assimilated in a dialectical synthesis, or what he calls "*assimilating* assimilation. It is a question of assimilating, not being assimilated."[35] Senghor raises an important point, a key to his theory of negritude and the civilization of the universal. Colonialism forced the colonized to assimilate into the culture of the colonizer, and yet it totally rejected the idea that the colonizer too needed to assimilate the culture of the colonized. When Senghor discusses the question of passive assimilation, he is referring to the one-way assimilation of the colonizers' culture by the colonized. "Assimilating assimilation," or active assimilation, is quite different. Here the assimilators are free to choose what to assimilate, and the assimilation is mutual, that is, the assimilator is assimilated, and the assimilated in turn assimilates. Just as African culture assimilates European culture, European culture assimilates African culture. In this notion of reciprocal assimilation, the racialism of Senghor's negritude evaporates into thin air. What started as negritude, as racial negation of the West, ends up in the harmonious higher unity of the "civilisation of the universal." By themselves, neither African nor European cultures are whole. They are incomplete particularities that attain true humanist universality only by incorporating, and by in turn being incorporated, other cultural particularities. In such a way, Senghor dialectically overcomes the one-sidedness of racism. For Senghor, racism is not universalism because it is a nonassimilating assimilator.[36]

For "assimilating assimilation" to exist, all parties should be both receivers and givers. Africa gives to Europe what it lacks, and Europe does the same. Per Senghor, Europeans "brought to us Africans logical reasoning; we bring to you Europeans, to you Latins, intuitive reasoning by which Negritude is defined." Furthermore, to Europe's "atheistic materialism we oppose spiritualistic materialism."[37]

In one of his most profound reflections on the subject of "assimilating assimilation," Senghor writes, "So that the civilization of tomorrow's world will not finish in a planetary catastrophe—and a moral dissolution would be worse than an atomic one—so that Europe's virtues can ripen into harvests for all, it is necessary that Europe appear at the catholic rendezvous of giving and taking. It is necessary for her to *assimilate*. . . . And those others must assimilate Europe."[38]

By arguing for reciprocal cultural assimilation, by advocating for a planetary civilization rich with concrete diversity, by invoking the metaphor of the "catholic rendezvous of giving and taking," Senghor opposes all forms of racial exclusivism. Senghor stands for racial equality. Herein lies his greatest contribution to modern African thought. He does not negate white culture for sake of black culture, per se, but tries to overcome and yet keep them both. Echoing Blyden, he states that Africans "shall begin by returning to our West African sources—Negro-African and Berber—to imbibe there deeply. This presupposes a prior inventory of our virtues and *defects*. With this as a starting point, we shall make our own choices."[39] In short, Senghor advocates nothing short of the hybridization of the world's cultures.[40]

With a theoretical depth, literary beauty, passionate mysticism, universalistic knowledge, and critical mind, Senghor is Fanon turned conformist.[41] The mastery of his material—be it Marxism, French thought, or African history—is outstanding. His advocacy of the "civilization of the universal" is informed by a critique of Eurocentrism: that the global hegemony of Western culture, material as well as ideological, cannot be read as the creation of universalism. For Senghor, the geographical expansion of Western culture is not to be taken as the creation of global culture. True universalism is not the non-Western world following in the footsteps of the West. For Senghor, the question is, which internationalism is humanity to follow: internationalism as the globalization of Western culture or internationalism as the voluntary union of various cultures and traditions, wherein all of them learn from and teach one another.[42] In all these questions, Senghor is deep in the abode of the Blydenian paradigm.

Frantz Fanon and the Question of Colonial Racial Hegemony

We see in this text Blyden's detailed and nuanced depiction of the alienation of the westernized "Negro" in Africa, and more so in the American diaspora. This is the same theme Fanon wrestled with in his intellectual productions spanning less than half of Blyden's life. Blyden lived to be eighty. Fanon died at thirty-six!

Fanon provides a sophisticated sociopsychological intervention in demystifying the cultural alienation of colonized peoples, by focusing on the colonialism and racism that affect the peoples of the non-Western world.[43] He describes the dialectic of the colonial world in all his writings. In his most famous work, the *Wretched of the Earth*, he declares, "The colonial world is a world divided into compartments. . . . The colonial world is a world cut into two. The dividing line, the frontiers are shown by barracks and police stations."[44] The two zones meet, but they don't mix. "The zone where the natives live is not complementary to the zone inhabited by the settlers. The two zones are opposed, but not in the service of a higher unity. Obedient to the rules of pure Aristotelian logic, they both follow the principle of reciprocal exclusivity. No conciliation is possible, for of the two terms, one is superfluous."[45]

Fanon calls the racially bifurcated structure of the colonial order, "Manichaean delirium." He writes, "Good-Evil, Beauty-Ugliness, White-Black, such are the characteristic pairings of the phenomena that, making use of an expression of Dide and Guiraud, we shall call 'Manichaean delirium.'"[46] "The colonial world is a Manichaean world. It is not enough for the settler to delimit physically, that is to say with the help of the army and the police force, the place of the native. As if to show the totalitarian character of colonial exploitation, the settler paints the native as a sort of quintessence of evil."[47] Fanon is not alone in his virulent condemnation of the world that colonialism created. Like him, Césaire too revolts against this Manichaean delirium by shouting, "Take me as I am. I don't adapt to you."[48] In these two sentences, Césaire summarizes what W. E. B. Du Bois calls the problem of the twentieth century, the problem of the color line, the race problem. The premise of Fanon's revolt against colonial racism is his refusal to abide by the rules of the colonial and racial hierarchies.

In *Toward the African Revolution*, Fanon, with his training in psychoanalysis, describes the colonial project in psychocultural terms. Much like Blyden's incisive, piercing disclosure of the cultural deracination of the Western-trained African, Fanon sees the colonial project as an "enterprise of deculturation."[49] Racism is embedded in the very structure of colonialism. "Racism . . . is only one element of a vaster whole: that of the systematized oppression of a people." In colonialism "we witness the destruction of cultural values, of ways of life. Language, dress, techniques are devalorized." For colonialism the "enslavement, in the strictest sense, of the native population is the prime necessity." The outcome is that "the social panorama is destructured; values are flaunted, crushed, emptied" (33).

For Fanon racism is "the shameless exploitation of one group of men by another which has reached a higher stage of technical development. This is why military and economic oppression generally precedes, makes possible, and legitimizes racism" (37–38). Fanon sees racism as a power relationship of domination and subjection. Racism is more than mere prejudice. Both whites and blacks could be racially prejudiced, but it is the former's power over the latter that Fanon defines as racism. That is why he disagrees with Sartre's catching description of negritude as "antiracist racism."[50]

Fanon writes, "It is not possible to enslave men without logically making them inferior through and through. And racism is only the emotional, affective, sometimes intellectual explanation of this inferiorization" (*Toward the African Revolution*, 40). In quite Blydenian fashion, he describes the internalization of racist-ascribed inferiorization of oppressed people in the following powerful words: "Having judged, condemned, abandoned his cultural forms, his language, his food habits, his sexual behavior, his way of sitting down, of resting, of laughing, of enjoying himself, the oppressed *flings himself* upon the imposed culture with the desperation of a drowning man" (39).

Fanon continues, "Race prejudice in fact obeys a flawless logic. A country that lives, draws its substance from the exploitation of other peoples, makes these peoples inferior. Race prejudice applied to those peoples is normal." He further notes, "A society has race prejudice or it has not. There are no degrees of prejudice. One cannot say that a given country is racist but that lynchings or extermination camps are not to be found there. The truth is that all that and still other things exist on the horizon. These virtualities, these latencies circulate, carried by the lifestream of psycho-affective, economic relations" (40–41).[51]

In an analysis similar to Blyden's plea of turning toward the African of the interior and to Cabral's call for a "return to the source," Fanon provides a fascinating picture of the moment the oppressed "natives" turn against racism and search for their roots. "Discovering the futility of his alienation, his progressive deprivation, the inferiorized individual, after this phase of deculturation, of extraneousness, comes back to his original positions." He goes on to say, "This culture, abandoned, sloughed off, rejected, despised, becomes for the inferiorized an object of passionate attachment. There is a very marked kind of overvaluation that is psychologically closely linked to the craving for forgiveness" (41). He echoes Senghor, "In conclusion, universality resides in this decision to recognize and accept the reciprocal relativism of different cultures, once the colonial status is irretrievably excluded" (44).

Like Blyden, but with a twist, Fanon sees a commonality between blacks and Jews as victims of racism. But he also sees fundamental differences between anti-Semitism and negrophobia. "In the case of the Jew, one thinks of money and its cognates. In that of the Negro, one thinks of sex. It is because he takes over the country that the Jew is a danger." Negrophobia is "to be found on an instinctual, biological level. At the extreme, I should say that the Negro, because of his body, impedes the closing of the postural schema of the white man—at the point, naturally, at which the black man makes his entry into the phenomenal world of the white man."[52]

Black is "authentic"; it cannot pass or be mistaken. By contrast, the Jew is "a white man, and, apart from some rather debatable characteristics, he can sometimes go unnoticed."[53] Sartre states that it is the anti-Semite who creates the Jew.[54] Similarly, Fanon declares that "it is the white man who creates the Negro. But it is the Negro who creates Negritude."[55] Traversing through the dark alleys of negrophobia, Fanon describes the racist construction of the image of the Negro: "The Negro is an animal, the Negro is bad, the Negro is mean, the Negro is ugly. . . . Mamma, the nigger's going to eat me up."[56]

Fanon is the Gramsci of the non-Western world. He, more than any other thinker of the twentieth century, lays bare the foundation of Western hegemony on the non-Western world. By his superb analysis of the colonial situation through the eyes of psychoanalysis, by his indefatigable struggle against colonial racism, Fanon opens up a highly sophisticated theoretical space of cultural studies.[57]

Fanon is the most prominent black cultural theorist of total decolonization—economic, political, social, cultural, and psychological—in the twentieth century. Now that we live in an intellectual era of postmodernism and cultural studies, we are witnessing a Fanon renaissance worldwide. Fanon analyzes and synthesizes the cultural realm of power and resistance under the colonial situation. He integrates the dimensions of race and class in his analysis. Under the colonial situation, race is class. Colonialism is more than a mode of production; it is also a mode of deculturation, a mode of destruction of the culture of the colonized. Like many others of his time, Fanon does not dwell much on gender in his works.

Fanon diagnoses the symptoms of racism, as well as the disease itself. He also searches for the cause of the disease, and he discovers a historical cause that goes in history by the name of capitalism. What is left at the level of absolute negation in the scholarship of Chinweizu's *The West and the Rest of Us* finds its bridge of negotiation and the desire for ultimate reconciliation in Fanon's *Wretched of the Earth*. Beginning with a declaration of rage in the first few pages of his book, Fanon concludes with an open call for reconciliation with Europe. Here is how he begins his book of violence and forgiveness: "National liberation, national renaissance, the restoration of nationhood to the people, commonwealth: whatever may be the headings used or the new formulas introduced, decolonization is always a violent phenomenon." The humanist heart of the reconciliatory last sentence of *Wretched of the Earth* reads, "For Europe, for ourselves, and for humanity, comrades, we must turn over a new leaf, we must work out new concepts, and try to set afoot a new man."[58] The dialectical opposition between "for Europe" and "for ourselves" is overcome in the global synthesis of "for humanity." This is Fanon's version of the Senghorian "civilization of the universal"; it is his global humanism. This is Fanon's synthesis, overcoming the thesis of Western colonial racism and the antithesis of violent struggle against Western domination. Fanon plays the role of a historical mirror that reflects back to Europe its deeds in the colonial world. He does not reject Europe in toto.[59] He is attracted to its spirit of humanism, its democracy, and its technological genius. Like Blyden, Fanon sees Europe as having a lot to offer humanity, especially black humanity.

Fanon is not a prophet of violence per se. His advocacy of violence is not out of love of violence for its own sake but out of the conviction that violence is the only way left for the attainment of true national liberation of the colonized. In Algeria, Kenya, Zimbabwe, Namibia, Guinea Bissau and Cape Verde, Mozambique, Angola, Congo, Namibia, and South Africa, African and European blood has reddened the African earth. In all these cases, Fanon's reflections on the colonial condition came remarkably true. Fanon's greatest contribution to the freedom of humanity of color lies in his genius of piercing through the veil of racism, especially as it has been internalized by its victims. It is in this sphere that we find powerful Blydenian themes, perspectives, and reflections.

Chiekh Anta Diop and the Two Cradle Theory

Blyden acknowledges ancient Egypt as a "Negro" civilization, one that Africans should be proud of. But he also remarks that no conceit is thereby justified on the part of the African. Diop goes further than any African scholar in giving critical importance to ancient Egypt and its historical significance for African history. In what is considered his magnum opus, *The African Origin of Civilization,* he states that any work on African history should take ancient Egypt as the origin and highest achievement of African civilization. His most quoted statement reads, "Ancient Egypt was a Negro civilization. The history of black Africa will remain suspended in air and cannot be written correctly until African historians dare to connect it with the history of Egypt." He goes on to say, "The African historian who evades the problem of Egypt is neither modest nor objective, nor unruffled; he is ignorant, cowardly, and neurotic." He draws an analogy with Europe to make his case: "Imagine, if you can, the uncomfortable position of a western historian who was to write the history of Europe without referring to Greco-Latin Antiquity and try to pass that off as a scientific approach."[60]

Ancient Egypt occupies a central place in Diop's historical paradigm. We read in his major work, *Civilization or Barbarism: An Authentic Anthropology,*

> For us, the return to Egypt in all domains is the necessary condition for recon-
> ciling African civilizations with history, in order to be able to construct a body
> of modern human sciences, in order to renovate African culture. Far from
> being a reveling in the past, a look toward the Egypt of antiquity is the best
> way to conceive and build our cultural future. In reconceived and renewed
> African culture, Egypt will play the same role that Greco-Latin antiquity plays
> in Western culture.[61]

Diop's views about the place of ancient Egypt in African history are also
found in the writings of other black scholars, including Blyden.[62]

Diop is a comparative world historian. He sees ancient Egypt as "the distant mother of Western cultures and sciences." Hence, "most of the ideas that
we call foreign are oftentimes nothing but mixed up, reversed, modified,
elaborated images of the creations of our African ancestors, such as Judaism,
Christianity, Islam, dialectics, the theory of being, the exact sciences, arith-
metic, geometry, mechanical engineering, astronomy, medicine, literature
(novel, poetry, drama), architecture, the arts, etc." He cautions, "how fundamentally improper is the notion, so often repeated, of the importation of
foreign ideologies in Africa. It stems from a perfect ignorance of the African
past. Just as modern technologies and sciences came from Europe, so did, in
antiquity, universal knowledge stream from the Nile Valley to the rest of the
world, particularly to Greece, which would serve as a link."[63]

Diop's views about ancient Egypt and African history at large are based
on a grand, global comparative historical paradigm. In his work, *The
Cultural Unity of Black Africa*, he provides a global comparative historical
anthropology in which he divides world history in the distant past into
two major cradles: the southern cradle, which he also calls the African
cradle, and the northern cradle, which he also calls the Aryan cradle. He
adds an intermediary cradle that combines elements of both, located in
the Middle East. This is the world of the Semites. He writes, the "Semites
are basically Indo-Europeans, that they served as a cushion, as a buffer
between the two cradles in the same way as the Slavs between the Aryan
world and the Far East."[64]

Diop traces the origins of the two cradles as one of difference between
the agrarian sedentary civilization of the southern cradle, primarily Africa,
and the pastoral nomadic lifestyles of the northern cradle, primarily the
Aryan or Indo-European. His studies on ancient Egypt are framed within
this larger historical anthropology. Ancient Egypt belongs to the southern or African cradle. It does not belong to either the Aryan or Semitic
cradles. His reflections on the distant African past are similar to that of
Blyden's own writings.

Diop provides a summary of his findings regarding the two cradles. He
first describes the southern cradle:

In conclusion, the Meridional cradle, confined to the African continent, is characterised by the matriarchal family, the creation of the territorial state, in contrast to the Aryan city-state, the emancipation of woman in domestic life, xenophilia, cosmopolitanism, a sort of social collectivism having as corollary a tranquility going as far as unconcern for tomorrow, a material solidarity of right for each individual, which makes moral or material misery unknown to the present day; there are people living in poverty, but no one feels alone and no one is in distress. In the moral domain, its shows an ideal of peace, of justice, of goodness and an optimism which eliminates all notion of guilt or original sin in religious and metaphysical institutions. The types of literature most favored are the novel, tales, fables and comedy.

In contrast with the southern cradle,

> The Northern cradle, confined to Greece and Rome, is characterised by the patriarchal family, by the city-state. . . . Individualism, moral and material solitude, a disgust for existence, all the subject-matter of modern literature, which even in its philosophic aspects is none other than the expression of the tragedy of a way of life going back to the Aryans' ancestors, are all attributes of this cradle. An ideal of war, violence, crime and conquests, inherited from nomadic life, with as a consequence, a feeling of guilt and of original sin, which causes pessimistic religious or metaphysical systems to be built, is the special attribute of this cradle.

Diop gives his own account of a diffusionist perspective when he writes, "it is easily seen that it is on contact with the Southern world that the Northerners broadened their conception of the state, elevating themselves to the idea of a territorial state and of an empire."[65] We should not lose sight of the fact that Diop's two-cradle theory, as well as his overall philosophy of history, is a gendered, comparative, global paradigm.[66]

Whether one agrees with Diop or not, his greatest contribution to the study of history is contained in his two-cradle theory, not in the idea that ancient Egypt was a black African civilization, something that was not in doubt even among Europeans up until the eighteenth century.[67] There may still be a problem with Diop's perspective, though. His argument that ancient Egypt is to Africa what ancient Greece is to the West is based on the uncritical appropriation of the Eurocentric construction of ancient Greek history, that it is the foundation of Western civilization. What if one were to argue that this view is wrong, that ancient Greece was as Eastern as it was Western, perhaps even more so? What of the argument that Eurocentrism, an Enlightenment invention, came up with the ideology of Greece as the foundation of Western specificity, while in fact ancient Greece had more to do with the Orient than the Occident? And what of Rome? Wasn't the Roman Empire the quintessential Mediterranean Empire, not just European? Even as Diop pushes the idea that ancient Greece was the pupil of ancient Egypt, he nevertheless takes at face value the ideology that sees ancient Greece as the foundation of Western civilization, distinct from that of Africa or the Orient.[68]

The Lure of African Socialism

African socialism is not a product of a single thinker. The argument of African socialism is that precolonial Africa was essentially classless. Here one is within the intellectual domain of Blyden's last major work, *African Life and Customs*.

Julius Nyerere provides the most sympathetic and detailed case for African socialism in his work, *Ujamaa*:

> In traditional African society *everybody* was a worker. There was no other way of earning a living for the community. Even the Elder, who appeared to be enjoying himself without doing any work and for whom everybody else appeared to be working, had, in fact, worked hard all his younger days. The wealth he now appeared to possess was not *his*, personally; it was only "his" as the Elder of the group which had produced it.

Nyerere explains what he means by the term "worker": "When I say that in traditional African society everybody was a worker, I do not use the word 'worker' simply as opposed to 'employer' but to 'loiterer' or 'idler.'"[69] He adds, "In our traditional African society we were individuals within a community. We took care of the community, and the community took care of us. We neither needed nor wished to exploit our fellow men" (6–7). Just as "traditional" Africa was socialistic, so was it democratic. "We in Africa, have no more need of being 'converted' to socialism than we have of being 'taught' democracy. Both are rooted in our own past—in the traditional society which produced us" (12).

Nyerere's conception of African socialism is opposed to both Marxist socialism and capitalism. It is based instead on the notion of familyhood. "'Ujamaa,' then or 'Familyhood,' describes our socialism. It is opposed to capitalism, which seeks to build a happy society on the basis of the exploitation of man by man; and it is equally opposed to doctrinaire socialism [i.e., Marxism] which seeks to build its happy society on a philosophy of inevitable conflict between man and man" (12).

Senghor, like Nyerere, is an advocate of African socialism. Like Nyerere, he argues for avoiding both capitalism and communism, and instead searching for a middle course, one he calls "*democratic socialism*." Unlike Nyerere, whose socialism draws from the traditional way of life of precolonial Africa,

Senghor stresses the European origin of his socialist thinking, especially French non-Marxist socialism and his ties with the French Socialist Party. What identifies Senghor with Nyerere is their rejection of class struggle, as Senghor explains, "In our NegroBerber society . . . there are no classes at war, but only social groups struggling for influence." He cautions, "Tomorrow they will be at war with one another unless we are careful, if we allow the intellectuals—liberal professionals, civil servants, employees, and even laborers—to form a class that oppresses by misleading peasants, shepherds and artisans."[70]

Kwame Nkrumah is the most outspoken critic of the theory of African socialism. For him, there is only one socialism, the scientific socialism of Marx and Lenin, whose principles are universally applicable. In *Class Struggle in Africa*, he writes,

> The term "African Socialism" is meaningless and irrelevant. It implies the existence of a form of socialism peculiar to Africa derived from communal and egalitarian aspects of traditional African society. The myth of African Socialism is used to deny the class struggle, and to obscure genuine socialist commitment. It is employed by those African leaders who are compelled—in the climate of African Revolution—to proclaim socialist policies, but who are at the same time deeply committed to international capitalism, and who do not intend to promote genuine socialist development.[71]

Nkrumah is also critical of Nyerere's conception of the classlessness of precolonial Africa, on which he bases his theory of African socialism. He writes, "All available evidence from the history of Africa, up to the eve of European colonization, shows that African society was neither classless nor devoid of a social hierarchy. Feudalism existed in some parts of Africa before colonization."[72]

In his philosophical manifesto of the African revolution, *Consciencism*, Nkrumah states his theory of Africa's "triple heritage": traditional African communalism, Islamic civilization, and European-derived Christianity. His triple heritage is in accord with what Blyden expresses unequivocally in his piece, *The Significance of Liberia*. Nkrumah notes, "African society has one segment which comprises our traditional way of life; it has a second segment which is filled by the presence of the Islamic tradition in Africa; it has a final segment which represents the infiltration of the Christian tradition and culture of Western Europe into Africa, using colonialism and neocolonialism as its primary vehicles." Like Blyden, he opts for a syncretic synthesis of these three segments, not a rejection of one or the other. "These different segments are animated by competing ideologies. But since society implies a certain dynamic unity, there needs to emerge an ideology which, genuinely catering for the needs of all, will take the place of competing ideologies, and so reflect the dynamic unity of society, and be the guide to society's continual progress."[73]

Amilcar Cabral and the Theory of National Liberation

Amilcar Cabral is the most original and most creative radical African thinker of the twentieth century.[74] In Cabral, Africa finds its most systematically developed marriage of Marxism and nationalism. His theory of national liberation begins with the statement that African history stopped with the coming of European colonialism. Like Blyden, Cabral sees history as central in peoples' identity. And like Blyden, he sees colonialism as a force undermining the history and identity of the colonized. "We therefore see that both in colonialism and in neocolonialism the essential characteristic of imperialist domination remains the same, the negation of the historical process of the dominated people by means of violent usurpation of the freedom of development of the national productive forces."[75] The identification of imperialism as a distorting, destabilizing, and destructive force for the independent development of the national history of the colonized peoples is one of Cabral's most important contributions to the theory of national liberation for the non-Western world.

Cabral rejects the identification of history with class struggle. He argues that history is the development of productive forces and production relations, hence embracing all human history.[76] He echoes Blyden's observations regarding the role of the West in silencing, erasing, and disfiguring African history. He states, "Our peoples have their own history regardless of the stage of their economic development. When they were subjected to imperialist domination, the historical process of each of our peoples . . . was subjected to the violent action of external factors." He identifies the essence of national liberation in Africa and the non-Western world at large as follows: "The basis of national liberation . . . is the inalienable right of every people to have its own history, and the objective of national liberation is to regain this right usurped by imperialism, that is to say, to free the process of development of the national-productive forces." This concept of "national productive forces" is critical for understanding national liberation. Cabral states, "the national liberation of a people is the regaining of the historical personality of that people, its return to history through the destruction of the imperialist domination to which it was subjected."[77] National liberation entails the regaining of national history.[78] This in turn entails three themes: the development of national productive forces, the development of national culture, and the "return to the source."

For Cabral, the denial of national history under colonial rule does not mean that colonialism is reactionary in the historical sense. It is one of the curious paradoxes of modern African intellectual history that Cabral, the most radical African thinker, shares with Blyden, whose ambiguities regarding European colonialism in Africa have been documented in this work, the same ambivalent attitude toward the colonial enterprise. Cabral sees the destruction of the political power of the African ruling groups as a progressive act. Trapped in the Marxist theory that considers capitalism as progress over precapitalist societies, Cabral identifies some of the progressive trends of colonial rule in Africa to include "the progressive loss of prestige of the ruling native classes and sectors, the forced or voluntary exodus of part of the peasant population to the urban centres, with the consequent development of new social strata; salaried workers, clerk, employers in commerce and the liberal professions, and an instable stratum of unemployed."[79]

Cabral's analysis of European colonialism in Africa is in many aspects similar to Marx's analysis of British rule in India. Marx writes, "England has to fulfill a double mission in India; one destructive, the other regenerating—the annihilation of old Asiatic society, and the laying of the material foundations of Western society in Asia." He adds, "Arabs, Turks, Tartars, Mongols, who had successively overrun India, soon became *Hinduized*, the barbarian conquerors being, by an eternal law of history, conquered themselves by the superior civilization of their subjects. The British were the first conquerors superior and, therefore, inaccessible to Hindu civilization."[80]

Marx sees Indian society as inferior to that of England. The measuring rod of the comparison was the "level of development" of productive forces. Marx is in no doubt of the progressive nature of the destruction of "Oriental despotism," which restrained "the human mind within the smallest possible compass, making it the unresisting tool of superstition, enslaving it beneath traditional rules, depriving it of all grandeur and historical energies," a system wherein the human "fell down on his knees in adoration of Hanuman, the monkey, and Sabbala, the cow."[81]

For Cabral, too, both the destruction of traditional African society and the creation of new social strata in colonial Africa was historically progressive. For him, traditional African society was materially and culturally backward compared with that of Western capitalism. Yet it is this very imperialism that negates the national history of the colonized. The kernel of Cabral's dialectical appraisal of imperialism in the non-Western world is, on one hand, the recognition of the progressive nature of imperialism in colonized societies and, on the other, that this very process brought about the negation of the national history of the colonized. Cabral is in the peculiar position of having it both ways: imperialism is the negation of the development of national productive forces in the colonized territories, while at the same time it brings about the development of imperialist productive forces in these same colonies. The contest, then, is not the development of productive forces per se, but their national origin, purpose, and orientation, that is, whether they are national or imperialistic. In a way, it seems that the development of national productive forces would go the same way as that found in the metropolitan colonial powers. Cabral, as a Marxist, cannot transcend the developmentalist paradigm.

Cabral sees Portuguese colonialism as an underdeveloped colonialism. As such, "the chronic and characteristic underdevelopment of Portugal which does not have a viable economic infrastructure" made it "incapable of imagining a process of decolonisation, in which the interests of the Portuguese ruling class would be safeguarded." In addition to the underdevelopment of Portuguese colonialism is the "inhibiting effects of almost half a century of the fascist regime over a society which, throughout its history, has never really (or significantly) known what human rights, freedom and democratic practice are." Like other colonial regimes, Portuguese colonial racism preached "the doctrine of the *superiority of the European* and the *inferiority of the African* as well as the myth of the 'civilising mission' of the Portuguese in regard to the African peoples deemed to be 'savages.'" Yet Portuguese colonial racism has its own unique specificities. "In spite of the fancies of the Portuguese colonialists concerning 'the creation of multiracial societies,' such a doctrine, to which they have lately added the bogey of 'Communist subversion,' ends in the crystallisation of a *primitive racism* often lacking any clear economic motivation."[82]

Cabral's description of Portuguese colonial racism as "primitive racism" is a reductionist argument: one based on the economic and political "underdevelopment" of Portuguese colonialism in Africa as compared with other colonialisms, such as that of the British or French. Cabral's approach here is similar to Perry Anderson's concept of "ultra-colonialism" in describing Portuguese colonialism in Africa.[83]

Interestingly enough, Blyden also charges colonialism as inhibiting the "development" of Africans according to their own idiosyncrasies and cultural conditionings. Yet he was firm in his belief that Africa's development was to be different from that of the West: Africa was to remain an agrarian, raw material producer for the industrial, materially affluent West. Africa need not, and cannot, reproduce the material civilization found in the Western world.

Very much like Blyden, Cabral takes culture to be the key to a society's identity. Indeed, it is the signifier of its very survival. All peoples' histories are inscribed in their culture. "Whatever may be the ideological or idealist characteristics of cultural expression, culture is an essential element of the history of a people." We see how much emphasis Blyden lays on "identity," that is, "Negro" race identity. Cabral discusses identity, too, though not on racial grounds. He situates it in determinate historical social relations. He refers to the identity and difference dialectic: "The dialectical character of identity lies in the fact that an individual (or a group) is only similar to certain individuals (or groups) if it is also different from other individuals (or groups)."[84]

Cabral's theory of imperialism as the negation of the national history of the colonized also extends to the cultural sphere. Sounding much like Blyden, he writes, "imperialist domination, by denying the historical development of the dominated people, necessarily also denies their cultural development." Through its cultural hegemony over the colonized, colonialism created a culturally alienated indigenous elite. Again, Cabral writes in a familiar Blydenian terrain:

> The experience of colonial domination shows that, in the effort to perpetuate exploitation, the colonizer not only creates a system to repress the cultural life of the colonized people, he also provokes and develops the cultural alienation of a part of the population, either by socalled assimilation of indigenous people, or be creating a social gap between the indigenous elites and the popular masses. As a result of this process of dividing or of deepening the divisions in the society, it happens that a considerable part of the population, notably the urban or peasant *petite bourgeoisie*, assimilates the colonizer's mentality, considers itself culturally superior to its own people and ignores or looks down their cultural values.[85]

The creation of hegemony in the colonial situation takes place through the formation of a Western-educated elite from among the colonized people that has internalized the paradigms of the colonial order. This évolué class, the petty bourgeoisie, as Cabral calls them, develops what he calls a "frustration complex." It is this class of people that bear the brunt of Blyden's powerful pen, the so-called civilized Negro.

Cabral is of the opinion that colonial cultural hegemony affected only the évolué class, the *assimilado*, mostly through the colonial education system. Sounding again like Blyden, he writes,

> All Portuguese education disparages the African, his culture and civilisation. African languages are forbidden in schools. The white man is always presented as a superior being and the African as an inferior. The colonial "conquistadors" are shown as saints and heroes. As soon as African children enter elementary schools, they develop an inferiority complex. They learn to fear the white man and to feel ashamed of being Africans. African geography, history and culture are either ignored or distorted, and children are forced to study Portuguese geography and history.[86]

The vast sea of African peasants, by contrast, remained hardly touched by the cultural productions of colonialism. African culture was hammered under colonialism but not destroyed. African culture took refuge from the colonial onslaught in the bushes among the masses. It was to this culture that Cabral turned to for national liberation and cultural renaissance. This too is a prominent feature of Blyden's cultural nationalism, the need to link up with the African interior, one not yet "spoiled" by European contact. This brings us to Cabral's famous "return to the source."

The "return to the source" is Cabral's pathway for the cultural renewal of colonized peoples. The retaining of national culture by the rural population, thanks in part to the unwillingness of the Portuguese colonialists to "raise" the cultural "level" of the colonized masses, left African culture "uncontaminated" by the colonialist "virus." Reminiscent of Blyden, Cabral writes, "Repressed, persecuted, humiliated, betrayed by certain social groups who have compromised with the foreign power, culture took refuge in the villages, in the forests, and in the spirit of the victims of domination." It is these rural masses "who are the repository of the culture and at the same time the only social sector who can preserve and build it up and make history."[87] Blyden's repeated plea to link up with the African of the interior, far away from the influences of Western ways, finds echo here in Cabral. Yet Cabral is not a simple radical reincarnation of Blyden. While he shares some astonishing similarities in national history and cultural domination, he is above all a revolutionary, which Blyden is not. Even his idea of "return to the source" is itself part of a larger process of fundamental revolutionary change.[88]

Cabral's original contribution to revolutionary theory lies in his analysis and radical conclusions of a predominantly precapitalist society. The development of capitalism in Guinea-Bissau and Cape Verde had been very marginal. There was no working class save dockworkers. This economic fact led Cabral to search for a new theory of revolution: the theory of national liberation led by the revolutionary petty bourgeoisie. His theory is that in a situation of a weak or nonexisting working class, the national liberation revolution has to be led by the revolutionary petty bourgeoisie.

Cabral divides the petty bourgeoisie in colonial countries into three class positions—assimilated, revolutionary, and vacillating.[89] The assimilated, nonrevolutionary petty bourgeoisie are done with their struggle against imperialism at the anticolonial phase. Once political independence is achieved, this class of people becomes an ally of foreign capital, including the former colonial power. This, for Cabral, is not what defines national liberation. National liberation is the struggle against neocolonialism. Its main objective is the regaining of national history through the development of the national productive forces. Indeed, "national liberation exists only when the national productive forces have been completely freed from every kind of domination."[90] National liberation is a revolution against neocolonialism: "*The principal aspect of national liberation struggle is the struggle against neo-colonialism.*" Hence, "*national liberation* necessarily corresponds to a *revolution.*" As for the agency of leading such revolution, Cabral says, "This alternative—to betray the revolution or to commit suicide as a class—constitutes the dilemma of the petty bourgeoisie in the general framework of the national liberation struggle."[91]

Cabral provides a powerful example of the extent that the newly formed African ruling elites, those who chose to "betray" the path of national liberation revolution, would go to maintain their power. He isolates what he calls "the so-called tribalism" as one such factor in the drive and maintenance of their power. He notes at the "reinvention" of tribalism as a mobilizing means for the elite in the drive for power. In a rage against those Africans who play tribalism for power's sake, he states, it has nothing to do with caring for their "tribe." Rather, it is "to have all the diamonds, all the gold, all those fine things in one's hand, to do as one pleases, to live well, to have all the women one wants in Africa or in Europe." It is "for the sake of touring Europe, being received as presidents, wearing expensive clothes—a morning coat or even great bubus to pretend that they are Africans. All lies, they are not Africans at all. They are lackeys or lapdogs of the whites."[92] Blyden would have felt vindicated reading these lines; they give testimony to his repeated warnings of the destructive force that could be unleashed on Africa by some of its own Western "mis-educated" elite.

Amilcar Cabral's works reflect the highest point reached in African radical thought. Blyden's repeated plea about the need to link up with the "native" of the African interior find powerful echo in Cabral's theory of "return to the source." Blyden's cry that history is written for Africans by others; that it is distorted, racist, and degrading; and that Africans should take the mantle away from Europeans in the representation of their history finds powerful seconding in Cabral's call for the need to regain national history that has been usurped by imperialist domination. Even in Marxist Cabral, the ghost of Blyden makes itself felt, and felt powerfully.

With the assassination of Cabral by Portuguese agents, Africa lost one of its most profound, fertile, and original radical thinkers in the history of its encounter with Western bourgeois modernity.

Let me close this epilogue with references from two of the most outstanding black intellectuals of the twentieth century: Césaire and Senghor. Césaire reminds humanity of its yet unfinished work. He writes in *Return to My Native Land,*

For it is not true that the work of man is finished,
That there is nothing for us to do in this world,
That we are parasites on this earth . . .
But the work of man has only just begun . . .
And no race has the monopoly on beauty, intelligence, or strength.[93]

Senghor seconds Césaire's humanism, adding the reminder of the role Africa shall play in the future realization of the "civilization of the universal": "The Negro African is not finished before he even gets started. Let him speak; above all, let him act. Let him bring, like a leaven, his message to the world in order to help build the Civilization of the Universal."[94]

Blyden's ideas live through the works of the intellectual giants glimpsed in this epilogue. They are not the only ones, of course. They are simply some of the most visible representations of Africa's refusal to fold in and shut up under the weight of Western hegemony. Perhaps the most paradoxical of the Blydenian paradigm is that the three outstanding African intellectuals with the most Blydenian themes in their works are Senghor, Fanon, and Cabral! And what makes their works closer to the Blydenian corpus than other prominent intellectuals such as Nkrumah or even Du Bois is their pertinent disclosure of the theme of cultural alienation that undergirded the Western hegemonic presence in Africa and the African diaspora. That neither Fanon nor Cabral mention Blyden is of no consequence. The epilogue shows the extent to which this paradigm is kept alive.

Blyden is to modern African thought what Hegel is to modern Western thought. Hegel, however, is acknowledged while Blyden is hardly recognized. Appropriated, transcended, or ignored, Blyden is the ancestor whose relevance to the present could not be but revered. The best way to transcend Blyden, if one were to opt for that, is to pay homage to the great intellectual that he was and to see the many strands of his thought in all their ramifications, including their contradictions and ambiguities. Ignoring Blyden would be almost sacrilegious. Not knowing him, we may end up repeating what he said and yet think we are saying something new.

Notes

Introduction

1. Walker, *David Walker's Appeal*; Douglass, *My Bondage*; Douglass, *Life and Times*; Douglass, *Narrative*; Truth, *Narrative of Sojourner Truth*.

2. See also Lemert, *Anna Julia Cooper*; and Hills, *Black Feminist Thought*.

3. See Litwack and Meier, *Black Leaders*.

4. Patterson, *Slavery and Social Death*, 13.

5. Jefferson, *State of Virginia*, 195–96.

6. Hahn, *Nation under Our Feet*.

7. Loewenberg and Bogin, *Black Women*.

8. Douglass, *Narrative*, 108.

9. Wood, *Arrogance of Faith*; Haynes, *Noah's Curse*.

10. W. James, *Banner of Ethiopia*.

11. Conrad, *Children of God's Fire*.

12. For the classic account of the Haitian Revolution, see C. James, *Black Jacobins*. See also Dubois, *Avengers*; Dubois and Garrigus, *Slave Revolution*; Geggus and Fiering, *Haitian Revolution*. For a focus on the slave revolution in Guadeloupe, see Dubois, *Colony of Citizens*.

13. Moitt, *Women and Slavery*, 128.

14. Du Bois, *World and Africa*; E. Williams, *Capitalism and Slavery*; Cox, *Capitalism as a System*; Cox, *Foundations of Capitalism*; Cox, *Capitalism and American Leadership*; Wallerstein, *Modern World-System*; Wallerstein, *World-Systems Analysis*.

15. Du Bois's "world-system" perspective actually goes much further back than the publication of *The World and Africa*. His pan-Africanist views and activism began at the turn of the century. His most famous work, *The Souls of Black Folk*, was first published in 1903, more than four decades before *The World and Africa*. In fact, Pan-Africanism by definition is a "world-system" perspective. As such, the formulators of the Pan-African idea and movement are in a way proponents of the "world-system" perspective. Henry Sylvester Williams is another example of a "world-systemist." For a comprehensive exploration of Henry Sylvester Williams's life and work, see Sherwood, *Origins of Pan-Africanism*.

16. Wallerstein began his academic career as an Africanist. His first three books were on Africa.

17. For an appraisal of Rodney's intellectual thought, see R. Lewis, *Walter Rodney's Intellectual Thought*.

18. See Hunter, "World-System Theory"; and Hier, "Forgotten Architect."

19. Drake, *Black Folk Here*.

20. In his excellent account of twentieth-century black literature, both in Africa and the diaspora, Abiola Irele writes about what he calls the "African imagination" as one "referring to a conjunction of impulses that have been given a unified expression

in a body of literary texts. From these impulses, grounded both in common experience and in common cultural references, Black texts have to assume a particular significance that is worth attempting to elucidate" (*African Imagination*, 4).

21. See Mudimbe, *Invention of Africa*; Rediker, *Slave Ship*; Kanneh, *African Identities*; Manning, *African Diaspora*; Gomez, *Reversing Sail*; Gilroy, *Black Atlantic*; Wright, *Becoming Black*; Holloway, *Africanisms in American Culture*; and G. Hall, *Slavery and African Ethnicities*.

22. Rediker, *Slave Ship*.

23. Baum, *Rise and Fall*, 22, 58.

24. Davis, *Problem of Slavery*, 447.

25. B. Lewis, *Muslim Discovery of Europe*, 18. For the significance of the rise of Islam for European history, see the celebrated work of the Belgian historian Henri Pirenne, *Mohammed and Charlemagne*. Pirenne's views have been known as the "Pirenne thesis." See also Hodges and Whitehouse, *Origins of Europe*.

26. Gibbon, *Decline and Fall*, 3:223, 64–65.

27. Islam, like its predecessor "Abrahamic" religions, has its own Manichaean view of the world: Dar al-Islam versus Dar al-Harb. Before the rise of Islam, Jews living in the midst of Christian Europe constituted its internal others. But this Jewish presence did not create the sense of unity within Christian Europe as that of the threat felt by the new, aggressive, and expansionist religion of Islam. For a discussion of European images of Jews, see Teshale, *Hegel and Anti-Semitism*.

28. Hegel, *Philosophy of World History*. For a comprehensive critique of Hegel's views on Africa, see Teshale, *Third World*.

29. Mudimbe, *Invention of Africa*; Mudimbe, *Idea of Africa*.

30. Mudimbe, *Invention of Africa*; Mazrui, *Africans*; Appiah, *In My Father's House*.

31. In my book, *Hegel and the Third World*, I call what befell peoples of the non-Western world in their encounter with Western modernity "negative modernity." It entails three domains: the American holocaust, African enslavement in the Americas, and colonialism (xvi).

32. For excellent accounts of modern African thought, see July, *Modern African Thought*; and Falola, *Nationalism and African Intellectuals*. For a tribute to the most remarkable intellectual achievements of Toyin Falola, one of the most productive African historians alive today, see Afolabi, *Man*.

33. For a discussion of the idea of progress in Western philosophy of history, see Teshale, *Third World*.

34. Hegel, *Science of Logic*, 119. Emphasis in original.

35. Thomson, *Works of James Thomson*, 2:191.

36. Lynch, *Edward Wilmot Blyden*, 3; Mudimbe, *Invention of Africa*, 115. Some of the other works on Blyden include Frenkel, "Edward Blyden"; Neuberger, "Early African Nationalism"; Pawlikova-Vilhanova, "African Personality"; Echeruo, "Edward W. Blyden"; and Sonderegger, "Anglophone Discourses."

37. Moses, *Classical Black Nationalism: From the American Revolution to Marcus Garvey*, 2. Hereafter cited in text.

38. Mazrui, *Africans*, 73–76. Mazrui writes, "Romantic gloriana . . . seeks to emphasise the glorious moments in Africa's history defined in part by European measurements of skill and performance, including the measurements of material monuments." By contrast, the idea behind "romantic primitivism" is "not to emphasise

past grandeur, but to validate simplicity and non-technical traditions. Romantic primitivism doers not counter European cultural arrogance by asserting civilisations comparable to that of ancient Greece. On the contrary, this school takes pride in precisely those traditions which European arrogance would seem to despise." Mazrui takes Diop as an example of the proponent of "romantic gloriana" and Aimé Césaire as that of "romantic primitivism" (73).

39. Cruse, *Negro Intellectual*, 564.

40. Moses, *Classical Black Nationalism*, 21.

41. Moses, *Afrotopia*, 131. Moses, alongside Tunde Adeleke, author of *The Case against Afrocentrism*, is one of the most vehement black critics of Afrocentrism. His *Afrotopia* is one such case. There is also Stephen Howe, author of *Afrocentrism*, who is white and also in the same camp. All these critics, among many others, use the term "Afrocentrism" to identify aspects of their criticisms. What is strange is that the most important scholar identified with Afrocentrism, Molefi Kete Asante, never uses the term himself to identify his perspective. He calls it not Afrocentrism but "Afrocentricity." Asante does not claim to have an "ism." Yet many, including Algernon Austin, author of *Achieving Blackness*, use the term "Afrocentrism." Sherman Jackson calls Asante's views on Arabs and Islam "black Orientalism." See "Black Orientalism."

42. Moses, *Afrotopia*, 134–35, 35.

43. Ibid., 131.

44. Lynch, *Edward Wilmot Blyden*, 78.

45. Moses, *Alexander Crummell*, 189, 151.

46. Ibid., 289.

47. Lynch, *Edward Wilmot Blyden*, 2–3. Hereafter cited in text.

48. Mudimbe, *Invention of Africa*. Hereafter cited in text.

49. Lynch, *Edward Wilmot Blyden*, 3.

50. I identify Blyden's central themes, as well as his overriding paradigm, at the end of this chapter.

51. See Frenkel, "Edward Blyden"; Garvey, *Philosophy and Opinions*; Martin, *Race First*; Brotz, *Political Thought*; Esedebe, *Pan-Africanism*; Moses, *Golden Age*; Moses, *Classical Black Nationalism*; Moses, *Afrotopia*; Moses, *Alexander Crummell*; Moses, *Liberian Dreams*; M. Price, *Dreaming Blackness*; Taylor, *Black Nationalism*; and Essien-Udom, *Black Nationalism*.

52. Edwards, *Practice of Diaspora*; Stephens, *Black Empire*.

53. B. Anderson, *Imagined Community*.

54. For an anthology of Delany's works, see Delany, *Martin R. Delany*. For studies on Delany, see, among others, Griffith, *African Dream*; R. Levine, *Representational Identity*; and Adeleke, *Without Regard to Race*.

55. Delany, "Political Destiny," 89–90.

56. Ibid., 90.

57. Delany, *Condition*, 11.

58. Ibid., 7.

59. Delany, "Political Destiny," 95.

60. Du Bois, *Negro*, 183.

61. Du Bois, *Souls of Black Folk*, 17–18. For a fascinating Hegelian reading of Du Bois's famous thesis of "double consciousness" in *Souls of Black Folk*, see Zamir, *Dark Voices*.

62. Derrick Bell calls racism the permanent face of America; see *Bottom of the Well.*
63. Blyden, *Christianity,* 227.
64. July, *Modern African Thought.* For Alexander Crummell, see Crummell, *Africa and America;* Crummell, *Future of Africa;* Crummell, *Destiny and Race;* Crummell, *Civilization and Black Progress;* Rigsby, *Alexander Crummell,* Oldfield, *Alexander Crummell;* and Moses, *Alexander Crummell;* for Martin Delany, see Delany, "Political Destiny"; Delany, *Condition;* Delany, *Races and Color;* Delany, *Martin R. Delany;* and Adeleke, *Without Regard to Race;* for Henry McNeal Turner, see Angell, *Bishop Henry McNeil Turner;* and Cummings, "Rhetoric."
65. Gellner, *Nations and Nationalism;* B. Anderson, *Imagined Community.*
66. Kanneh, *African Identities.*
67. Patterson, *Slavery and Social Death,* 13.
68. Rediker, *Slave Ship.*
69. For a discussion of memories on both sides of the black Atlantic, see Diouf, *Fighting the Slave Trade;* Araujo, Candido, and Lovejoy, *Crossing Memories;* Sansone, Soumonni, and Barry, *Trans Atlantic Identities;* Afolabi, *Afro-Brazilians;* Conniff and Davis, *Africans in the Americas;* Bailey, *African Voices;* and Fairhead, Geysbeek, Holsoe, and Leach, eds. *African-American Exploration.*
70. Lynch, *Edward Wilmot Blyden.*

Chapter 1

1. Blyden's view here is the opposite of what Mazrui calls "romantic gloriana." Yet it is not a view of "romantic primitivism" either. See Mazrui, *Africans,* 73–76. As noted in the introduction, Blyden shares both versions of romanticism about Africa and Africans.
2. Blyden, *Christianity,* 134. Hereafter cited in text.
3. For a discussion of the so-called Noah's curse and the theological argument rationalizing African servitude, see Haynes, *Noah's Curse;* and Goldenberg, *Curse of Ham.* See also St. Claire Drake's meticulous study, *Black Folk Here and There.* For a different contextualization of the Hamitic hypothesis in the European colonial discourse about Africa, see Seligman, *Races of Africa;* and Sanders, "Hamitic Hypothesis." For the specific Rwandan context of the Hamitic thesis and its dreadful genocide consequences, see Semujanga's brilliant work, *Origins of Rwandan Genocide.* For the origins of the racialized Hamitic thesis in nineteenth-century European travel discourse, see Speke, *Source of the Nile.*
4. Blyden's view expressed here is similar to Eric Williams's famous work published in 1944, *Capitalism and Slavery.* Williams' work deals with the links between Caribbean slavery and English industrial development. His view came to be known as the "Williams thesis." For a discussion of Williams's thesis, see Solow and Engerman, *British Capitalism.*
5. Blyden, *Selected Letters,* 476–77.
6. Blyden, *Christianity,* 138.
7. George Benjamin calls Blyden "messiah"; see *Edward W. Blyden.*
8. Blyden, *Liberia's Offering,* 6. Hereafter cited in text.

9. Blyden, *Voice from Bleeding Africa*, 6.

10. Ibid., 10.

11. Fage, "Slavery"; Thornton, *Africa and Africans*.

12. Rodney, *Upper Guinea Coast*; Rodney, *How Europe Underdeveloped Africa*.

13. See Miers and Kopytoff, *Slavery in Africa*.

14. Blyden, *Voice from Bleeding Africa*, 10.

15. Hegel, *Philosophy of World History*, 174. See also Teshale, *Third World*, chap. 6.

16. Amin, *Accumulation*; Amin, *Unequal Development*; Wallerstein, *Modern World-System*; Frank, *Development of Underdevelopment*; Rodney, *How Europe Underdeveloped Africa*; Blyden, *Voice from Bleeding Africa*, 11.

17. Teshale, *Third World*, xvi.

18. Blyden, *Voice from Bleeding Africa*, 12. Hereafter cited in text.

19. For African agency in the transatlantic slave trade, see Diouf, *Fighting the Slave Trade*; Thornton, *Africa and Africans*; and Bailey, *African Voices*.

20. Blyden, *Negro in Ancient History*, 20.

21. Ibid. See also Blaut, *Colonizer's Model*; and Abu-Lughod, *Before European Hegemony*.

22. Blyden, *Negro in Ancient History*, 20.

23. Blyden, *West Africa to Palestine*, 109–10.

24. Blyden, *Christianity, Islam, and the Negro Race*, 224. Hereafter cited in text.

25. See Rediker, *Slave Ship*; and Diouf, *Fighting the Slave Trade*.

26. Blyden, *West Africa before Europe*, 131. Hereafter cited in text.

27. See Snowden, *Blacks in Antiquity*; and Drake, *Black Folk Here*.

28. Blyden, *Black Spokesman*, 207. Hereafter cited in text.

29. The expression "rose in the cross" is from Hegel; see *Philosophy of Right*, 12.

30. Douglass, *Narrative*.

31. Blyden, *Selected Letters*, 462.

32. Ibid.

33. For a reflection on black liberation theology, see Cone, *Black Theology of Liberation*; Cone, *Black Theology*; Cone, *God of the Oppressed*; and Thurman, *Jesus and the Disinherited*. For a global view, see Lanternari, *Religions of the Oppressed*.

34. Blyden, *The Three Needs of Liberia*, 20. Hereafter cited in text.

35. For a history of the "communism" of early Christianity, see Kautsky, *Foundations of Christianity*.

36. For Douglass's incisive critique of American Christianity, see the appendix in his *Narratives*.

37. Blyden, *Significance of Liberia*, 25.

38. Ibid., 23.

39. Blyden, *Christianity*, 422.

40. See Haynes, *Noah's Curse*.

41. Blyden, *Significance of Liberia*, 26.

42. Blyden, *Christianity, Islam, and the Negro Race*, 135. Hereafter cited in text.

43. Blyden, *Problems Before Liberia*, 22.

44. Blyden, *Negro in Ancient History*, 24–25.

45. The "infant" Blyden is referring to here is Jesus.

46. Meisner, *Marxism, Maoism, and Utopianism*.

47. Blyden, *West Africa before Europe*, 148.

48. J. E. Casely Hayford made similar remarks about the service Africans are made to provide to Europeans, but under duress and by force. See his *Ethiopia Unbound*, 168.

49. Lynch, *Edward Wilmot Blyden*, 63–64.

50. Blyden, *Jewish Question*, 9. Hereafter cited in text.

51. For a discussion of Blyden's views on Jews and Zionism, see Lynch, "Black Nineteenth-Century Response"; Neuberger, "Early African Nationalism"; and Echeruo, "Edward W. Blyden." For a discussion of black Zionism and black views regarding Jews and Judaism, see Washington, *Jews in Black Perspectives*; and Essien-Udom, *Black Nationalism*, chap. 10.

52. Blyden, *Significance of Liberia*, 2. Hereafter cited in text.

53. Blyden, *Negro in Ancient History*, 26. Interestingly, Blyden's view of pharaoh is similar to that of enslaved Africans in America. Moses is the icon of freedom in African American theology, as in Blyden's; Pharaoh, by contrast, is the oppressor. Enslaved Africans in America saw the American slaveholder as the pharaoh of slave-holding modernity, while they depicted themselves as the comrades-in-suffering with the Hebrews. In *The Negro in Ancient History*, Blyden writes, "When we notice the scornful indifference in which the Negro is spoken of by certain politicians in America, we fancy that the attitude of Pharaoh and the aristocratic Egyptians must have been precisely similar toward the Jews."

54. Blyden, *Christianity*, 314.

Chapter 2

1. Woodson, *Mis-Education of the Negro*. The Nigerian nationalist leader, intellectual, and first president of independent Nigeria, Nnamdi Azikiwe, made similar comments about the "mis-education" of Africans under the Western educational system: "*Africans have been mis-educated. They need mental emancipation so as to be re-educated to the real needs of Renascent Africa*" (*Renascent Africa*, 135).

2. Blyden, *Christianity, Islam, and the Negro Race*, 43. Hereafter cited in text.

3. Fanon, *Wretched of the Earth*; Fanon, *Dying Colonialism*; Fanon, *Black Skin, White Masks*; Fanon, *Toward the African Revolution*.

4. Cabral, *Return to the Source*.

5. D. Levine, *Greater Ethiopia*, 64.

6. Hegel, *Philosophy of World History*.

7. Blyden, *Selected Letters*, 461.

8. Blyden, *Black Spokesman*, 194, 228.

9. Ibid., 252.

10. For a discussion of Hegel's views on the Semitic world, see Teshale, *Hegel and Anti-Semitism*.

11. Hegel, *Philosophy of Subjective Spirit*, vol. 2.

12. Blyden, *African Society*, 15.

13. Blyden, *Selected Letters*, 460–61.

14. Ibid., 461, 463.

15. Ibid., 465.

16. Blyden, *Religion for the African*, 18.

17. Ibid., 19.

18. Ibid., 17–18.

19. Blyden, *African Life and Customs*, 84, 85.

20. Blyden did not say much about Islam in the African diaspora in the Americas. He could not have been unaware of its presence there.

Chapter 3

1. Blyden, *Christianity*, 277–78.

2. Ibid., 278.

3. Ibid., 280–81. See Mazrui, *Euro-Jews and Afro-Arabs*, for an interesting discussion on crossbreedings of cultures that run contrary to Blyden's views expressed in the citation.

4. Blyden, *Christianity*, 297.

5. See Irele, *Negritude Movement*.

6. For a history and role of Islam in Africa, see Robinson, *Muslim Societies*; and Levtzion and Pouwels, *History of Islam*.

7. Blyden, *Christianity*, 266, 190. Hereafter cited in text.

8. Hegel, *Philosophy of World History*, 177. For Hegel's views on Islam, see Teshale, *Hegel and Anti-Semitism*, chap. 5.

9. There is extensive literature dealing with the subject of Islam and African enslavement. See Goldenberg, *Curse of Ham*; B. Hall, *History of Race*; Fisher and Fisher, *Black Muslim Africa*; and Mirzai, Montana, and Lovejoy, *Slavery, Islam, and Diaspora*.

10. For the history of Islam in the black Americas, see Diouf, *Servants of Allah*; GhaneaBassiri, *Islam in America*; S. Jackson, *Islam and the Blackamerican*; S. Jackson, *Problem of Black Suffering*; Turner, *Islam*; Dannin, *Black Pilgrimage to Islam*; Gomez, *Black Crescent*; Mirzai, Montana, and Lovejoy, *Slavery, Islam, and Diaspora*; Curtis, *Islam in Black America*; Curtis, *Black Muslim Religion*; and Marable and Aidi, *Black Routes to Islam*.

11. See Drake, *Black Folk Here*.

12. Hegel, *Philosophy of Religion*, vol. 3.

13. For a discussion of Ethiopian Christianity, see Teshale, *Making of Modern Ethiopia*.

Chapter 4

1. Blyden understood modernity to mean capitalism: "But what is modern civilisation, with all its activities and agencies? What is it, after all, but an extensive system of bargain and barter, in which the struggle is to see how much of intellectual, physical, or pecuniary power one man can get out of another for the little he may bestow upon that other?" *West Africa to Palestine*, 117–18.

2. For a historical analysis of liberalism, see Wallerstein, *Centrist Liberalism Triumphant*.

3. Blyden, *Christianity*, 251.

4. Blyden, *Voice from Bleeding Africa*, 28.

5. For a discussion of the idea of a black diaspora "civilizing mission" to Africa, see Jenkins, *Black Zion*; Adeleke, *UnAfrican Americans*; Harris, "Racial Identity"; and Collier-Thomas, *Jesus, Jobs, and Justice*.

6. For a discussion and critique of the Hegelian Eurocentric developmentalist paradigm, see Teshale, *Third World*.

7. Blyden, *Christianity*, 384–85.

8. Blyden, *Liberia's Offering*, 68.

9. Blyden, *Liberia*, 23.

10. Blyden, *Voice from Bleeding Africa*, 18–19. For an incisive indictment against the deliberate forbidding of education for the enslaved in American slavery, see Douglass, *Narratives*, 44.

11. The American Colonization Society's full name was the Society for the Colonization of Free People of Color of America. It was founded in 1816 in Washington, DC.

12. Blyden, *African Problem*, 14–15.

13. Ibid., 8, 10.

14. Hegel rationalizes the Native American genocide and African enslavement as being in tune with reason; see *Philosophy of World History*. For a critique, see Teshale, *Third World*.

15. Blyden, *Liberia's Offering*, 70–71.

16. Ibid., 27.

17. Blyden, *Origin, Danger, and Duties*, 39–40.

18. Ibid., 41.

19. For similar critique of white liberalism, see Biko, *What I Like*.

20. Blyden, *Liberia*, 23.

21. Blyden, *Liberia's Offering*, 27.

22. Blyden, *Origin, Danger, and Duties*, 41.

23. Ibid., 39.

24. Blyden, *Christianity*, 124–25.

25. Blyden, *African Problem*, 24.

26. Blyden, *Liberia's Offering*, 18–19, 27.

27. Ibid., 71–72.

28. Blyden, *African Problem*, 9. For similar view in the context of slavery in Brazil, see Conrad, *Children of God's Fire*.

29. Blyden, *Christianity*, 146.

30. Blyden, *Liberia's Offering*, 28. Hereafter cited in text.

31. Joseph, *Midnight Hour*.

32. Blyden, *Liberia's Offering*, v; Blyden, *Significance of Liberia*, 2.

33. Blyden, *Liberia's Offering*, 19.

34. Ibid., 21, 23.

35. Blyden, *Voice from Bleeding Africa*, 28–29.

36. Blyden, *Liberia's Offering*, 24–25.

37. Ibid., 90–91.

38. Hegel, *Philosophy of World History*, 174.

39. Blyden, *Inaugural Address*, 23, 25.

40. Ibid., 39–40.

41. Diop, *African Origin of Civilization*.

42. Blyden, *African Problem*, 16. Hegel similarly sees the Sphinx as the essential representation of the Egyptian spirit, one where spirit strives to come out of its immersion in nature, yet it is unable to attain that liberation (*Philosophy of History*, 199.) For Hegel, the liberation of spirit from its immersion in nature was first attained among the Greeks (*Aesthetics*, 1:360). For a critique of Hegel's Egyptology, see Teshale, *Third World*, 273–94. J. E. Casely Hayford cites Blyden's comments about Africa and the Sphinx in his *Gold Coast Native Institutions*, 8.

43. Blyden, *Liberian Scholar*, 52.

44. Blyden, *Liberia*, 15.

45. Ibid., 26–27.

46. Blyden, *Christianity*, 425, 430.

47. Blyden, *African Problem*, 20–21.

48. For a discussion of the republican racism of the founders of the American Colonization Society, see Streifford, "American Colonization Society."

49. Blyden, *Significance of Liberia*, 12.

50. Ibid., 8, 12.

51. Blyden, *Liberia's Offering*, 87.

52. Ibid.

53. See Conklin, *Mission to Civilize*; Worger, Clark, and Alpers, *From Colonialism to Independence*; Lugard, *Dual Mandate*; and R. Price, *Making Empire*.

54. Blyden, *Liberia's Offering*, 86.

55. Ibid., 87–88.

56. Ibid., 89.

57. Blyden, *African Problem*, 19, 20.

58. Blyden, *Black Spokesman*, 116–17, 114.

59. Blyden, *Liberian Scholar*, 42–43.

60. Ibid., 43.

61. Ibid., 44.

62. See Diouf, *Fighting the Slave Trade*; Rediker, *Slave Ship*; and Bailey, *African Voices*.

63. Blyden, *Liberian Scholar*, 45. Hereafter cited in text.

64. Blyden, *Christianity*, 124.

65. Ibid., 45.

66. Ibid., 125–26.

67. Ibid., 126.

68. See Holloway, *Africanisms in American Culture*.

69. Blyden, *Significance of Liberia*, 22.

70. Blyden, *Three Needs of Liberia*, 1. Hereafter cited in text.

71. Africanus Horton offers the same kind of praise to British rule in Africa. See his *Political Condition*, iii.

72. For a detailed account on the Liberian civil war, see Ellis, *Mask of Anarchy*.

73. One of the most pervasive of the Eurocentric views about Africa is its alleged isolation from the outside world. In *Christianity, Islam, and the Negro Race* Blyden writes against such a view, citing as an example the interactions between the peoples of Asia and Africa: "The people of Asia, and the people of Africa have been in constant intercourse. No violent social or political disruption has ever broken through this

communication. No chasm caused by war has suspended intercourse." The "greatest religious reforms the world has ever seen—Jewish, Christian, Mohammedan—originating in Asia, have obtained consolidation in Africa." The link between Asia and Africa continues through tens of centuries. "As in the days of Abraham and Moses, of Herodotus and Homer, so to-day, there is a constantly accessible highway from Asia to the heart of the Soudan. Africans are continually going to and fro between the Atlantic Ocean and the Red Sea" (131). It was such a link between the two sides of the Red Sea that made Africans feel at home in the various biblical narratives (132).

74. Blyden, *African Problem*, 16.

75. Here too, Blyden's view echoes that of Hegel, who opines that Islam is the only civilizing influence among Africans prior to Western contact; see Hegel, *Philosophy of World History*, 177.

76. Blyden, *Christianity*, 418.

77. Blyden, *Problems Before Liberia*, 8.

Chapter 5

1. Blyden, *Christianity, Islam, and the Negro Race*, 317. Hereafter cited in text.

2. For a discussion of the difference between racism and racialism, see Appiah, *In My Father's House*.

3. For a comprehensive study of the divine rationalization of race distinctions in American history, see Haynes, *Noah's Curse*.

4. Blyden, *African Problem*, 24.

5. Blyden, *Significance of Liberia*, 24.

6. For a study of the American Colonization Society, see Staudenraus, *African Colonization Movement*; and Burin, *Peculiar Solution*.

7. Blyden, *Selected Letters*, 72n.

8. Ibid., 84–85.

9. Blyden, Letter to William Coppinger, October 19, 1874, vol. 17.

10. Garvey was faced the same kind of problem when he met the Ku Klux Klan leaders. Almost all the prominent African American leaders condemned him for his actions; see Martin, *Race First*.

11. Blyden, *Selected Letters*, 197, 198.

12. Blyden, Letter to William Coppinger, April 23, 1879, vol. 19, pt. 1.

13. Blyden, *Selected Letters*, 322–23.

14. Blyden, Letter to William Coppinger, April 13, 1887, vol. 24, pt. 1.

15. Blyden, Letter to William Coppinger, October 3, 1887, vol. 24, pt. 2.

16. Garvey, *Philosophy and Opinions*.

17. Blyden, Letter to William Coppinger, October 3, 1887, vol. 24, pt. 2.

18. Blyden, Letter to William Coppinger, June 19, 1888, vol. 25, pt. 2.

19. Blyden, *Selected Letters*, 442. Hereafter cited in text.

20. For a discussion and critique of Hegel's geographical determinism of racial distinctions among human beings and how Africa is the natural domain custom tailored for the "Negro," see Teshale, *Third World*.

21. Blyden, *Selected Letters*, 467.

22. Blyden, *Christianity*, 373.

23. Blyden, *Three Needs of Liberia*, 15.

24. By "equalitarian" I mean a view that articulates race difference wherein all racial categories are seen as equal. "Hegemonic," by contrast, refers to not only race difference but race hierarchy, that is, racism.

25. Blyden, *Black Spokesman*, 189.

Chapter 6

1. Blyden, *West Africa before Europe*, 73–74. Hereafter cited in text.

2. For a different recourse on the black "struggle for recognition," see Teshale, *Third World*, 349.

3. Hegel, *Philosophy of Subjective Spirit*.

4. Blyden, *West Africa before Europe*, 99.

5. Blyden, *African Society*, 17–18.

6. For the most comprehensive study of the Gikuyu revolt, see Elkins, *Imperial Reckoning*.

7. For a discussion of Roume and French colonialism in West Africa, see Conklin, *Mission to Civilize*.

8. Blyden, "Africa and the Africans," 33–34.

9. Ibid., 35–36.

10. Ibid., 45.

11. Hegel, *Philosophy of Right*, 10.

12. Hegel, *Philosophy of World History*, 69.

13. Ibid., 91.

14. Blyden, *West Africa before Europe*, 25.

15. Blyden, *Christianity*, 267.

16. Ibid., 267–68.

17. Hegel, *Philosophy of World History*, 174.

18. Hegel, *Philosophy of Religion*, vol. 3.

19. Blyden, *Christianity*, 425, 426.

20. Blyden, *Jewish Question*, 22. Hereafter cited in text.

21. Alex Lubin charges Blyden of Orientalism for his views regarding Jews, especially Zionism; see "Locating Palestine," 22–24. Jacob Dorman claims that Blyden's views about Islam were informed by black Christian Orientalism; see Dorman, "Lifted."

22. Blyden, *African Life and Customs*, 73.

23. In my book *Hegel and the Third World*, I showed Hegel's three Ds concerning Africa: "defamation, degradation, and dehumanization" (Teshale, *Third World*, 171).

24. For a sympathetic, anticolonial defense of an African social system, see Jomo Kenyatta's classic work, *Facing Mount Kenya*.

25. Blyden, *Significance of Liberia*, 18.

26. Ibid., 20.

27. Ibid.

28. Blyden, *Christianity*, 126–27.

29. Ibid., 127.

30. Ibid., 128.

31. See Hegel, *Philosophy of World History*; Pieterse, *White on Black*; and Teshale, *Third World*.

32. For an insightful look at black Hegelianism, see Camara, "Falsity of Hegel's Theses."

33. Blyden, *Three Needs of Liberia*, 20, 14.

34. Blyden, *Arabic Bible*, 19.

35. Blyden, *Significance of Liberia*, 20. Hereafter cited in text.

36. The last sentence is written in capital letters in the original.

37. Ethiopian modernist intellectuals during the first few decades of the twentieth century took Japan as a model for Ethiopia's quest for modernity. Addis Hiwet calls them "Japanizers" (*Ethiopia*, 68–77.) Their efforts to bring about Ethiopia's sovereign modernity were interrupted by the fascist invasion and occupation of Ethiopia, 1935–41. Many of them were deliberately targeted and eliminated by Mussolini's forces. For a history of these Japanizers, see Bahru, *Pioneers of Change*. For a discussion of the ambiguities of Ethiopian identity in Western scholarship, see Teshale, "Ethiopia." Joseph Clarke explores the relations between Ethiopia and Japan in the early part of the twentieth century; see *Alliance*.

38. Blyden, *Elements of Permanent Influence*, 4.

39. Blyden, *Significance of Liberia*, 8.

40. For an incisive, critical reconceptualization of black diaspora discourses, see Zeleza, "Rewriting African Diaspora."

Epilogue

1. The most prominent scholar of Afrocentricity is Molefi Kete Asante of Temple University. He has written extensively on the subject. Some of his most important works on Afrocentricity include *Kemet* and *Afrocentric Idea*.

2. Lynch, *Edward Wilmot Blyden*, 248.

3. Ibid., 252.

4. In his excellent book *Nations and Nationalism since 1780*, Hobsbawm argues that terms such as "African nationalism" are misnomers, because Africa is composed of many nations, not one. To talk of nationalism in the non-Western world, as we do here, sounds even more ludicrous. And yet we should not lose sight of the fact that there is a shared vision in the fight against French colonialism in "French" Indo-China, Algeria, Senegal, or Martinique, namely, the quest for freedom from French colonial rule. In that sense, we can talk of tricontinental nationalism, defined by what it considers as its nemesis, Western colonialism, and by what it aspires after, freedom from colonial rule. Once sovereign status in the interstate system is achieved, such extra-large nationalism shrinks into its many small- and medium-size nationalist components. Moreover, we should not forget that nationalism is an "invented tradition," an "imagined community," in this case of non-Western peoples oppressed by the same foe, Western colonialism. The 1955 Bandung Conference is a reflection of this tricontinental imagined community (see Prashad, *Darker Nations*; see also Lee, *Making a World*; and Ahmad, *In Theory*, chap. 8).

For an interpretation of nationalism different from Hobsbawm's, see Gellner, *Nations and Nationalism*; and Hastings, *Construction of Nationhood*. Abdel-Malek coined the term "nationalitarian phenomena" to describe the unique aspects of non-Western nationalisms and reserved the term "nationalism" for the European nation-making process (*Social Dialectics*, 2:13). For an excellent anthology of works on nationalism across the globe, see Eley and Suny, *Becoming National*.

5. Abdel-Malek, *Social Dialectics*, 1:72–73.

6. Amin, *Eurocentrism*. For an Ethiopian contribution to the critique of Eurocentrism, see my work, *Third World*.

7. Balandier, *Sociology of Black Africa*, 83, 37, 52.

8. Nkrumah, *Neo-Colonialism*, xii.

9. Senghor, *On African Socialism*, 10.

10. Ibid., 33, 68–69.

11. Memmi, *Colonizer and the Colonized*, 71.

12. Ibid., 71–72.

13. Ibid., 85; Sartre quoted on xxvi.

14. Césaire, *Collected Poetry*, 59.

15. Césaire, *My Native Land*, 105.

16. Ibid., 103.

17. Mazrui, *Africans*, 73; Césaire, *My Native Land*, 72. For a discussion of the Hegelian developmentalist paradigm, see Teshale, *Third World*.

18. Césaire, *Discourse on Colonialism*, 9.

19. Arnold, *Modernism and Negritude*, 159.

20. Irele, "Negritude or Black Cultural Nationalism," 321.

21. Caute, *Frantz Fanon*, 21.

22. Mudimbe, *Invention of Africa*, 132.

23. For an excellent synopsis of the origins of Césaire's philosophy of negritude, see Tomich, "Colonialism and Culture." For one of the most authoritative studies on negritude, see Irele, *Negritude Movement*. For a discussion of Senghor's and others' negritude, see Ba, *Concept of Negritude*; Hymans, *Léopold Sédar Senghor*; Vaillant, "Dilemmas"; Vaillant, *Black, French, and African*; Spleth, *Léopold Sédar Senghor*; Spleth, *Critical Perspectives*; Markovitz, *Politics of Negritude*; Kluback, *Léopold Sédar Senghor*; English, *What We Say*; Kesteloot, *Black Writers in French*; Jack, *Francophone Literatures*; Wilder, *French Imperial Nation-State*; Thomas, "Senghor and Negritude"; and Berrian and Long, *Negritude*.

24. Senghor, "Black Host," in Kennedy, *Negritude Poets*, 136, 138.

25. The journal *Présence Africaine* played a critical role in disseminating ideas by radical black thinkers dealing with discourses of power and othering, including Senghor; see Mudimbe, *Surreptitious Speech*.

26. Senghor, "Psychology of the African Negro," 50. Hereafter cited in text.

27. Senghor repeats this quote verbatim in *On African Socialism*, 72–73.

28. Hegel, perhaps the best representation of the "European white man," calls it "the eye of the concept, the eye of reason" (*Philosophy of World History*, 30).

29. Camara, *Reason in History*, 22–24. For Gobineau's views on race, see his *Human Races*.

30. Senghor, cited in Hymans, *Léopold Sédar Senghor*, 71. For the most comprehensive account of Egypt as the foundation of African history, see Diop, *African Origin of Civilization*; and Diop, "Ancient Egyptians."

31. See Biko, *I Write What I Like*. The comparative historian of racism, George Fredrickson, writes, "racism exists when one ethnic group or historical collectivity dominates, excludes, or seeks to eliminate another on the basis of differences that it believes are hereditary and unalterable" (*Racism*, 170).

32. Satrtre, *Black Orpheus*, 59–60.

33. The transcendence of negritude in the "civilization of the universal" is an act of Hegelian sublation. The term "sublation" is central to Hegel's dialectic. It means cancellation and preservation at a higher phase. See Hegel, *Science of Logic*, 106–8.

34. Senghor, cited in Hymans, *Léopold Sédar Senghor*, 85.

35. Ibid., 90.

36. See Teshale, *Third World*.

37. Senghor, cited in Hymans, *Léopold Sédar Senghor*, 99.

38. Ibid., 103.

39. Ibid., 83.

40. For a discussion of Senghor's advocacy of global cultural hybridization, see Badiane, "Léopold Sédar Senghor"; Mortimer, "Sine and Seine." For reflections on Senghor's life and works, see Irele, ed. *Research in African Literatures*.

41. For critical reflections on race discourses and Fanon's views on negritude, see McCulloch, *Black Soul, White Artifact*, 40, 46–47; Zahar, *Colonialism and Alienation*; Caute, *Frantz Fanon*; Hansen, *Frantz Fanon*; and Macey, *Frantz Fanon*.

42. See also Césaire, who has similar views to Senghor regarding the "civilization of the universal" (*My Native Land*, 109).

43. For one of the best accounts of Fanon's life and works, see Macey, *Frantz Fanon*.

44. Fanon, *Wretched of the Earth*, 37–38.

45. Ibid., 38–39.

46. Fanon, *Black Skin, White Masks*, 183.

47. Fanon, *Wretched of the Earth*, 41.

48. Cited in Tomich, "Colonialism and Culture," 382.

49. Fanon, *Toward the African Revolution*, 31. Hereafter cited in text.

50. Sartre, *Black Orpheus*, 15, 59. For an excellent review of the intellectual relations between Sartre and Fanon, see Haddour, "Sartre and Fanon."

51. For a powerful indictment against American antiblack racism, see Bell, *Bottom of the Well*.

52. Fanon, *Black Skin, White Masks*, 160.

53. Ibid., 115.

54. Sartre, *Anti-Semite and Jew*.

55. Fanon, *Dying Colonialism*, 47.

56. Fanon, *Black Skin, White Masks*, 113–14. Hegel calls the African "animal man" (*Philosophy of World History*, 177). For a critique, see Teshale, *Third World*.

57. One of the most prominent cultural theorists is Stuart Hall, the Jamaican-born intellectual working in England; see Morley and Chen, *Stuart Hall*.

58. Fanon, *Wretched of the Earth*, 35, 316.

59. Ira Katznelson wrongly charges Fanon of being an anti-Western racial exclusivist (*Liberalism's Crooked Circle*, 184–85). For a response to this charge, see Teshale, *Third World*, 334–38.

60. Diop, *African Origin of Civilization*, xiv.

61. Diop, *Civilization or Barbarism*, 3. For a fascinating critique of the view of the ancient Greeks as the foundation of Western civilization, see Vlassopoulos, *Unthinking the Greek Polis*.

62. See Ben-Jochannan, *Black Man*; Ben-Jochannan, *Africa*; Higgins and Jackson, *Introduction to African Civilizations*; DeGraft-Johnson, *African Glory*; Du Bois, *World and Africa*; Blayechettai, *Hidden Mystery of Ethiopia*; C. Williams, *The Destruction of Black Civilization*; J. Jackson, *Introduction to African Civilizations*; Snowden, *Blacks in Antiquity*; and G. James, *Stolen Legacy*.

63. Diop, *Civilization or Barbarism*, 3. For one of the most powerful claims on the Egyptian origins of Greek philosophy, see Onyewuenyi, *African Origin*.

64. Diop, *Cultural Unity*, 180. See also Diop, *African Origin of Civilization*, xv.

65. Diop, *Cultural Unity*, 195.

66. Two of the African female scholars who agree with Diop's gender analysis of his two-cradle theory are Amadiume, *Re-inventing Africa*; and Oyewumi, *Invention of Women*.

67. See Bernal, *Fabrication of Ancient Greece*.

68. See Vlassopoulos, *Unthinking the Greek Polis*; and Bernal, *Fabrication of Ancient Greece*.

69. Nyerere, *Ujamaa*, 4–5. Hereafter cited in text.

70. Senghor, *On African Socialism*, 46, 87. For the origins of Senghor's idea of African socialism, see Hymans, "African Road to Socialism."

71. Nkrumah, *Class Struggle in Africa*, 26. Marx and Engels write about the possibility of direct transition from "primitive" communalism to "advanced" socialism without having to go through a long gestation period of capitalist development. They had the Russian Mir as their example. See Marx and Engels, *Russian Menace to Europe*, 217–22. For the most detailed Marxist historical sociology of the development of capitalism in Russia, see Lenin, *Development of Capitalism*.

72. Nkrumah, *Revolutionary Path*, 440.

73. Nkrumah, *Consciencism*, 68.

74. Some of the works on Cabral include Chabal, *Amilcar Cabral*; Lopes, *Africa's Contemporary Challenges*; Fobanjong, *Life, Thought, and Legacy*; Dhada, *Warriors at Work*; Chilcote, *Amicar Cabral's Revolutionary Theory*; and Peterson, *DuBois, Fanon, Cabral*.

75. Cabral, *Revolution in Guinea*, 102.

76. In Marxist theory the thesis that history is the history of class struggles is meant only for class societies. Engels qualifies the statement as applicable to class-divided societies only. He notes that societies without classes have history too (Marx and Engels, *Manifesto*).

77. Cabral, *Revolution in Guinea*, 102, 98, 102.

78. Joseph Ki-Zerbo gives credence to the critical importance of national history. Calling history "the memory of nations," he writes, "for Africans, the history of Africa is not some narcissistic mirror or a subtle excuse for avoiding the tasks and burdens of today. . . . All the evils that afflict Africa today, as well as all the possibilities for the

future, are the result of countless forces transmitted by history" ("General Introduction," 30).

79. Cabral, *Revolution in Guinea*, 99.
80. Marx and Engels, *On Colonialism*, 82.
81. Ibid., 40–41.
82. Cabral, *Unity and Struggle*, 262.
83. P. Anderson, "Portugal."
84. Cabral, *Return to the Source*, 42, 64.
85. Ibid., 42–43, 45.
86. Cabral, *Unity and Struggle*, 63.
87. Ibid., 60–61.
88. Ibid., 63.
89. Cabral, *Revolution in Guinea*, 106.
90. Ibid., 102.
91. Ibid., 103, 110.
92. Cabral, *Unity and Struggle*, 97.
93. Césaire, *Collected Poetry*, 77.
94. Senghor, *On African Socialism*, 65.

Bibliography

Abdel-Malek, Anouar. *Social Dialectics.* 2 vols. Albany: State University of New York Press, 1981.

Abu-Lughod, Janet. *Before European Hegemony: The World System A.D. 1250–1350.* New York: Oxford University Press, 1989.

Addis Hiwet. *Ethiopia: From Autocracy to Revolution.* London: Merlin, 1975.

Adeleke, Tunde. *The Case against Afrocentrism.* Jackson: University Press of Mississippi, 2009.

———. *UnAfrican Americans: Nineteenth-Century Black Nationalists and the Civilizing Mission.* Lexington: University Press of Kentucky, 1998.

———. *Without Regard to Race: The Other Martin Robinson Delany.* Jackson: University Press of Mississippi, 2003.

Afolabi, Niyi. *Afro-Brazilians: Cultural Production in a Racial Democracy.* Rochester, NY: University of Rochester Press, 2009.

———. *The Man, the Mask, the Muse.* Edited by Toyin Falola. Durham, NC: Carolina Academic Press, 2010.

Ahmad, Aijaz. *In Theory: Nations, Classes, Literatures.* London: Verso, 2008. First published 1992.

Amadiume, Ifi. *Re-Inventing Africa: Matriarchy, Religion, and Culture.* London: Zed, 1998.

Amin, Samir. *Accumulation on a World Scale.* New York: Monthly Review, 1974.

———. *Eurocentrism.* 2nd ed. New York: Monthly Review, 2010.

———. *Unequal Development.* New York: Monthly Review, 1976.

Anderson, Benedict. *Imagined Communities: Reflections on the Origin and Spread of Nationalism.* Rev. ed. London: Verso, 2006.

Anderson, Perry. "Portugal and the End of Ultra-Colonialism." *New Left Review* 1, no. 15 (May-June, 1962): 83–102; no. 16 (July-August, 1962): 88–123; no. 17 (Winter 1962): 85–114.

Angell, Stephen Ward. *Bishop Henry McNeil Turner and African-American Religion in the South.* Knoxville: University of Tennessee Press, 2001.

Appiah, Kwame Anthony. *In My Father's House: Africa in the Philosophy of Culture.* New York: Oxford University Press, 1992.

Araujo, Ana Lucia, Mariana Candido, and Paul Lovejoy, eds. *Crossing Memories: Slavery and African Diaspora.* Trenton, NJ: Africa World, 2011.

Arnold, James. *Modernism and Negritude: The Poetry and Poetics of Aimé Césaire.* Cambridge, MA: Harvard University Press, 1981.

Asante, Molefi Kete. *The Afrocentric Idea.* Rev. ed. Philadelphia: Temple University Press, 1998.

———. *Kemet, Afrocentricity, and Knowledge.* Trenton, NJ: Africa World, 1990.

Austin, Algernon. *Achieving Blackness: Race, Black Nationalism, and Afrocentrism in the Twentieth Century.* New York: New York University Press, 2006.

Austin, Allan. *African Muslims in Antebellum America: Transatlantic Stories and Spiritual Struggles.* Rev. ed. New York: Routledge, 1997.

Azikiwe, Nnamdi. *Renascent Africa.* London: Cass, 1968.

Ba, Washington Sylvia. *The Concept of Negritude in the Poetry of Léopold Sédar Senghor.* Princeton, NJ: Princeton University Press, 1973.

Badiane, Mamadou. "Léopold Sédar Senghor and Nicolas Guillen: Two Poets of Hybridization." *Journal of Caribbean Literatures* 6, no. 2 (Fall 2009): 101–23.

Bahru Zewde. *Pioneers of Change in Ethiopia: Reformist Intellectuals of Early Twentieth Century.* Athens: Ohio University Press, 2002.

Bailey, Anne. *African Voices of the Atlantic Slave Trade: Beyond the Silence and Shame.* Boston: Beacon, 2006.

Baum, Bruce. *The Rise and Fall of the Caucasian Race: A Political History of Racial Identity.* New York: New York University Press, 2006.

Bell, Derrick. *Faces at the Bottom of the Well: The Permanence of Racism.* New York: Basic Books, 1992.

Benjamin, George. *Edward W. Blyden: Messiah of Black Revolution.* New York: Vintage, 1979.

Ben-Jochannan, Yoseph. *Africa: Mother of Western Civilization.* Baltimore: Black Classic, 1997. First published 1971.

———. *Black Man of the Nile.* Baltimore: Black Classic, 1996. First published 1972.

Bernal, Martin. *The Fabrication of Ancient Greece, 1785–1985.* Vol. 1 of *Black Athena: The Afroasiatic Roots of Classical Civilization.* New Brunswick, NJ: Rutgers University Press, 1987.

Berrian, Albert, and Richard Long, eds. *Negritude: Essays and Studies.* Hampton, VA: Hampton Institute Press, 1967.

Beyan, Amos. *African American Settlements in West Africa: John Brown Russwurm and the American Civilizing Efforts.* New York: Palgrave Macmillan, 2005.

Biko, Steve. *I Write What I Like: Selected Writings.* Chicago: University of Chicago Press, 2002. First published 1978.

Balandier, Georges. *The Sociology of Black Africa: Social Dynamics in Central Africa.* New York: Praeger, 1970.

Blaut, Jim. *The Colonizer's Model of the World: Geographical Diffusionism and Eurocentric History.* New York: Guilford, 1993.

Blayechettai, Joseph Emanuel. *The Hidden Mystery of Ethiopia.* New York: New York Public Library (microfilm), first published in 1922.

Blyden, Edward. "Africa and the Africans." In *Africa and the Africans: Proceedings on the Occasion of a Banquet Given at the Holborn Restaurant, August 15th, 1903, to Edward W. Blyden, LL.D., by West Africans in London,* 32–48. London: Phillips, 1903.

———. *African Life and Customs.* Baltimore: Black Classic, 1994. First published 1908.

———. *The African Problem, and the Method of Its Solution.* Washington, DC: Gibson, 1890.

———. *The African Society and Miss Mary H. Kingsley.* London: Scott, 1901.

———. *The Arabic Bible in the Soudan: A Plea for Transliteration.* London: Phillips, 1910.

———. *Black Spokesman: Selected Published Writings of Edward Wilmot Blyden.* Edited by Hollis Lynch. New York: Humanities, 1971.

——. *Christianity, Islam, and the Negro Race.* 2nd ed. With an introduction by Samuel Lewis. London: Whittingham, 1888.

——. *The Elements of Permanent Influence: Discourse Delivered in the Fifteenth Street Presbyterian Church, Washington, D.C., Sunday, February 16, 1890.* Washington, DC: Pendleton, 1890.

——. *From West Africa to Palestine.* Freetown, Sierra Leone: Sawyer, 1873.

——. *Inaugural Address: Proceedings at the Inauguration of Liberia College at Monrovia.* Monrovia: Legislature of the Republic of Liberia, 1862.

——. *The Jewish Question.* Liverpool: Hart, 1898.

——. Letters to William Coppinger. Part I, Series B. American Colonization Society Papers, 1874–88. Washington, DC: Library of Congress.

——. *The Liberian Scholar: An Address, Delivered at the Inauguration of Rev. G. W. Gibbon, D. D., President-Elect of Liberia College, at Monrovia, February 21st, 1900.* Monrovia, 1900.

——. *Liberia: Past, Present, and Future.* Washington, DC: McGill and Witherow, 1869.

——. *Liberia's Offering.* New York: Gray, 1862.

——. *The Negro in Ancient History.* Washington, DC: McGill and Witherow, 1869.

——. *Our Origin, Danger, and Duties.* New York: Gray and Green, 1865.

——. *The Problems Before Liberia: A Lecture Delivered in the State Chamber at Monrovia, January 18, 1909.* London: Phillips, 1909.

——. *The Religion for the African.* New York: Schomburg, 1903.

——. *Selected Letters.* Edited by Hollis Lynch. Millwood, NY: KTO, 1978.

——. *The Significance of Liberia: An Address Delivered in the State Chamber, Monrovia, Liberia, 20th May, 1906.* 2nd ed. Liverpool: Richardson and Sons, 1907.

——. *The Three Needs of Liberia: A Lecture Delivered at Lower Buchanan, Grand Bassa County, Liberia, January 26, 1908.* London: Phillips, 1908.

——. *A Voice from Bleeding Africa on Behalf of Her Exiled Children.* Monrovia: Killian, 1856.

——. *West Africa before Europe, and Other Addresses.* With an introduction by Casely Hayford. London: Phillips, 1905.

Brotz, Howard, ed. *Negro Social and Political Thought, 1850–1920: Representative Texts.* New York: Basic Books, 1966.

Burin, Eric. *Slavery and the Peculiar Solution: A History of the American Colonization Society.* Gainesville: University of Florida Press, 2005.

Cabral, Amilcar. *Return to the Source.* New York: Monthly Review, 1973.

——. *Revolution in Guinea: Selected Texts.* New York: Monthly Review, 1969.

——. *Unity and Struggle: Selected Speeches and Writings.* 2nd ed. Pretoria, South Africa: UNISA; Hollywood, CA: Tsehai, 2007.

Camara, Babacar. "The Falsity of Hegel's Theses on Africa." *Journal of Black Studies* 36, no. 1 (September 2005): 82–96.

——. *Reason in History: Hegel and Social Change in Africa.* Lanham, MD: Lexington Books, 2011.

Caute, David. *Frantz Fanon.* New York: Viking, 1970.

Césaire, Aimé. *The Collected Poetry.* Translated by Clayton Eshleman. Berkeley: University of California Press, 1983.

————. *Discourse on Colonialism.* Translated by Dan Pinkham. With a new introduction by Robin D. G. Kelley. New York: Monthly Review, 2011. First published in French 1955.

————. *Return to My Native Land.* Paris: Présence Africaine, 1968.

Chabal, Patrick. *Amilcar Cabral: Revolutionary Leadership and People's War.* Trenton, NJ: Africa World, 2003. First published 1983.

————. "The Social and Political Thought of Amilcar Cabral: A Reassessment." *Journal of African History* 19, no. 1 (1981): 31–56.

Chilcote, Ronald. *Amilcar Cabral's Revolutionary Theory and Practice: A Critical Guide.* Boulder: Lynne Rienner, 1991.

Chinweizu. *The West and the Rest of Us: White Predators, Black Slavers, and the African Elite.* New York: Vintage Books, 1975.

Chireau, Yvonne, and Nathaniel Deutsch, eds. *Black Zion: African American Religious Encounters with Judaism.* Rev. ed. New York: Oxford University Press, 2000.

Clarke, Joseph. *Alliance of the Colored Peoples: Ethiopia & Japan before World War II.* Woodbridge: James Currey, 2011.

Clegg, Claude. *The Price of Liberty: African Americans and the Making of Liberia.* Chapel Hill: University of North Carolina Press, 2003.

Collier-Thomas, Bettye. *Jesus, Jobs, and Justice: African American Women and Religion.* New York: Knopf, 2010.

Collins, Patricia Hill. *Black Feminist Thought: Knowledge, Consciousness, and the Politics of Empowerment.* Rev. 2nd ed. New York: Routledge, 2000.

Cone, James. *Black Theology and Black Power.* New York: Orbis Books, 1999. First published 1969.

————. *A Black Theology of Liberation.* New York: Orbis Books, 2010. First published 1970.

————. *God of the Oppressed.* New York: Orbis Books, 1997. First published 1975.

Conklin, Alice. *A Mission to Civilize: The Republican Idea of Empire in France and West Africa, 1895–1930.* Stanford: Stanford University Press, 1997.

Conniff, Michael, and Thomas Davis, eds. *Africans in the Americas: A History of the Black Diaspora.* New York: St. Martin's Press, 1994.

Conrad, Robert, ed. *Children of God's Fire: A Documentary History of Black Slavery in Brazil.* University Park: Pennsylvania State University Press, 1997.

Cooper, Anna Julia. *A Voice from the South by a Black Woman of the South.* With an introduction by Mary Helen Washington. New York: Oxford University Press, 1990. First published 1892.

Cox, Oliver. *Capitalism and American Leadership.* New York: Philosophical Library, 1962.

————. *Capitalism as a System.* New York: Monthly Review, 1964.

————. *The Foundations of Capitalism.* New York: Philosophical Library, 1959.

Crummell, Alexander. *Africa and America: Addresses and Discourses.* Miami, FL: Mnemosyne, 1969.

————. *Civilization and Black Progress: Selected Writings of Alexander Crummell on the South.* Charlottesville: University of Virginia Press, 1995.

————. *Destiny and Race: Selected Writings, 1840–1898.* Amherst: University of Massachusetts Press, 1992.

————. *The Future of Africa: Being Addresses, Sermons, etc., etc., Delivered in the Republic of Liberia.* New York: Negro Universities Press, 1969.

Cruse, Harold. *The Crisis of the Negro Intellectual*. New York: Quill, 1984. First published 1967.

Cummings, Melbourne. "The Rhetoric of Bishop Henry McNeil Turner." *Journal of Black Studies* 12, no. 4 (June 1982): 457–67.

Curtis, Edward. *Black Muslim Religion in the Nation of Islam, 1960–1975*. Chapel Hill: University of North Carolina Press, 2006.

———. *Islam in Black America*. Albany: State University of New York Press, 2002.

Dannin, Robert. *Black Pilgrimage to Islam*. New York: Oxford University Press, 2005.

Davis, David Brion. *The Problem of Slavery in Western Culture*. Ithaca: Cornell University Press, 1975.

Delany, Martin. *The Condition, Elevation, Emigration and Destiny of the Colored People of the United States, Politically Considered*. Baltimore: Black Classic, 1993. First published 1852.

———. *Martin R. Delany: A Documentary Reader*. Edited by Robert S. Levine. Chapel Hill: North Carolina University Press, 2007.

———. *The Origin of Races and Color*. Baltimore: Black Classic, 1997. First published as *Principia of Ethnology* in 1879.

———. "Political Destiny of the Colored Race, on the American Continent." In *Black Nationalism in America*, edited by John Bracey, August Meier, and Elliott Rudwick, 87–110. Indianapolis: Bobbs-Merrill, 1970.

Diop, Chiekh Anta. *The African Origin of Civilization: Myth or Reality*. Edited and translated from the French by Mercer Cook. Westport, CT: Hill, 1974.

———. *Civilization or Barbarism: An Authentic Anthropology*. Edited by Harold Salemson and Marjolijn de Jager. Translated from the French by Yaa-Lengi Meema Ngemi. Brooklyn: Lawrence Hill Books, 1991. First published in French 1981.

———. *The Cultural Unity of Black Africa: The Domains of Patriarchy and of Matriarchy in Classical Antiquity*. With an introduction by John Henrik Clarke. Foreword by James Spady. Chicago: Third World, 1990. First published in French 1959.

———. "Origin of the Ancient Egyptians." In *Ancient Civilizations of Africa*, edited by G. Mokhtar, 27–51. Vol. 2 of *UNESCO General History of Africa*. Berkeley: University of California Press, 1981.

Diouf, Sylviane, ed. *Fighting the Slave Trade: West African Strategies*. Athens: Ohio University Press; London: Currey, 2003.

———. *Servants of Allah: African Muslims Enslaved in the Americas*. New York: New York University Press, 1998.

DeGraft-Johnson, J. C. *African Glory: Study of Vanished Negro Civilisations*. London: Watts, 31954.

Dhada, Mustafah. *Warriors at Work: How Guinea Was Really Set Free*. Boulder: University Press of Colorado, 1993.

Dorman, Jacob. "Lifted Out of the Commonplace Grandeur of Modern Times: Reappraising Edward Wilmot Blyden's Views of Islam and Afrocentrism in Light of His Scholarly Black Christian Orientalism." *Souls* 12, no. 4 (October 2010): 398–418.

Douglass, Frederick. *Life and Times of Frederick Douglass*. In *The Oxford Frederick Douglass Reader*, edited by Williams Andrews, 227–311, 316–38. New York: Oxford University Press, 1996.

———. *My Bondage and My Freedom*. Edited by Philip Foner. New York: Dover, 1969. First published 1855.

———. *Narrative of the Life of Frederick Douglass, an American Slave*. In *Narrative of the Life of Frederick Douglass, an American Slave, and Incidents in the Life of a Slave Girl*, 1–113. Introduction by Kwame Anthony Appiah. Notes and Biographical Note by Joy Viveros. New York: Modern Library, 2000.

Drake, St. Clair. *Black Folk Here and There: An Essay in History and Anthropology*. Vol. 2. Los Angeles: Center for Afro-American Studies/University of California at Los Angeles, 1990.

Dubois, Laurent. *Avengers of the New World: The Story of the Haitian Revolution*. Cambridge, MA: Belknap Press of Harvard University Press, 2005.

———. *A Colony of Citizens: Revolution and Slave Emancipation in the French Caribbean, 1787–1804*. Chapel Hill: University of North Carolina Press, 2004.

Dubois, Laurent, and John Garrigus, eds. *Slave Revolution in the Caribbean, 1789–1804: A Brief History with Documents*. New York: Bedford/St. Martin, 2006.

Du Bois, W. E. B. *The Negro*. Houston, TX: Africa Diaspora, 2010. First published 1915.

———. *The Souls of Black Folk*. New York: Simon and Schuster, 2005. First published 1903.

———. *The World and Africa: An Inquiry into the Part Which Africa Has Played in World History*. Rev. ed. New York: International, 1979. First published 1946.

Echeruo, Michael. "Edward W. Blyden, 'the Jewish Question,' and the Diaspora: Theory and Practice." *Journal of Black Studies* 40, no. 3 (March 2010): 544–65.

Edwards, Brent Hayes. *The Practice of Diaspora: Literature, Translation, and the Rise of Black Internationalism*. Cambridge, MA: Harvard University Press, 2003.

Eley, Geoff, and Ronald Suny, eds. *Becoming National: A Reader*. New York: Oxford University Press, 1996.

Elkins, Caroline. *Imperial Reckoning: The Untold Story of Britain's Gulag in Kenya*. New York: Henry Holt, 2005.

Ellis, Stephen. *The Mask of Anarchy: The Destruction of Liberia and the Religious Dimension of an African Civil War*. Rev. ed. New York: New York University Press, 2007.

English, Parker. *What We Say, Who We Are: Léopold Sédar Senghor, Zora Neale Hurston, and the Philosophy of Language*. Lanham, MD: Lexington Books, 2009.

Esedebe, Olisanwuche. *Pan-Africanism: The Idea and Movement, 1776–1991*. 2nd ed. Washington, DC: Howard University Press, 1994.

Essien-Udom, E. U. *Black Nationalism: The Search for an Identity in America*. Chicago: University of Chicago Press, 1971.

Fage, David. "Slavery and the Slave Trade in the Context of African History." *Journal of African History* 10 (1969): 393–404.

Fairhead, James, Tim Geysbeek, Svend E. Holsoe, and Melissa Leach, eds. *African-American Exploration in West Africa: Four Nineteenth-Century Diaries*. Bloomington: Indiana University Press, 2003.

Falola, Toyin. *Nationalism and African Intellectuals*. Rochester: University of Rochester Press, 2004.

Fanon, Frantz. *Black Skin, White Masks*. New York: Grove, 1967.

———. *Studies in a Dying Colonialism*. New York: Monthly Review, 1965.

———. *Toward the African Revolution*. New York: Monthly Review, 1967.

————. *Wretched of the Earth.* New York: Grove, 1963.

Fisher, Allan, and Humphrey Fisher. *Slavery in the History of Black Muslim Africa.* New York: New York University Press, 2001.

Fobanjong, John, ed. *The Life, Thought, and Legacy of Cape Verde's Freedom Fighter Amilcar Cabral (1924–1973): Essays on His Liberation Philosophy.* Lewiston, NY: Mellen, 2006.

Frank, Andre Gunder. *Development of Underdevelopment.* New York: Monthly Review, 1966.

Fredrickson, George. *Racism: A Short History.* Princeton, NJ: Princeton University Press, 2002.

Frenkel, M. Yu. "Edward Blyden and the Concept of African Personality." *African Affairs* 38, no. 292 (July 1974): 277–89.

Garvey, Marcus. *The Philosophy and Opinions of Marcus Garvey.* Compiled by Amy J. Garvey. Dover, MA: Majority, 1986.

Geggus, David, and Norman Fiering, eds. *The World of the Haitian Revolution.* Bloomington: Indiana University Press, 2009.

Gellner, Ernest. *Nations and Nationalism.* 2nd ed. Ithaca: Cornell University Press, 1983.

GhaneaBassiri, Kambiz. *A History of Islam in America: From the New World to the New World Order.* New York: Cambridge University Press, 2010.

Gibbon, Edward. *The Decline and Fall of the Roman Empire.* 3 vols. New York: Modern Library, 1977.

Gilroy, Paul. *The Black Atlantic: Modernity and Double-Consciousness.* Cambridge, MA: Harvard University Press, 1993.

Gobineau, Arthur. *The Inequality of the Human Races.* Translated by Adrian Collins. New York: Fertig, 1967. First published 1915.

Goldenberg, David. *The Curse of Ham: Race and Slavery in Early Judaism, Christianity, and Islam.* Princeton, NJ: Princeton University Press, 2003.

Gomez, Michael. *Black Crescent: The Experience and Legacy of African Muslims in the Americas.* New York: Cambridge University Press, 2005.

————. *Reversing Sail: A History of the African Diaspora.* New York: Cambridge University Press, 2004.

Griffith, Cyril. *The African Dream: Martin R. Delany and the Emergence of Pan-African Thought.* University Park: Pennsylvania State University Press, 1975.

Haddour, Azzedine. "Sartre and Fanon: On *Negritude* and Political Participation." In *Sartre Today: A Centenary Celebration,* edited by Adrian van den Hoven and Andrew Leak, 286–301. New York: Berghahn Books, 2005.

Hahn, Steven. *A Nation under Our Feet: Black Political Struggles in the Rural South from Slavery to the Great Migration.* Cambridge, MA: Belknap Press of Harvard University Press, 2005.

Hall, Bruce. *A History of Race in Muslim West Africa, 1600–1960.* New York: Cambridge University Press, 2011.

Hall, Gwendolyn. *Slavery and African Ethnicities in the Americas: Restoring the Links.* Chapel Hill: University of North Carolina Press, 2007.

Hansen, Emmanuel. *Frantz Fanon: Social and Political Thought.* Columbus: Ohio State University Press, 1977.

Harris, Paul. "Racial Identity and the Civilizing Mission: Double-Consciousness at the 1895 Congress on Africa." *Religion and American Culture: A Journal of Interpretation* 18, no. 2 (Summer 2008): 145–76.

Hastings, Adrian. *The Construction of Nationhood: Ethnicity, Religion, and Nationalism.* Cambridge, UK: Cambridge University Press, 1997.

Hayford, J. E. Casely. *Ethiopia Unbound: Studies in Race Emancipation.* London: Cass, 1969.

———. *Gold Coast Native Institutions.* London: Cass, 1970.

Haynes, Stephen. *Noah's Curse: The Biblical Justification of American Slavery.* New York: Oxford University Press, 2002.

Hegel, G. W. F. *Hegel's Aesthetics: Lectures on Fine Art.* Translated by Thomas M. Knox. 2 vols. Oxford: Clarendon, 1998–99.

———. *Hegel's Philosophy of Subjective Spirit.* Translated and edited by Michael J. Petry. 3 vols. Boston: Reidel, 1979.

———. *Lectures on the Philosophy of Religion.* Translated by Robert F. Brown, Peter C. Hodgson, and Jon M. Stewart, with the assistance of John P. Fitzer and Henry S. Harris. Edited by Peter C. Hodgson. 3 vols. Berkeley: University of California Press, 1995–98.

———. *Lectures on the Philosophy of World History: Introduction; Reason in History.* Translated by Hugh B. Nisbet. Cambridge, UK: Cambridge University Press, 1998.

———. *Phenomenology of Spirit.* Translated by Arnold V. Miller. Oxford: Oxford University Press, 1977.

———. *The Philosophy of History.* Translated by Joseph Sibree. New York: Dover, 1956.

———. *Philosophy of Right.* Translated with notes by Thomas M. Knox. Oxford: Clarendon, 1967.

———. *Science of Logic.* Translated by Arnold V. Miller. Atlantic Highlands, NJ: Humanities, 1991.

Hier, Sean. "The Forgotten Architect: Cox, Wallerstein and World-System Theory." *Race and Class* 42, no. 3 (January 2001): 69–86.

Higgins, Willis, and John Jackson. *An Introduction to African Civilizations, with Main Currents in Ethiopian History.* Chicago: Third World, 1999. First published 1937.

Hobsbawm, Eric. *Nations and Nationalism since 1780: Programme, Myth, Reality.* 2nd ed. New York: Cambridge University Press, 2012.

Hodges, Rich, and David Whitehouse. *Mohammed, Charlemagne, and the Origins of Europe.* Ithaca: Cornell University Press, 1983.

Holden, Edith. *Blyden of Liberia: An Account of the Life and Labors of Edward Wilmot Blyden, LL.D. as Recorded in Letters and in Print.* New York: Vantage, 1966.

Holloway, Joseph, ed. *Africanisms in American Culture.* Bloomington: Indiana University Press, 1991.

Horton, Africanus. *Letters on the Political Condition of the Gold Coast.* London: Cass, 1970.

Howe, Stephen. *Afrocentrism: Mythical Pasts and Imagined Homes.* London: Verso, 1998.

Hunter, Herbert. "The World-System Theory of Oliver C. Cox." *Monthly Review* 37, no. 5 (October, 1985): 43–55.

Hymans, Jacques. *Léopold Sédar Senghor: An Intellectual Biography.* Edinburgh: Edinburgh University Press, 1971.

————. "The Origins of Leopold Senghor's African Road to Socialism." *Genève Afrique* 6, no. 1 (1966): 33–48.

Irele, Abiola. *The African Imagination: Literature in Africa and the Black Diaspora.* New York: Oxford University Press, 2001.

————. *The Negritude Movement: Explorations in Francophone African and Caribbean Literature and Thought.* Trenton, NJ: Africa World, 2010.

————. "Negritude or Black Cultural Nationalism." *Journal of Modern African Studies* 3, no. 3 (1965): 321–48.

————. ed. *Research in African Literatures.* Special Issue: Léopold Sédar Senghor. 33, no. 4 (Winter 2002).

Jack, Belinda. *Francophone Literatures: An Introductory Survey.* New York: Oxford University Press, 1997.

Jackson, John. *Introduction to African Civilizations.* New York: Citadel, 2001. First published 1937.

Jackson, Sherman. "Black Orientalism: Its Genesis, Aims, and Significance for American Islam." In *Black Routes to Islam,* edited by Manning Marable and Hishaam Aidi, 33–48. New York: Palgrave Macmillan, 2009.

————. *Islam and the Blackamerican: Looking toward the Third Resurrection.* New York: New York University Press, 2005.

————. *Islam and the Problem of Black Suffering.* New York: Oxford University Press, 2009.

Jacobs, Harriet. *Incidents in the Life of a Slave Girl.* In *Narrative of the Life of Frederick Douglass, an American Slave, and Incidents in the Life of a Slave Girl.* Introduction by Kwame Anthony Appiah. Notes and Biographical Note by Joy Viveros, 115–353. New York: Modern Library, 2000.

James, C. L. R. *Black Jacobins: Toussaint L'Overture and the San Domingo Revolution.* 2nd rev. ed. New York: Vintage, 1989.

James, George. *Stolen Legacy.* New York: Classic House Books, 2009.

James, Winston. *Holding Aloft the Banner of Ethiopia: Caribbean Radicalism in Early Twentieth-Century America.* London: Verso, 1998.

Jefferson, Thomas. *Notes on the State of Virginia.* Edited by David Waldstreicher. New York: Palgrave Macmillan, 2002. First published 1782.

Jenkins, David. *Black Zion: The Return of Afro-Americans and West Indians to Africa.* London: Wildwood House, 1975.

Johnson, Robert. *Returning Home: A Century of African-American Repatriation.* Trenton, NJ: Africa World, 2010.

Joseph, Peniel. *Waiting 'Til the Midnight Hour: A Narrative History of Black Power in America.* New York: Owl Books, 2007.

July, Robert. *The Origins of Modern African Thought: Its Development in West Africa during the Nineteenth and Twentieth Centuries.* Trenton, NJ: Africa World, 2004. First published 1967.

Kanneh, Kadiatu. *African Identities: Race, Nation, and Culture in Ethnography, Pan-Africanism and Black Literatures.* London: Routledge, 1998.

Katznelson, Ira. *Liberalism's Crooked Circle: Letters to Adam Michnik.* Princeton, NJ: Princeton University Press, 1996.

Kautsky, Karl. *The Foundations of Christianity.* Translated by Jacob W. Hartmann. New York: Monthly Review Press, 1972. First published in 1908.

Kennedy, Ellen, ed. *The Negritude Poets: An Anthology of Translations from the French.* Edited by Ellen Conroy Kennedy. New York: Thunder's Mouth, 1989.

Kenyatta, Jomo. *Facing Mount Kenya.* New York: Vintage, 1963.

Kesteloot, Lilyan. *Black Writers in French: A Literary History of Negritude.* Rev. ed. Washington, DC: Howard University Press, 1991. First published in French 1963.

Ki-Zerbo, Joseph. "General Introduction." In *Methodology and African Prehistory*, edited by Joseph Ki-Zerbo, 1–23. Vol. 1 of *UNESCO General History of Africa*. Berkeley: University of California Press, 1981.

Kluback, William. *Léopold Sédar Senghor: From Politics to Poetry.* Bern: Peter Lang, 1997.

Lanternari, Vittorio. *Religions of the Oppressed: A Study in Modern Messianic Cults.* New York: Knopf, 1963.

Lee, Christopher, ed. *Making a World after Empire: The Bandung Moment and Its Political Afterlives.* Athens: Ohio University Press, 2010.

Lemert, Charles. *The Voice of Anna Julia Cooper: Including a Voice from the South and Other Important Essays, Papers, and Letters.* Lanham, MD: Rowman and Littlefield, 1998.

Lenin, Vladimir. *The Development of Capitalism in Russia.* Moscow: Progress, 1977.

Levine, Donald. *Greater Ethiopia: The Evolution of a Multiethnic Society.* Chicago: University of Chicago Press, 2000. First published 1974.

Levine, Robert Steven. *Martin Delany, Frederick Douglass, and the Politics of Representative Identity.* Chapel Hill: North Carolina University Press, 1997.

Levtzion, Nehemia, and Randall Pouwels, eds. *History of Islam in Africa.* Athens: Ohio University Press, 2000.

Lewis, Bernard. *The Muslim Discovery of Europe.* New York: Norton, 1982.

Lewis, Rupert. *Walter Rodney's Intellectual Thought.* Detroit: Wayne State University Press, 1999.

Litwack, Leon, and August Meier, eds. *Black Leaders of the Nineteenth Century.* Urbana: University of Illinois Press, 1988.

Loewenberg, Bert James, and Ruth Bogin, eds. *Black Women in Nineteenth-Century American Life: Their Words, Their Thoughts, Their Feelings.* University Park: Pennsylvania State University, 1993.

Lopes, Carlos, ed. *Africa's Contemporary Challenges: The Legacy of Amilcar Cabral.* London: Routledge, 2009.

Lubin, Alex. "Locating Palestine in Pre-1948: Black Internationalism." In *Black Routes to Islam*, edited by Manning Marable and Hishaam Aidi, 17–32. New York: Palgrave Macmillan, 2009.

Lugard, Frederick. *The Dual Mandate in British Tropical Africa.* Ithaca: Cornell University Press, 2009. First published 1922.

Lynch, Hollis. "A Black Nineteenth-Century Response to Jews and Zionism: The Case of Edward Wilmot Blyden." In *Jews in Black Perspectives: A Dialogue*, edited by Joseph R. Washington Jr. Lanham, MD: University Press of America, 1989.

———. *Edward Wilmot Blyden: Pan-Negro Patriot, 1832–1912.* London: Oxford University Press, 1967.

Macey, David. *Frantz Fanon: A Biography.* New York: Picador, 2000.

Manning, Patrick. *The African Diaspora: A History through Culture.* New York: Columbia University Press, 2009.

Marable, Manning, and Hishaam Aidi, eds. *Black Routes to Islam*. New York: Palgrave Macmillan, 2009.

Markovitz, Irving. *Léopold Sédar Senghor and the Politics of Negritude*. Portsmouth: Heinemann Educational Books, 1990.

Martin, Tony. *Race First*. Dover, MA: Majority, 1976.

Marx, Karl, and Fredrick Engels. *Manifesto of the Communist Party*. Radford, VA: Wilder, 2008.

———. *On Colonialism*. New York: International, 1972.

———. *The Russian Menace to Europe*. Glencoe: Free Press, 1952.

Mazrui, Ali. *The Africans: A Triple Heritage*. London: BBC, 1986.

———. *Euro-Jews and Afro-Arabs: The Great Semitic Divergence in World History*. Lanham, MD: Hamilton Books, 2008.

McCulloch, Jack. *Black Soul, White Artifact: Fanon's Clinical Psychology and Social Theory*. New York: Cambridge University Press, 1983.

———. *In the Twilight of Revolution: The Political Thought of Amilcar Cabral*. London: Routledge/Kegan Paul, 1983.

Meisner, Maurice. *Marxism, Maoism and Utopianism*. Madison: University of Wisconsin Press, 1982.

Memmi, Albert. *The Colonizer and the Colonized*. Exp. ed. Boston: Beacon, 1991.

Miers, Suzanne, and Igor Kopytoff, eds. *Slavery in Africa: Historical and Anthropological Perspectives*. Madison: University of Wisconsin Press, 1979.

Mirzai, Behnaz, Ismael Musah Montana, and Paul Lovejoy, eds. *Slavery, Islam and Diaspora*. Trenton, NJ: Africa World, 2009.

Moitt, Bernard. *Women and Slavery in the French Antilles, 1635–1848*. Bloomington: Indiana University Press, 2001.

Morley, David, and Kuan-Hsing Chen, eds. *Stuart Hall: Critical Dialogues in Cultural Studies*. London: Routledge, 1996.

Mortimer, Mildred. "Sine and Seine: The Quest for Synthesis in Senghor's Life and Poetry." *Research in African Literatures* 33, no. 4 (Winter 2002): 38–50.

Moses, Wilson Jeremiah. *Afrotopia: The Roots of African American Popular History*. New York: Cambridge University Press, 1998.

———. *Alexander Crummell: A Study of Civilization and Discontent*. Amherst: University of Massachusetts Press, 1992.

———, ed. *Classical Black Nationalism: From the American Revolution to Marcus Garvey*. New York: New York University Press, 1996.

———. *The Golden Age of Black Nationalism, 1850–1925*. New York: Oxford University Press, 1978.

———, ed. *Liberian Dreams: Back-to-Africa Narratives from the 1850's*. University City: Penn State University Press, 1998.

Mudimbe, Valentin Y. *The Idea of Africa*. Bloomington: Indiana University Press; London: Currey, 1994.

———. *The Invention of Africa: Gnosis, Philosophy, and the Order of Knowledge*. Bloomington: Indiana University Press; London: Currey, 1988.

———, ed. *The Surreptitious Speech: Présence Africaine and the Politics of Othering, 1947–1987*. Chicago: University of Chicago Press, 1992.

Neuberger, Benyamin. "Early African Nationalism, Judaism and Zionism: Edward Wilmot Blyden." *Jewish Social Studies* 47, no. 2 (Spring 1985): 151–66.

Nkrumah, Kwame. *Africa Must Unite.* New York: Praeger, 1963.

————. *Class Struggle in Africa.* New York: International, 1970.

————. *Consciencism: Philosophy and Ideology for Decolonization.* New York: Monthly Review, 1970.

————. *Neo-Colonialism, the Last Stage of Imperialism.* New York: International, 1965.

————. *Revolutionary Path.* New York: International, 1973.

Novati, Giampaolo Calchi. "At the Source of the Contemporary African State: Late XIX Century Polity and Society in Monrovia and Freetown." *Journal of Pan African Studies* 1, no. 8 (June 2007): 52–76.

Nyerere, Julius K. *Ujamaa: Essays on Socialism.* Dar es Salaam: Oxford University Press, 1968.

Oldfield, John. *Alexander Crummell (1819–1898) and the Creation of an African-American Church in Liberia.* Lewiston, NY: Mellen, 1990.

Onyewuenyi, Innocent. *The African Origin of Greek Philosophy: An Exercise in Afrocentrism.* Charleston, SC: Booksurge, 2005.

Oyewumi, Oyeronke. *Invention of Women: Making an African Sense of Western Gender Discourses.* Minneapolis: University of Minnesota Press, 1997.

Parka, Daniel. *The Athens of West Africa: A History of International Education at Fourah Bay College, Freetown, Sierra Leone.* New York: Routledge, 2003.

Patterson, Orlando. *Freedom in the Making of Western Culture.* Vol. 1 of *Freedom.* New York: Basic Books, 1992.

————. *Slavery and Social Death.* Cambridge, MA: Harvard University Press, 1983.

Pawlikova-Vilhanova, Viera. "The African Personality or the Dilemma of the Other and Self in the Philosophy of Edward W. Blyden, 1832–1912." *Asian and African Studies* 7, no. 2 (1998): 162–75.

Peterson, Charles. *DuBois, Fanon, Cabral: The Margins of Elite Anti-colonial Leadership.* Lanham, MD: Lexington Books, 2007.

Pieterse, Jan Nederveen. *White on Black: Images of Africa and Blacks in Western Popular Culture.* New Haven, CT: Yale University Press, 1998.

Pirenne, Henri. *Mohammed and Charlemagne.* Mineola, NY: Dover, 2001. First published in French 1937.

Prashad, Vijay. *The Darker Nations: A People's History of the Third World.* New York: New Press, 2007.

Price, Melanye. *Dreaming Blackness: Black Nationalism and African American Public Opinion.* New York: New York University Press, 2009.

Price, Richard. *Making Empire: Colonial Encounters and the Creation of Imperial Rule in Nineteenth-Century Africa.* New York: Cambridge University Press, 2008.

Rediker, Marcus. *The Slave Ship: A Human History.* New York: Penguin, 2008.

Redkey, Edwin. *Black Exodus: Black Nationalism and Back to Africa Movements, 1890–1919.* New Haven, CT: Yale University Press, 1969.

Rigsby, Gregory. *Alexander Crummell: Pioneer in Nineteenth-Century Pan-African Thought.* New York: Greenwood, 1987.

Robinson, David. *Muslim Societies in African History.* New York: Cambridge University Press, 2004.

Rodney, Walter. *A History of the Upper Guinea Coast, 1545–1800.* Oxford: Clarendon, 1970.

————. *How Europe Underdeveloped Africa*. Washington, DC: Howard University Press, 1974.

Sanders, Edith. "The Hamitic Hypothesis: Its Origin and Functions in Time Perspective." *Journal of African History* 10, no. 4 (1969): 521–32.

Sansone, Livio, Elise Soumonni, and Boubacar Barry, eds. *Africa, Brazil and the Construction of Trans Atlantic Identities*. Trenton, NJ: Africa World, 2008.

Sartre, Jean-Paul. *Anti-Semite and Jew*. Translated by George Becker. New York: Schocken Books, 1948.

————. *Black Orpheus*. Translated by S. W. Allen. Paris: Présence Africaine, 1963.

Seligman, Charles. *Races of Africa*. London: Oxford University Press, 1966.

Semujanga, Josias. *Origins of Rwandan Genocide*. Amherst, NY: Humanity Books, 2003.

Senghor, Léopold Sédar. "Black Host." In *The Negritude Poets: An Anthology of Translations from the French*, edited by Ellen Conroy Kennedy, 136–39. New York: Thunder's Mouth, 1989.

————. Foreword to *Selected Letters*, by Edward Blyden. Millwood, NY: KTO Press, 1978.

————. *On African Socialism*. Translated by Mercer Cook. New York: Praeger, 1964.

————. "The Psychology of the African Negro." In *Negritude: Essays and Studies*, edited by Albert H. Berrian and Richard A. Long, 48–55. Hampton, VA: Hampton Institution Press, 1967.

Sherwood, Marika. *Origins of Pan-Africanism: Henry Sylvester Williams, Africa, and the African Diaspora*. London: Routledge, 2012.

Snowden, Frank. *Blacks in Antiquity: Ethiopians in the Greco-Roman Experience*. Cambridge, MA: Belknap Press of Harvard University Press, 1970.

Solow, Barbara, and Stanley Engerman, eds. *British Capitalism and Caribbean Slavery: The Legacy of Eric Williams*. Cambridge, UK: Cambridge University Press, 2004.

Sonderegger, Arno. "Anglophone Discourses on Race in the 19th Century: British and African Perspectives." *Stichproben: Wiener Zeitschrift für kritische Afrikastudien* 16, no. 9 (2009): 45–85.

Speke, John Hanning. *Journal of the Discovery of the Source of the Nile*. New York: Harper and Brothers, 1864.

Spleth, Janice. *Critical Perspectives on Léopold Sédar Senghor*. Colorado Springs: Three Continents, 1993.

————. *Léopold Sédar Senghor*. New York: Twayne, 1985.

Staudenraus, P. J. *The African Colonization Movement, 1816–1825*. New York: Columbia University Press, 1961.

Stephens, Michelle Ann. *Black Empire: The Masculine Global Imaginary of Caribbean Intellectuals in the United States, 1914–1962*. Durham, NC: Duke University Press, 2005.

Streifford, David. "The American Colonization Society: An Application of Republican Ideology to Early Antebellum Reform." *Journal of Southern History* 45, no. 2 (May 1979): 201–20.

Taylor, James L. *Black Nationalism in the United States: From Malcolm X to Barack Obama*. Boulder: Lynne Rienner, 2011.

Teshale Tibebu. "Ethiopia: The 'Anomaly' and 'Paradox' of Africa." *Journal of Black Studies* 26, no. 4 (March 1996): 414–30.

————. *Hegel and Anti-Semitism*. Pretoria: University of South Africa Press, 2008.

———. *Hegel and the Third World: The Making of Eurocentrism in World History.* Syracuse, NY: Syracuse University Press, 2011.

———. *The Making of Modern Ethiopia, 1896–1974.* Lawrenceville, NJ: Red Sea, 1995.

Thomas, L. V. "Senghor and Negritude." *Présence Africaine* 26, no. 54 (1965): 102–33.

Thomson, James. *Works of James Thomson.* Vol. 2. London: Millar, 1763.

Thornton, John. *Africa and Africans in the Making of the Atlantic World.* New York: Cambridge University Press, 1988.

Thurman, Howard. *Jesus and the Disinherited.* Boston: Beacon, 1996. First published 1949.

Tocqueville, Alexis de. *Democracy in America, and Two Essays on America.* Translated by Gerald Bevan. Introduction and Notes by Isaac Kramnick. London: Penguin, 2003.

Tomich, Dale. "The Dialectics of Colonialism and Culture: The Origins of the Negritude of Aimé Césaire." *Review* 2, no. 3 (Winter 1979): 351–85.

Truth, Sojourner. *Narrative of Sojourner Truth: A Northern Slave.* New York: Penguin Classics, 1998.

Turner, Richard. *Islam in the African-American Experience.* 2nd ed. Bloomington: Indiana University Press, 2003.

Vaillant, Janet. *Black, French, and African: A Life of Léopold Sédar Senghor.* Cambridge, MA: Harvard University Press, 1990.

———. "Dilemmas of Anti-Western Patriotism: Slavophilism and Negritude." *Journal of Modern African Studies* 12, no. 3 (1974): 377–93.

Vlassopoulos, Kostas. *Unthinking the Greek Polis: Ancient Greek History beyond Eurocentrism.* New York: Cambridge University Press, 2007.

Walker, David. *David Walker's Appeal: To the Coloured Citizens of the World.* Edited by Peter Hinks. University Park: Pennsylvania State University, 2000.

Wallerstein, Immanuel. *Capitalist Agriculture and the Origins of the European World-Economy in the Sixteenth Century.* Vol. 1 of *The Modern World-System.* New York: Academic Press, 1974.

———. *Centrist Liberalism Triumphant, 1789–2011.* Vol. 4 of *The Modern World-System.* Berkeley: University of California Press, 2011.

———. *Mercantilism and the Consolidation of the European World-Economy, 1600–1750.* Vol. 2 of *The Modern World-System.* New York: Academic Press, 1980.

———. *The Modern World-System.* 4 vols. New York: Academic Press, 1974–89; Berkeley: University of California Press, 2011.

———. *The Second Era of Great Expansion of the Capitalist World-Economy, 1730s–1840s.* Vol. 3 of *The Modern World-System.* San Diego: Academic Press, 1989.

———. *World-Systems Analysis: An Introduction.* Durham, NC: Duke University Press, 2005.

Washington, Joseph, ed. *Jews in Black Perspectives: A Dialogue.* Lanham, MD: University Press of America, 1989.

Wilder, Gary. *The French Imperial Nation-State: Negritude and Colonial Humanism between the Two World Wars.* Chicago: University of Chicago Press, 2005.

Williams, Chancellor. *The Destruction of Black Civilization: Great Issues of a Race from 4500 B.C. to 2000 A.D.* Chicago: Third World. First published 1976.

Williams, Eric. *Capitalism and Slavery.* Chapel Hill: University of North Carolina Press, 1994. First published 1944.

Wood, Forrest. *The Arrogance of Faith: Christianity and Race in America from the Colonial Era to the Twentieth Century.* New York: Knopf, 1990.

Woodson, Carter. *The Mis-Education of the Negro.* Trenton, NJ: Africa World, 1998.

Worger, William, Nancy Clark, and Edward Alpers, eds. *From Colonialism to Independence, 1875 to the Present.* Vol. 2 of *Africa and the West: A Documentary History.* New York: Oxford University Press, 2010.

Wright, Michelle. *Becoming Black: Creating Identity in the African Diaspora.* Durham, NC: Duke University Press, 2004.

Zahar, Renate. *Colonialism and Alienation: Concerning Frantz Fanon's Political Theory.* Benin City: Ethiopia, 1974.

Zamir, Shamoon. *Dark Voices: W. E. B. Dubois and American Thought, 1888–1903.* Chicago: University of Chicago Press, 1995.

Zeleza, Paul Tiyambe. "Rewriting African Diaspora: Beyond the Black Atlantic." *African Affairs* 104, no. 414 (2005): 35–68.

Index

Douglass, Frederick, work of: *Narrative of
the Life of Frederick Douglass*, 2, 29
Drake, St. Claire, 48
Du Bois, W. E. B.: pan-Africanism of, 12,
147; parentage of, 125; on race problem, 15, 158; world-system perspective of, 3, 173n15
Du Bois, W. E. B., works of: *The Negro*,
15; *The Souls of Black Folk*, 15; *The
World and Africa*, 3

education: of black Christians in
Africa, 61–62; of black Christians in
America, 50–53, 57–58, 75, 79–80,
178n1; curriculum at Liberia College, 54–57; establishment of African
colleges, 93–94; of freedmen, 78; in
Portuguese colonies, 169
egalitarianism, 183n24
Egypt: Africans' connection to, 32; Afrocentrists' reference to, 10; Blyden
on enslavement of Negroes in, 34;
Blyden's view of, 91; Christianity/
Islam in, 45; as home of Abraham,
48; as Negro civilization, 34, 155,
161; place in Diop's historical paradigm, 161–62; as refuge for Jesus, 43,
45; as refuge for Jews, 140
Egyptians, 91
Einstein, Albert, 154
emigration to Africa, 78, 80–86
England: abolition of Atlantic slave
trade, 128–29; Blyden's praise of
colonial system in Africa, 128, 130,
132; commerce, development of,
130–31; link to Caribbean slavery,
176n4; railway construction, 127–28.
See also Anglo-Saxons; colonialism
Engels, Fredrick, 187n71, 187n76
English language, 59, 94, 96, 104, 136,
147
Enlightenment, 4, 6, 163
enslaved men: Blyden on education of,
31; emasculation of in America, 85;
Haitian Revolution, 2–3; Moses as
icon of freedom for, 178n53; opposition to racism/slavery in Caribbean/

Brazil, 2; response to enslavement in
America, 1–2. *See also* African American men; slavery
enslaved women, 1, 3, 24
enslavement of Africans: black responses
to in America, 1–2; Blyden's view of
benefits of for Africans, 26–27, 34–36;
Blyden's lament over, 26, 27–28, 104;
Blyden's view of as divine calling, 11,
21–23, 26, 83, 84; creation of unity,
3–4; development of concept of
freedom, 7; effect on Africa's development, 28, 29, 31, 32, 34; effect
on Blyden's political philosophy, 13;
Haitian Revolution, 2–3; Jefferson's
view of, 2; as means to progress,
23–24, 77, 124; mixing of African
tribes/classes, 32–33; myth of inferiority of Negroes as validation of,
11; as negative modernity, 174n31; as
outcome of Columbian project,
28; response to in Caribbean, 2; as
source of division in Africa, 28–29; as
tool for enlightenment, 31; unifica-
tion of Africans, 3–4. *See also* black
burden of existence in America;
slavery; transatlantic slave trade
environmental theory, 131
Ethiopia: Christianity/Islam in, 45, 68,
74; fascist invasion/occupation of,
184n37; Jews in, 140; modernity,
quest for, 184n37; place in history,
44–45, 64, 87; resistance to coloniza-
tion/foreign religions, 145
Ethiopians, 91
Eurocentrism: Blyden's critique of, 10,
11, 19, 50, 54–58, 60–62, 147; creation of "West," 6–7; education of
Africans, 20, 50–53, 57–58, 61–62,
171; effect on Africans, 60–62; protests against, 148–49; Senghor's critique of, 157; view of Africa, 181n73
European identity, 4–7
European imperialism. *See* colonialism
Europeanization, 59, 61–62
Europe/Europeans: Africa as savior
of, 45–46; assimilation of African

culture, 156–57; Blyden's advice to colonizers, 127–28, 132; Blyden's praise of, 30, 60; Blyden's view of, 37, 138; Christianity of, 63–64; development of concept of freedom, 7; effect on Africa, 44–45; effects on Africans, 40; enslavement of Africans in, 26, 28; Fanon's view of, 161; link to Africa, 24; mis-education of blacks in, 61–62; motivations for emigration to Africa, 100; natural abode of, 100–101; occupation of North America, 78; Senghor's view of, 156–57; study of Africa/not Africans, 60; underdevelopment of Africa, 31; view of Negro, 108. *See also* colonialism

familyhood, 164
Fanon, Frantz: Blyden's ideas found in, 16, 20, 172; call for reconciliation, 160–61; on concept of alienation, 150; on concept of West, 7; on deculturation by colonial racial hegemony, 157–61; Eurocentrism, critique of, 19, 147; Katznelson's opinion of, 187n59; on mis-education of Africans, 52, 61
Fanon, Frantz, works of: *Toward the African Revolution*, 158–59; *Wretched of the Earth*, 158, 160
France: Blyden's praise of colonial system in Africa, 130, 133; negritude movement in, 12, 147, 148, 153; quest for freedom from colonial rule by, 184n4; railway construction, 127–28; Senghor's prayer for, 153
Fredrickson, George, 186n31
free trade, 131
freedom, 7, 13–14, 104, 144
freemen. *See* African Americans: as agents of civilizing mission; black burden of existence in America
frustration complex, 169

Gambia, 135
Garvey, Marcus, 16, 77, 117, 147, 182n10

Gellner, Ernest, 17
genocide of Native Americans, 78, 174n31
geoenvironmental racial determinism, 100–101, 107, 131, 145
Germany, 130
Gibbon, Edward, 5
global capitalism, 24
Gobineau, Arthur, 12, 155
God: Blyden's view of role in civilizing mission, 82–83, 84, 86, 90–91; Blyden's view of role in slavery, 8, 11, 26, 34–35, 83, 84, 92, 98; classical black nationalist view of role in history, 8; as creator of race, 108, 111, 122; relationship with violence by men, 99; role in colonization of Africa, 130, 133, 134
Greece/Greeks, 48, 49, 91, 163–64

Haiti, 2–3, 66, 72, 116, 124
Hall, Stuart, 186n57
Ham: as ancestor of Muhammed, 22; enslavement of descendants of, 21; as father of Negroid race, 59, 91, 118, 137; Jesus's identification with, 41; mixing of blood of descendants of, 22, 122
Harrison, Frederick, 54
Haven, Bishop, 80
Hayford, J. E. Casely, 16, 147
Hebrews. *See* Jews
Hegel, G. W. F.: acknowledgment of, 172; on civilizing influence of Islam, 65; classification of history, 54; developmentalist paradigm, 152; on identity, 7; influence on black thinkers, 77; on Islamic civilizing mission in Africa, 182m75; racial theory of, 60, 131; on struggle for recognition, 128; sublation, definition of, 186n33; view of Africa, 6, 28, 88, 183n23; view of Africans, 143; view of Christianity, 29, 72, 73; view of Sphinx, 181n42; on wrongs done in history, 134

CPSIA information can be obtained
at www.ICGtesting.com
Printed in the USA
LVHW101335190822
726300LV00024B/39